The Marketing / Acco

When marketing managers and financial managers join forces within any business, the result can often be poor communication on financial criteria and goals. The risk of this situation occurring is inevitably present when those with different professional backgrounds and roles are working in accordance with their own norms.

In his seminal 1956 paper on general systems theory, the economist Kenneth Boulding referred to the phenomenon of *"specialised ears and generalised deafness"*, which can be seen to exist when marketing managers are financially illiterate or when financial managers lack the necessary insights to design, implement and operate accounting systems which are useful to marketing managers in carrying out their roles.

It is increasingly difficult to attach credence to the idea of marketing managers who lack financial skills, or financial managers who fail to relate to the context in which marketing managers operate. Understanding the marketing/accounting interface is therefore important in generating emergent properties from the interaction of marketers and accountants whereby the whole is greater than the sum of the parts. The chapters in this volume seek to address this challenge.

This book was originally published as a special issue of the *Journal of Marketing Management*.

Robin Roslender is Professor of Accounting and Finance at the University of Dundee, UK, where he is also Director of Research in the School of Business. He pursues research interests in both mainstream and critical accounting, with most of his contributions in the field of managerial accounting. His work at the marketing/accounting interface dates back to the mid 1990s. Since 2008 he has been the Editor of the *Journal of Human Resource Costing and Accounting*.

Richard M.S. Wilson is Professor of Business Administration and Financial Management (Emeritus) at Loughborough University, UK. He holds degrees and professional qualifications in both marketing and accounting, has held academic and commercial appointments in each of these subject areas, and has published extensively on their interface as well as in the fields of marketing and accounting more broadly. He is the founding Editor of *Accounting Education: an international journal* (of which he is currently Editor-in-Chief).

Key Issues in Marketing Management

The *Journal of Marketing Management* was founded in 1985 by Michael J. Baker to provide a forum for the exchange of the latest research ideas and best practice in the field of marketing as a whole, in an accessible way.

Currently edited by Mark Tadajewski and Paul Hewer, the *Journal of Marketing Management* is the official Journal of the Academy of Marketing and has an international reputation for publishing influential and original contributions which blend the best of theory and practice. It is concerned with all aspects of the management of marketing, and seeks to meet the needs of a wide but sophisticated audience comprising senior marketing executives and their advisors, senior line managers, teachers and researchers in marketing, and undergraduate and postgraduate students of the subject.

The *Key Issues in Marketing Management* book series contains a wide range of the journal's special issues. These special issues are an important contribution to the work of the journal, where leading theoreticians and practitioners bring together articles dedicated to a key topic in the industry. Through publishing these special issues as a series of books, Westburn Publishers and Taylor & Francis hope to allow a wider audience of scholars, students and professionals to engage with the work of the *Journal of Marketing Management*.

Titles in the series include:

The Marketing/Accounting Interface
Edited by Robin Roslender and
Richard M. S. Wilson

New Horizons in Arts, Heritage,
Nonprofit and Social Marketing
Edited by Roger Bennett, Finola Kerrigan and
Daragh O'Reilly

New Developments in Online
Marketing
Edited by Jim Hamill, Stephen Tagg,
Alan Stevenson and Tiziano Vescovi

Multicultural Perspectives in
Customer Behaviour
Edited by Maria G. Piacentin and Charles C. Cui

The Marketing / Accounting Interface

Edited by
Robin Roslender and Richard M.S. Wilson

Routledge
Taylor & Francis Group
LONDON AND NEW YORK

First published 2012
by Routledge
2 Park Square, Milton Park, Abingdon, Oxfordshire OX14 4RN

Simultaneously published in the USA and Canada
by Routledge
711 Third Avenue, New York, NY 10017

First issued in paperback 2016

Routledge is an imprint of the Taylor & Francis Group, an informa business

British Library Cataloguing in Publication Data
A catalogue record for this book is available from the British Library

ISBN 13: 978-1-138-19288-1 (pbk)
ISBN 13: 978-0-415-62886-0 (hbk)

Typeset in Baskerville
by Taylor & Francis Books

Publisher's Note
The publisher would like to make readers aware that the chapters in this book may be referred to as articles as they are identical to the articles published in the special issue. The publisher accepts responsibility for any inconsistencies that may have arisen in the course of preparing this volume for print.

Contents

CONTENTS

Notes on Contributors

Tim Ambler is now retired from London Business School where he taught international marketing. Books include *The Sage Handbook of Advertising* (co-edited with Gerard Tellis), *Marketing and the Bottom Line*, and *Doing Business in China* (with Morgen Witzel). He is a Senior Fellow of Adam Smith Institute, Marketing Society and Australian Marketing Institute. Previously Joint Managing Director of IDV, now part of Diageo plc, he launched Baileys, Malibu and Archers and developed Smirnoff vodka worldwide.

Ken Bates is a Lecturer in Accounting at Victoria University of Wellington, New Zealand, where he teaches management and financial accounting on a variety of undergraduate and postgraduate courses. Ken's research interests include: financial analysis and valuation; strategic management accounting; performance measurement and cost management systems; customer accounting; and accounting education. Ken is also an Associate Fellow of the Warwick Business School, having lectured in the School for 17 years, during which time Ken was a key participant in MBA programmes and served as the Distance Learning MBA Academic Director. Ken has also lectured on a variety of executive courses through the WBS executive development programme and externally. Ken is a Fellow of the ICAEW and has worked for two of the UK's (then) big 6 professional accountancy firms. Ken gained experience in industry as a Company Secretary and Finance Director of companies within the Caparo Group.

Jamie Burton is a Lecturer in Marketing at Manchester Business School. He teaches at every level, directed the MSc in Marketing and MSc Corporate Communications and Reputation Management (2006-2011) and currently teaches core MBA and MSc, Marketing courses. His main research interests focus on customer management: feedback, relationships and services marketing. Following his PhD, he was awarded the Littlewoods Post-Doctoral Fellowship at Manchester Business School. He is co-author of the book *Converting Customer Value* and has published in various marketing journals and conference proceedings. He has worked extensively with and presented for, a range of large organisations on customer management issues. He has led an Excellence research project for the British Quality Foundation and is Research Director for the Customer Management Leadership Group. Prior to joining Manchester Business School Jamie worked in a number of service and retail management roles for various organisations including HMV and Best Western and studied at Cardiff Business School.

Nevine El-Tawy, at the time of writing, was a PhD student at Brunel University, UK, investigating asset recognition criteria using a grounded theory approach.

Robin Gleaves was a Management Consultant specialising in the measurement and management of customer profitability and lifetime value as part of marketing strategy development. He was a Visiting Fellow of Manchester Business School (MBS) and a regular guest lecturer on its MBA programme and other executive programmes. His main research interests focused on customer management and reporting, especially non-financial performance measures and intangibles, but he had a capability to quickly master almost any key management topic. He had an MBA from Manchester Business School and is co-author of the book *Converting Customer Value*. As well as a wide range of private client work he has also undertaken multiple research projects for Manchester Business School's Customer Management Leadership Group, a non-competing customer management benchmarking group covering a wide range of areas including customer profitability measurement, customer satisfaction measurement and the relevance of value statements. Robin sadly passed away in November 2011 whilst teaching for MBS.

Chris Guilding is a Professor at Griffith Business School, Griffith University, Australia. He has a long-standing research interest in the accounting-marketing interface. He has conducted research concerned with valuing brands, accounting for competitors, trade credit management, customer accounting and pricing. He has more than 50 refereed journal publications and is sole author of the Elsevier text *Accounting Essentials for Hospitality Decision Makers*.

Sue Vaux Halliday is Professor of Marketing at the University of Hertfordshire, UK. Before joining academia she held management posts in several services firms, ultimately as the Director of Marketing for a City law firm.

Robert M. Inglis is an Associate Professor in the School of Accounting at RMIT University, Melbourne, Australia. He has postgraduate degrees in marketing from the University of Strathclyde and University of Stirling and an accounting degree and PhD from RMIT University. His research interests include the marketing and management accounting interface, accounting education and business strategy.

Jan Kitshoff is a Management Consultant specialising in the measurement and management of customer profitability and lifetime value as part of strategy development. He is a regular guest lecturer on the MBA programme at Manchester Business School. His main research interests focus on customer profitability analysis segmentation and customer portfolio analysis. He has an MBA from Manchester Business School and is co-author of the book *Converting Customer Value*. As well as a wide range of private client work he has also undertaken four research projects for the Customer Management Leadership Group. Prior to completing his MBA he held a number of positions in BHP Billiton, the last being a member of a Senior Management Team at one of their operations.

Lisa McManus is an Associate Professor at Griffith Business School, Griffith University, Australia. She has a strong interest in the intersection of accounting and marketing, particularly in relation to accounting for customers, having a number of refereed journal publications in this area. She also researches in the areas of management accounting, control systems and accounting education.

Paul Phillips is Professor of Strategic Management and Director of the Kent Business School, University of Kent, UK. He is a qualified accountant and marketer and holds a PhD in strategic planning systems from Cardiff University, in Wales. With more than 15 years experience of strategic management, performance management and more recently e-business strategy, Paul acts as a conduit for those organisations who are trying to address technological and business change management issues. He has specialised experience for private sector, Governments and Government Agencies, and has published extensively in national and international academic journals.

John R. Roberts holds a joint appointment as Professor of Marketing at the Australian National University and London Business School. He is a winner of the American Marketing Association's John Howard Award, William O'Dell Award and Advanced Research Techniques Best Paper Award, and the Australian Marketing Institute's Sir Charles McGrath Award.

Robin Roslender is Professor of Accounting and Finance at the University of Dundee, UK, where he is also Director of Research in the School of Business. A trained social scientist, he initially taught sociology, behavioural science and organisation studies at Napier University, Edinburgh, before taking up a lectureship in accountancy at the University of Stirling in 1989, moving to Heriot-Watt University, Edinburgh as Professor in Accountancy in 2005. He pursues research interests in both mainstream and critical accounting, with most of his contributions in the field of managerial accounting. His work at the marketing/accounting interface dates back to the mid 1990s, since which time he has produced a range of published outputs with Susan Hart. Dr Roslender is also currently engaged in researching workforce health and well-being as a constituent of primary intellectual capital, and since 2008 has been the Editor of the *Journal of Human Resource Costing and Accounting*.

Lynette Ryals specialises in key account management and marketing portfolio management, particularly in service businesses, and has completed a PhD on customer profitability. She came into marketing from a financial background and much of her work focuses on the marketing/accounting interface. She is a Registered Representative of the London Stock Exchange and a Fellow of the Society of Investment Professionals. Lynette is the Director of Cranfield's Key Account Management Best Practice Research Club and of the Demand Chain Management community, which includes faculty in Marketing, Sales and Supply Chain Management. As well as the *Journal of Marketing Management*, her work has been published in the *Journal of Marketing*, *European Journal of Marketing*, and *Industrial Marketing Management*.

Baljit K. Sidhu is Professor of Accounting at the University of New South Wales, Australia, and Editor-in-Chief of the *Australian Journal of Management*. Her research interests reflect issues of concern to Accounting Standard setters and regulators, focusing on corporate reporting and especially the informational role of accounting constructs in contracting and firm valuation.

Tony Tollington is a Chartered Management Accountant and Senior Lecturer at Brunel University, UK. He has published extensively on the interface between marketing and accounting, notably in respect of brand assets.

Kenneth Weir, at the time of writing, was a PhD student at Heriot-Watt University, UK, where he also received his Masters degree in Accountancy and Finance in 2006. Prior to undertaking a postgraduate appointment, he provided research assistance for a study on employee wellness. His research interests include developments in management accounting practice, its links with other disciplines, and more generally critical accounting.

Mark Whittington is a Senior Lecturer in Accountancy and Finance at the University of Aberdeen, Scotland, UK. He teaches undergraduate and postgraduates specialising in financial analysis, management accounting and personal finance. Over the years he has also been responsible for running MBA programmes. His research interests include: financial analysis, strategic management accounting, performance measurement, customer accounting, corporate responsibility and accounting education. Before joining Aberdeen in 2003, Mark previously worked in industry as an accountant, then as a management trainer and for over a decade as an academic at Warwick Business School. In the past he has undertaken a wide variety of executive education assignments with organisations ranging from banks to engineering to advertising agencies.

Richard M.S. Wilson is Professor of Business Administration and Financial Management (Emeritus) at Loughborough University, having previously held chairs in these disciplines in several other universities. He holds degrees and professional qualifications in both marketing and accounting, has held academic and commercial appointments in each of these subject areas, and has published extensively on their interface as well as in the fields of marketing and accounting more broadly. For almost 40 years, on an international basis, he has been active in educational policy-making within marketing and accounting professional bodies relating to pre-qualifying and post-qualifying education. He is the founding Editor of *Accounting Education: an international journal* (of which he is currently Editor-in-Chief). During his career Professor Wilson has worked in more than a dozen countries, covering all five continents and, amongst other honours, has received two Lifetime Achievement Awards.

Introduction
The marketing / accounting interface

Robin Roslender, *Heriot Watt University, UK*
Richard M. S. Wilson, *Loughborough University, UK*

Abstract

Given: one marketing manager and one accounting manager. Finding: poor communication on financial criteria and goals.

(Berry 1977: 125)

The risk of this situation occurring is inevitably present when those with different professional roles are working in accordance with their own norms.

In his seminal paper on general systems theory, the economist Kenneth Boulding (1956) referred to the phenomenon of *"specialised ears and generalised deafness"*, which can be seen to exist when, for example, marketing managers are financially illiterate or accountants lack the necessary insights to design, implement and operate accounting systems which are useful to marketing managers in carrying out their roles. It is increasingly difficult to attach credence to the idea of marketing managers who lack financial skills, or accountants who fail to relate to the context in which marketing managers operate, hence understanding the marketing/accounting interface is important in generating emergent properties from the interaction of marketers and accountants (whereby the whole is greater than the sum of the parts).

As Hopwood noted (1976: 227):

It is paradoxical that whilst many of the most significant financial and accounting activities within any company start with the forecasts of market opportunities, sales volumes, prices and anticipated revenues, the explicit role of accounting and finance in the control of the marketing function itself has been neglected.

Those studying for an undergraduate degree or a master's degree in business administration or management studies will almost certainly be required to take courses in both Marketing and Accounting – although it is unlikely that the academic curriculum will focus on the interface of these two disciplines.

Some years ago, within two UK professional bodies (both of which have many registered students around the world) there was an explicit recognition within the respective curricula/examinations of the Chartered Institute of Marketing (CIM) on the one hand, and the Chartered Institute of Management Accountants (CIMA) on the other, of the importance of avoiding *generalised deafness* due to *specialised ears*. The CIM syllabus included a paper entitled "Financial Aspects of Marketing", and the CIMA syllabus included a paper entitled "Organization and Marketing Management". Neither of these papers has survived as a separate component of either curriculum, however; financial awareness is currently deemed to be implicit in the CIM's syllabus, as is marketing awareness within the CIMA's syllabus. This seems grossly unsatisfactory given the relative importance of having financially aware marketers, and accountants who recognise the imperatives of marketing orientation, if the effectiveness of organisations is to be enhanced.

The literature on the marketing/accounting interface can be traced back over many years – as is evident in Harrison's 1981 review. Early contributions were made by US-based authors such as Culliton, Goodman, Longman, Mossman, Sevin, Schiff, Bursk, with Canadian contributions from Shapiro, Australian contributions from Ratnatunga, and more recent British contributions being provided by Simmonds, Guilding, Piercy, Ambler, Shaw, Doyle, Roslender, Ward and Wilson.

In 2006 a *Call for Papers* was issued (see Appendix), the responses to which included the papers collected in this themed double issue of *JMM*. These papers could be located within the schematic framework of five key managerial questions which provides the structure of Wilson and Gilligan (2005), namely:

- Where are we now?
- Where do we want to be?
- How might we get there?
- Which way forward is best?
- How can we ensure arrival?

The second and third of these five key questions are the concerns of top management and senior/middle management respectively in specifying **ends** and **means**. The interface between marketing and accounting is more evident in relation to Question 1 (re *Planning*), Question 4 (re *Decision-making*) and Question 5 (re *Control*).

However, given the clustering of the accepted papers we thought it more appropriate for the purposes of this collection of papers to locate them as follows, with an increasing emphasis on metrics and customers as one works through the collection:

Studies on the marketing/accounting interface

Baljit K. Sidhu and John H. Roberts
The marketing/accounting interface - lessons and limitations

This paper explores the issues giving rise to the challenges on the interface and urges a stronger marketing-financial analyst dialogue, underpinned by a stronger marketing accounting shared language.

Robert M. Inglis
Exploring accounting and market orientation: an inter-functional case study

The findings from an inter-functional case study highlight a number of factors which potentially moderate the adoption of market-oriented accounting (MOA), and reveal a space in conceptual linkages between market orientation and contemporary management accounting techniques.

Nevine El-Tawy and Tony Tollington
The recognition and measurement of brand assets: an exploration of the accounting / marketing interface

The asset recognition criteria presented in this paper break free from the narrow, definitional and rule-based perspective of accounting epistemology to offer an alternative view based on the recognition of artefacts and the related notion of separability.

Applications

Tim Ambler and John H. Roberts
Assessing marketing performance: don't settle for a silver metric

This paper starts with the premise that marketing should be accountable, and considers by which measure (or measures) it should be held to account. It proceeds to rigorously evaluate alternative 'silver metrics' and comes out in favour of multiple metrics for assessing marketing performance.

Paul A. Phillips and Sue Vaux Halliday
Marketing / accounting synergy: a discussion of its potential and evidence in e-business planning

This paper sheds light on how e-business planning is taking place and identifies the key areas which are, together, acting as barriers to aligning organisational design, structures and people in the digitised world. It presents empirical evidence of *de facto* leadership being taken by the IT function, to the detriment of what might otherwise have been developed (i.e. a synergistic relationship between the marketing/ accounting planning interface and business performance).

Focusing on the customer

Christopher Guilding and Lisa McManus
Exploring the potential of customer accounting: a synthesis of the accounting and marketing literatures

In this paper a review of the marketing and accounting literatures shows that, to date, no previous study has examined the intersection of the marketing and accounting literatures pertinent to customer accounting (CA). It provides a synthesis of these two literatures in exploring the potential of CA.

Kenneth Weir
Examining the theoretical bases of customer valuation metrics

In this paper the intensification of marketing activity in the last 20 years, giving rise to greater needs for customer valuation and profitability metrics, is explored. The author seeks to clarify the theoretical influences underpinning alternative approaches, and offers some implications for the future development of customer valuation metrics.

Robin Gleaves and Jamie Burton
Accounting is from Mars, marketing is from Venus: counselling both disciplines to improve conceptualisation of customer profitability in business management

Marketing and management accounting have traditionally been poles apart in terms of both focus and approach, which highlights the need for greater synergy. In this paper a case is made (via a novel conceptual model) to establish a common 'platform of understanding' both within and between the two disciplines in order that further progress might be made.

Lynette Ryals
Determining the indirect value of a customer

This paper examines the development and application of three processes to determine indirect value in business-to-business and business-to-consumer contexts. It shows that indirect value has a measurable monetary impact which is not captured by conventional financial tools, and that understanding this fact changes the way in which customers are managed.

Conclusion

Robin Roslender and Richard M. S. Wilson
Accounting / marketing synergy: a final word but certainly not the last word

In this *Editorial Essay* the Guest Editors offer some concluding comments, while emphasising that there is a continuing need for developing a closer relationship between marketing and accounting in the interests of enhanced organisational effectiveness.

ACKNOWLEDGEMENTS

We would like to thank the Editor of *JMM*, Professor Susan Hart, for both facilitating and encouraging this themed issue, and the editorial staff at Westburn Publishers (especially Laura Hemming).

Our appreciation is also due to those who have helped by acting as referees for submissions received in response to the *Call for Papers* (which is reproduced at the end of this Editorial).

When we embarked on this venture in 2006, Tim Ambler of the London Business School was part of the team of Guest Editors, but he withdrew from this role during 2007 due to the pressure of his other commitments. Nevertheless, we are grateful to him for his contribution to setting up the project and his valuable role in reviewing several submissions.

It is our hope that this collection might make a modest contribution to achieving closer links and greater mutual understanding between accountants and their marketing colleagues in the interests of enhanced organisational effectiveness.

REFERENCES

Ambler, T. (2000), *Marketing and the Bottom Line: the marketing metrics to pump up cash flow*, London: FT/Prentice Hall.

Ambler, T., Barwise, P. and Higson, C. (2001), *Market Metrics: What shall we tell the shareholder?* London: ICAEW – Centre for Business Performance.

Ambler, T. and Kokkinaki, F. (1997), "Measures of Marketing Success", *Journal of Marketing Management*, Vol. 13, No. 7, pp. 665-78.

Berry, D. (1977), "Profit contribution: accounting and marketing interface", *Industrial Marketing Management*, Vol. 6, No. 2, pp. 125-8.

Boulding, K. (1956), General Systems Theory: The Skeleton of Science, *Management Science*, 1(1), April, pp. 197-208.

Bursk, E.C. (1966), View Your Customers as Investments, *Harvard Business Review*, Vol. 44, No. 3, May-June, pp. 91-4.

Culliton, J.W. (1948) *The Management of Marketing Costs*, Boston: Division of Research, Harvard Business School.

Doyle, P. (2000), *Value-Based Marketing*, Chichester: Wiley.

Goodman, S.R. (1970), *The Marketing Controller Concept: An Inquiry into Financial/ Marketing Relationships in Selected Consumer Companies*, Cambridge, Mass.: Marketing Science Institute (Special Report).

Guilding, C.J. and Pike, R.H. (1990), "Intangible Marketing Assets: A Managerial Accounting Perspective", *Accounting and Business Research*, Vol. 21, No. 18, pp. 41-9.

Harrison, G.L. (1981), "The Accountant's Role in Marketing: a Bibliographic Study and Analysis of its Origins and Development" pp 22-57 in Wilson, R.M.S. (ed.) (1981).

Hopwood, A.G. (1976), "Corporate Finance and Management Accounting", pp. 211-34 in *Use of Management and Business Literature*, London: Butterworth.

Longman, D.R. and Schiff, M. (1955) ,*Practical Distribution Cost Analysis*, Homewood, Illinois: Irwin.

Mossman, F.H., Crissy, W.J.E. and Fischer, P. M. (1978), *Financial Dimensions of Marketing Management*, New York: Wiley.

Piercy, N.J. (1987), "The Marketing Budgeting Process: Marketing Management Implications", *Journal of Marketing*, Vol. 51, No. 4, pp. 45-59.

Ratnatunga, J.T.D. (1988), *Accounting for Competitive Marketing*, London: CIMA (Occasional Paper Series)

Roslender, R. and Hart, S.J. (2002a), *Marketing and Management Interfaces in the Enactment of Strategic Management Accounting Practices: An Exploratory Investigation*, London: CIMA.

Roslender, R. and Hart, S.J. (2002b), "Integrating marketing and management accounting in the pursuit of competitive advantage: the case for strategic management accounting", *Critical Perspectives on Accounting*, Vol. 13, No. 2, pp. 255-277.

Roslender, R. and Hart, S.J. (2003), "In search of strategic management accounting: theoretical and field study perspectives", *Management Accounting Research*, Vol. 14, No. 3, pp. 255-279.

Roslender, R. and Hart, S.J. (2006), "Interfunctional cooperation in progressing accounting for brands. the case for brand management accounting", *Journal of Accounting and Organizational Change*, Vol. 2, No. 3, pp. 229-247.

Schiff, M. and Mellman, M. (1962), *Financial Management of the Marketing Function*, New York: FERF.

Sevin, C.H. (1965), *Marketing Productivity Analysis*, New York: McGraw-Hill.

Shapiro, S.J. and Kirpalani, V.H. (eds.) (1984), *Marketing Effectiveness: Insights from Accounting and Finance*, Boston: Allyn & Bacon.

Shaw, R. (1998), *Improving Marketing Effectiveness*, London: *The Economist* in association with Profile Books.

Simmonds, K. (1982), "Strategic Management Accounting for Pricing: A Case Example", *Accounting and Business Research*, Vol. 12, No. 47, pp. 206-14.

Simmonds, K. (1986), "The Accounting Assessment of Competitive Position", *European Journal of Marketing*, Vol. 20, No. 1, pp. 16-31.

Ward, K. (1989), *Financial Aspects of Marketing*, Oxford: Heinemann.

Wilson, R.M.S. (1973), *Management Controls in Marketing*, London: Heinemann/CIM.

Wilson, R.M.S. (ed.) (1981), *Financial Dimensions of Marketing*, (two volumes) London: Macmillan/CIMA.

Wilson, R.M.S. (1999), *Accounting for Marketing*, London: International Thomson Business Press.

Wilson, R.M.S. (ed.) (2001), *Marketing Controllership*, Aldershot: Ashgate. (A volume in the Dartmouth International Library of Management).

Wilson, R.M.S and Bancroft, A.L. (1983), *The Application of Management Accounting Techniques to the Planning and Control of Marketing of Consumer Non-durables*, London: CIMA (Occasional Paper Series).

Wilson, R.M.S. and Gilligan, C. (2005), *Strategic Marketing Management,* 3rd edition, Oxford: Elsevier.

APPENDIX: CALL FOR PAPERS

Promoting an Improved Marketing/Accounting Synergy

Work in the space covered by both marketing and accounting has increased in recent years. As both disciplines have expanded their activities, they have identified a coincidence of interests resulting in developments including strategic management accounting, corporate performance measurement, marketing accountability, customer relationship management and intellectual capital. These developments have built upon longer established interests in marketing controllership, brand accounting and pricing approaches. It therefore is opportune to assemble a collection of papers that provides a comprehensive survey of the state of the art of research and practice in the marketing-accounting joint space, including how this relates to previous developments and the prospect of further developments given the expansion of direct marketing, e-commerce and the central role attributed to relational capital assets.

With growing attention being given to performance measurement and management in both the marketing and management disciplines, this is also an ideal opportunity to record the current state of research in this important area.

Potential contributions are envisaged as being characterised by a significant degree of interdisciplinarity, mirroring a progressive abandonment of traditional silo or exclusive approaches to management. Submissions are therefore invited from researchers and practitioners in either discipline, or in other aspects of management, whose work is at or close to the interface with the other discipline. An indicative list of the topics that might be addressed in the special issue is:

- marketing accountability
- marketing controllership
- marketing efficiency and effectiveness
- marketing investment
- marketing performance measurement and reporting
- marketing productivity analysis
- the continuing use of PIMS data
- approaches to customer valuation
- valuing/managing marketing assets
- strategic management accounting
- preparing business/marketing/brand plans
- linking marketing activities with corporate goals

The marketing accounting interface – lessons and limitations

Baljit K. Sidhu, *University of New South Wales, Australia*
John H. Roberts, *University of New South Wales, Australia, and London Business School, UK*

Abstract The disciplines of Marketing and of Accounting are facing challenges that threaten their respective roles in the firm and beyond; the Marketing profession faces renewed threats to its place at the boardroom table, while the Accounting profession is beset by calls for indicators of shareholder value well beyond what is permitted under the traditional accounting model.

Much has been written about the need for marketing and accounting to get more in tune with the financial value of the firm. Little has been written about the need (or opportunity) for marketing to work more closely with the accounting function in reporting value creation or performance enhancements achieved through its activities. And yet, the accounts represent the primary and formal mechanism by which the firm reports its past financial performance, for internal control purposes and to the financial community. In the face of a widening accounting-finance gap (evidenced by growing Market to Book ratios) a closer marketing-accounting communication may allow accounting to increase its relevance to shareholder value without compromising its aversion to numbers involving uncertainty and judgment.

This paper explores the issues giving rise to these challenges and urges a stronger marketing-financial analyst dialogue underpinned by a stronger marketing-accounting shared language. We address some of the obstacles on this path, given that both groups have different objectives, methods and metrics, and discuss ways in which each discipline can leverage off the other.

INTRODUCTION

Marketing is losing its seat at the boardroom table (Kumar 2004) and accounting is losing its influence as an indicator of shareholder value. Much has been written about the need for marketing and accounting to get more in tune with the financial value of the firm. For example, in marketing Srivastava et al. (1999) argue for the process mapping of marketing activity all the way to shareholder value, while in accounting Lev (2004) describes the danger to accounting of using measurements that do not speak to the market-based value of the firm. Little has been written about the need (or opportunity) for marketing to work more closely with the reported accounting performance of the firm. And yet, the accounts represent the primary and formal mechanism by which the firm reports its past financial performance, for internal control purposes and to the financial community.

Therefore, even if a better marketing-finance understanding underpins a stronger marketing-financial analyst dialogue, it stands to reason a stronger marketing-accounting shared language must underpin a Marketing Director-CFO one. Similarly, the widening accounting-finance gap (evidenced by growing Market to Book ratios and often driven by the rise of marketing intangibles) means that a closer marketing-accounting communication may allow accounting to increase its relevance to shareholder value without compromising its aversion to numbers involving uncertainty and judgment.

Such a shared marketing-accounting language is not without its problems. Both groups have different objectives and vehicles by which to achieve them, and therefore tend to focus on different metrics. In this paper we look at some of the issues that need to be addressed in improving the marketing-accounting interface and how they might be addressed by actions on both sides. We also look at accounting practices and marketing practices and see what there is to be learned in the approaches of the one that might benefit the other.

To examine potential benefits of a closer marketing-accounting relationship and the areas in which that might occur we examine the nature of marketing, the nature of accounting and relevant issues currently vexing the practitioners and stakeholders of both. Because of the central role of shareholder value analysis (SVA), we also give a brief review of that area and its relation to marketing and accounting. In this paper our primary purpose is not to provide an exhaustive review of challenges facing all aspects of marketing, accounting and shareholder value analysis, but rather to bring together those parts that relate to an improved accounting-marketing interface.

MARKETING AS A DISCIPLINE

The leading marketing text, Kotler and Keller (2006, p. 6), quotes the American Marketing Association's definition of marketing;

an organization function or set of processes for creating, communicating, and delivering value to customers and for managing customer relationships in ways that benefit the organization and its stakeholders.

We are more drawn to Ambler and Roberts' (2006a) more ambitious definition of marketing as *"what the whole firm does to source and harvest cash flow"* since this moves emphasis to what marketing does, as opposed to who does it, finessing the need for turf fights. That is, marketing's job is to generate income streams. It uses resources (inputs) to create current and future outputs. It incurs expenses to develop revenue.[1]

Marketers have not been perceived as unambiguously successful in this quest. And they are currently under attack on a variety of fronts. Problems often identified as facing marketers include:

- They lack a voice in the board room. For example, Doyle (2000, p. 1) notes that only 12 top 100 U.K. CEOs in 2000 had marketing experience and only 57% of companies had marketing represented on their board.

- Marketing is seen as an expense, and a discretionary one at that. When marketing is seen as an expense it is subject to the vagaries of arbitrary budget cuts. Kaplan and Atkinson (1989, p. 531) state *"examples of discretionary expense centres are some marketing activities such as advertising, promotion and warehousing. For marketing functions often no strong relation exists between inputs and outputs. We are unable to determine whether they are operating efficiently. Given the difficulty of measuring the efficiency of discretionary expense centres, a natural tendency may arise for their managers to desire a very high quality department even though a somewhat lower quality department would provide almost the same service at significantly lower costs"*.

- Marketing is not seen to be accountable. In an environment with a growing need for accountability, Kotler and Keller (2006, p557) point out that *"senior managers want to know the outcomes and revenues relating from communications investments. Too often, however, their communications directors supply only outputs and expenses: press clipping counts, number of ads placed, media costs"*. To quote Dominic Cadbury, Chairman of Cadbury Schweppes, *"There is growing pressure from shareholders to make marketing more accountable. Investors are becoming more active in analysing and questioning marketing expenditures"* (in Doyle 2000, p. 295).

- A result of this lack of accountability can be a loss of visibility. To quote Ambler (2003, p 5), *"Brand equity, for many companies, is by far their biggest and most valuable asset. It lacks the attention it deserves because it is not on the balance sheet and it is hard to measure"*. Marketing is thus perceived as unimportant or non-central. A survey for Accenture by O'Halloran and Mosher (2004) found that just 23 per cent of executives in their sample said that marketing makes a very significant contribution and of those that considered marketing one of their three most important functions, only 28 per cent thought that their marketing department performed any better than those of their competitors.

- Even where visibility is high, satisfaction with the marketing function does not always follow. Ambler (2003, p 17) quotes a Marketing Leadership Council survey which suggests that 63 per cent of members are dissatisfied with the marketing measurement systems and that on average they felt they were wasting 26% of their marketing budget (an improvement of the legendary 50% of waste claimed by Lord Leverhulme, founder of Unilever PLC).

This combination of factors leads to a number of negative outcomes both for marketing and for its stakeholders, including the CEO and shareholders. Perhaps the major

---

[1] It is not relevant to our discussion whether marketing is **the** customer-facing function within the firm that generates customers and cash flows or one of the functions.

one of these is potential under-investment due to imperfect understanding of causal mechanisms. This can be manifested in at least two ways. First, if there is information uncertainty that is resolvable a priori but is not resolved, some projects which could have been shown to be worth undertaking will not be undertaken. Second if only part of the resultant returns stream is identified (as would be the case, for example, if advertising had both a contemporaneous and a carry over effect but only the former were measured) then under-investment will also occur.

ACCOUNTING AS A DISCIPLINE

Accounting may also be defined is a variety of ways. The Miriam Webster on line dictionary (2007) defines it as *"the system of recording and summarizing business and financial transactions and analyzing, verifying, and reporting the results"*. This definition applies to accounting irrespective of whether it pertains to internal reporting (management accounting) or reporting to external stakeholders (financial accounting). Firms are largely free to devise internal reporting or management accounting systems to suit their individual needs. In contrast, external (financial) reporting is highly regulated by bodies such as the Financial Accounting Standards Board (FASB) in the United States and similar bodies elsewhere. It is the shortcomings in external reporting that are central to many of the arguments in this paper. More formally, the FASB states that

> *Financial reporting is not an end in itself but is intended to provide information that is useful in making business and economic decisions—.for making reasoned choices among alternative uses of scarce resources in the conduct of business and economic activities*

(FASB, 2008 paragraph 9)

The statement is telling because it provides a criterion against which we can measure the success of accounting; is it assisting in the efficient allocation of resources? Accounting is often used in a more narrow sense to report on the generation of (mainly historical) income and cash flow streams and assessments of financial position to various stakeholders. The difference is an important one. Past income streams are considerably less ambiguous than future ones and so much less open to manipulation in reporting. Much of accounting focuses on the past because the criterion of reliability makes accountants very wary of uncertain promises of cash – and that includes the future to a greater or lesser extent.

However, different users have different requirements and thus need different measures. Like marketing, accounting is also under siege, but for very different reasons. Some of the problems facing accountants that are relevant to our concerns of the marketing-accounting interface include:

- Pressure to value the intangible assets of the firm. *"Accounts measure monetary flows well. Intangibles challenge this"* (European Commission 2003). That is, the rise of intangibles reduces the relative relevance of past cash flows because intangible assets by their very definition are indicators of the ability to generate *future* cash flows. If we ignore this factor, we do not include the full value of the firm. However, accountants are suspicious of intangibles. They recognise the danger of capitalising marketing costs (into intangible assets). The dot com bubble exacerbated this fear. For example, Penman (2007, p.653) cites the example of AOL that capitalised its customer acquisition costs and saw its share price drop from $ 35 to almost $ 10 when retention rates were lower than anticipated, leading to reduced expected customer lifetime values. Penman (2007, p.51) explains the danger of such practices by saying, *"but the critique was one of accounting that allowed speculation to enter the financial statements (and of the deviance of compromised management, directors, and auditors who wished to inflate profits). So fundamental analysts have a maxim: **Don't mix what you know with what you don't know**"* (emphasis added). Financial statements contain only "concrete information" (p. 640), as specified by the reliability criterion.

- Difficulties in applying the matching principle. Balanced against the reliability criterion is the matching principle: that revenues should be matched with the expenses incurred to generate them. Even the advocates of conservative accounting recognise the difficulty of reconciling these two principles. Penman (2007, p. 52) notes that *"there is a tension between the matching principle and reliability criterion and, in the case of R&D and advertising, GAAP [Generally Accepted Accounting Principles] comes down on the side of mismatching"*. One of the consequences is less than relevant valuation of assets (in the sense of reflecting market price). Penman (2007, p.82) acknowledges that, *"there may be so-called intangible assets – such as brand assets, knowledge assets and managerial assets – missing from the balance sheet because accountants find their values too hard to measure under the GAAP 'reliability' criterion. The accounting profession has essentially given up on this idea and placed it in the 'too difficult basket'"*.

While this problem may indeed be very difficult, those using financial statements do need a reliable answer to it. Burgeoning Market to Book ratios have greatly exacerbated this problem. For example, Ambler (2003, p. 208) shows how quickly these have grown. We calculate it to be a rate of 11% per annum over the past twenty years and 14% per annum over the past ten. With the ratio currently sitting at well over 6, this means that what the accounts are explaining in terms of the market's view of the value of the firm is only a fifth as important as what they are not explaining (except to the extent that other elements can be inferred from the firm's accounts). For many firms the problem is more extreme. For example, while Penman (2007, p. 556) notes that Coca Cola is a *"brand management firm"* since brands are the key drivers of value creation in the firm, he acknowledges that fundamental accounting cannot help in the assessment of that value. Many of these firms have negative shareholder equity if brands are not included on their balance sheet (Ambler 2003, p 209). Brand values often represent the majority of their market capitalisations (reaching as high as 81% in the case of Nestlé according to Ambler 2003). These points apply equally well to other intangibles termed by Srivastava et. al. (1998) *"market based assets"*, including customer and collaborator relationships, as well as non-marketing intangibles. They also apply to many of the tangible assets of the firm.

Lev (2003b, p. 521) talks of *"the growing disconnect between market values and financial information"* and suggests that accounting as a profession is at risk (Lev 2000). Lev (2003a) claims that conservative accounting is not always conservative and is often inconsistent. He suggests that, *"the accounting rules for intangibles do not make much economic sense or common sense"*. He outlines the problems of recognising intangibles and regards failure to address them as continuing the decline of accounting. What Lev (2004) calls the *"information brown out"* leads

Doyle (2000, p. 43) to note that *"book value nowadays is a poor measure of the real value of a company's assets"*. It is worth pointing out that some accountants still question the wisdom of recognising intangibles (or even disclosing them), even if the implementation problems could be addressed. For example, Kanodia et al. (2003) develop a stylised model in which, for some situations (primarily related to noise in measurement), the disadvantages of such recognition outweigh the advantages. Meanwhile, others show that the decline in "value relevance" of accounting reports is worst in companies which are *less* (rather than *more*) conservative in the recognition of intangible assets. (Balachandran and Mohanram 2006).

By and large, the problem of dealing with intangibles does not present a problem in acknowledging that past cash flows have been made for particular purposes such as brand building or customer acquisition. The real problem arises in determining what portion of cash outlays should be formally recognised ("booked") as signalling a reasonable expectation of future benefits. At one level, this may involve capitalising rather than expensing past costs, acknowledging that revenue is likely to arise from them and so according to the matching principle these costs should be carried forward (capitalised) and expensed against revenue in some future period(s). At a more fundamental level, it may involve trying to ascertain the future earning potential of intangible assets (discounted appropriately by time and the probability of them not eventuating) which may be substantially more (or less) than the expense (cost) involved in generating them. That is, the core of the debate is around valuation and the statement of assets, although that then affects the profit and loss statement. The problem is that under the current regime, the relationship between what accountants report as the book value of the firm and what the market regards as the (expected net present) value of the firm is weakening quite quickly. For example, Lev (2001, Figure 4-2) shows that from 1980 to 1996 the fit of the relationship went from an $\bar{R}^2$ 0.82 to 0.54. We infer from this a drop of 0.02 each year (t=-5.5 and $\bar{R}^2 = 0.67$).

While recent IFRS and FASB changes recognise this problem, they do not solve it. Internally generated intangible assets are still not recognised. To quote McLannahan (2003): *"The new rules alone aren't able to provide the "full picture" of how a company is creating value from its intangibles"*.

VALUE BASED MANAGEMENT AS A MANAGEMENT APPROACH

Shareholder Value Analysis (SVA) while not the central focus of this paper, provides a vehicle by which we can establish a common language and set of metrics that have currency in both the accounting and the marketing literatures. In marketing channel terms, SVA may provide a push to marketers to demonstrate their contribution and a pull to accountants to prove the relevance of their numbers. We do not aim to give a comprehensive overview of SVA here. Rather our objective is to use SVA as an integrative tool to help establish a marketing activity-accounting performance shared currency.

Doyle (2000) summarises the philosophy behind SVA well when he says, *"The heart of SVA is that economic value is created only when the business earns a return on investment that exceeds its cost of capital"*. What puts SVA proponents in conflict with conservative accountants is often around when that return is recognised. SVA's preparedness to estimate and recognise uncertain future net income streams tends to be based on a decision analytic framework, which attempts to cope with uncertainty by calculating expected values. This push to market valuation has put its proponents at loggerheads with conservative accountants, who have concerns about a moral hazard problem of using firms' estimates of their future earnings. As Lev (2003a, p. 520) says, *"some of the limitations of accounting-based information are rooted in the structure of accounting, which essentially reflects legally binding transactions with third parties"*. He notes that this was relevant in agricultural and industrial societies, but in a knowledge-based economy, *"much of the value-creation or destruction precedes, sometimes by years, the occurrence of transactions"*. The result can lead to goals inconsistent with the interests of many stakeholders. Doyle (2000, p 3), for example, says *"many managers have confused maximising shareholder value and maximising profitability. The two are completely different. Maximising profitability is short term and invariably erodes a company's long-term market competitiveness"*.

While financial analysts are creating challenges for marketers (in terms of demonstrating their return) and accountants (in terms of providing a realistic view to enable optimal resource valuations and allocations noted earlier in this section), they have their own problems too. These include:

- Information about a large part of the firm's assets is missing. Market to Book ratios of 6 show that only a small part of the firm's value is visible. This average is slightly better than the 10% of an iceberg that is visible, but for many firms the proportion is less than the tip of an iceberg. The measurement error (variance) of components not covered in the accounts can be quite high.

- Credibility of information. While the firm gives analysts earnings and cash flow information, Eccles and his colleagues (2001, p. 128) found that in order of importance as performance measures these ranked only 5th and 9th respectively. Other information may be available, but it is not subject to the same quality control as earnings or cash flow numbers. In fact, with such limited amount of formal information on intangibles, analysts must read as much as they can into earnings and company's estimates of future earnings. This leads to what Eccles et al. (2001, p. 70) call "The Earnings Game", with a National Investor Relations Institute survey finding a 90 per cent participation rate. That is, there may be bias in estimates as well as high variance further increasing the mean squared error of non-recognised value components.

In this environment, from a financial analyst's perspective there is a need for financially based tools that identify how increased (or decreased) marketing expenditure can grow (or not commensurately shrink) earnings now and in the future and a need for process-based accounting that is better able to account for the value of the firm, as recognised by financial markets.

Focusing on value-based management is not new, but it may be new to many marketers and accountants. Its adoption has benefits that accrue to a variety of stakeholders. Increased information leads to better valuations, lower risk for investors and lower cost of capital for investors. This was demonstrated experimentally in a PwC study (McLannahan 2003) and in the marketplace by Lev (2004, p. 116). Managerially, this should lead to better resource allocation and so greater wealth creation. Furthermore, benefits are both diagnostic and prognostic. By understanding the relative performance of resources across time more accurately, better deployment of them is possible. However, from a forecasting perspective, not only might accuracy be increased (McLannahan 2003), it may be received earlier. Both Urban and Hauser (1983, p520-21) in marketing and Ittner and Larcker (2003) in accounting demonstrate that intermediate variables lead financial outcomes and therefore detect trends before them. Finally, the problems of not recognising intangible assets as an integrated part of the financial reporting basis are well argued by Lev (2004).

Having looked at both marketing and accounting, and their relation to shareholder value analysis, we proceed to examine the three links between the three groups.

THE MARKETING-ACCOUNTING INTERFACE

The most surprising thing about the marketing-accounting dialogue is that there is no dialogue. The leading marketing text, Kotler and Keller (2006) devotes all of 5 of its 729 pages to accounting. In return, Penman's authoritative text on financial analysis devotes 1 page to marketing outlays and that is merely a warning on the dangers of not expensing it (Penman 2007). Accounting provides the respected and accepted means by which past financial transactions of the firm are calibrated. It is inexcusable for marketers not to understand the basis on which that is done. No one is going to seriously suggest that accounting does not have something important to say about the economic progress of the firm. Conversely, our colleague, Tim Ambler, is very fond of pointing out that accountants count cash. Marketers generate cash (and spend it too). Again, it seems obvious that some understanding on the part of accountants of the transformation process by which money spent is turned into money earned is essential if they are to do their job properly.

THE ACCOUNTING-VALUATION INTERFACE

The mutuality of need between accountants and those who value the firm and its actions is similarly reasonably self-evident. Accountants' task to provide information for resource allocation and financial valuation is an important scorecard by which progress is calibrated. (One could argue that it has become something of a holy grail, for better or worse in that respect.) If valuers are to do their job accurately they are going to have to rely heavily on financial records, at least as a starting point for their analysis.

As far as performance of this link goes, Doyle (2000, p. 20) is damning in his assessment of the influence of accounting on market valuation, claiming *"accounting profits encourage an excessively short term view of business. They also encourage under-investment in information based assets – staff, brands and customer and supplier relationships"*. These are exactly the means of production that Srivastava et. al. (1998) term market-based assets and argue are the future life-blood of the firm. Indeed, Doyle (2000, p. 22) goes so far as to say *"if the market value of the shares exceeds the book value of the firm, it has created value"*. That is, Doyle thinks of value created not as that reflected in the books, but that **not** reflected in the books!

THE MARKETING-VALUATION INTERFACE

The final link is that between marketing and financial valuation. Given that marketing aims to both generate contemporaneous net cash flow and long term market-based assets (Srivastava et al. 1998) one can argue that, given current accounting treatment of internally generated intangible assets, SVA presents an ideal opportunity to make

FIGURE 1 Main functions of marketing, accounting, and financial valuation

MARKETING ACTIVITIES	ACCOUNTING RECORDS	MARKET VALUATION

Product Management
  Features
  New products
  Product range
 	
Communications
 	
Distribution
 	
Pricing
	Profit and loss
	  Income recognition
	  Expense recognition
	
	Balance sheet reports
	  Assets
	  Liabilities
	  Equity
	
	Cash flow reports
		Market capitalisation
		
		Revenue stream
		  persistence
		Risk profile
		Growth opportunities
		Timing of cash flows
		Volatility

the case for the long term contribution of marketing efforts. Marketing's performance, however, is less fulsome. Doyle (2000, p. 19) sees marketing's failure to incorporate shareholder value principles as fundamental to its loss of influence. *"Because the link between marketing strategy and shareholder value has not been made, boards have tended to look at two more transparent strategies [cost reduction and acquisition]".* Doyle (2000, p. 21) sees SVA as the way for marketers to break accountants' lock on an overly conservative constraint on its potential in the future. He says

> *SVA encourages profitable marketing investments. Conventional accounting has treated marketing expenditures as costs rather than investments in intangible assets. Because the long-term profit streams generated by such assets are ignored, marketing is under-funded in many businesses. SVA, however, is future oriented. It encourages the long-term effects of marketing expenditures to be explicitly estimated. Brand building investments that would be discouraged under conventional accounting procedures because they reduce current profits are shown to be creating value under SVA.*

To some extent this separation of the valuation of intangibles from the formal accounts, advanced by Doyle, is already happening. At HIT Entertainment, for example, the CFO is *"taking the route that other CFOs are being forced down – moving beyond the realm of accounting standards to share with external stakeholders the impact that specific intangibles have on earnings"* (McLannahan 2002).

We can summarise the relationship between these three groups in Figure 1 above.

BARRIERS AND DRIVERS TO IMPROVING THE MARKETING – ACCOUNTING INTERFACE

We use our analysis of these three groups and the relation between them, particularly marketing and accounting, to understand the forces driving closer synergy and cooperation between the two, and barriers preventing it.

Drivers

There are real benefits for marketing if it learns to speak the language of business, as accounting has often been called. It leads to legitimacy and credibility. As Ambler (2003, p 73) puts it, *"Brand valuation gets the marketing foot in the Exec's door if it is not already there"*. For accountants and CFOs, the adoption of such techniques by marketers helps them with their budgeting and resource allocation, providing performance tools. For the CEO, the accountability for which many stakeholders (including not just financial analysts but also regulatory bodies, tax authorities, and community groups) have been calling is closer to hand. Disclosure is valued. Lev (2004, p 116) shows that fuller disclosure is associated with narrower bid-ask spreads, indicating a lower cost of capital and less share price volatility.

Barriers

What, then, are the barriers to this happening? Firstly, different groups have different objectives and different objectives lead to different philosophies. From an accounting perspective, barriers to increased disclosure by working with marketing to gain mutually acceptable indicators of marketing performance may lead to legal liability, loss of commercially sensitive information, and cost (Lev 2004). An examination of the cost of implementing Sarbanes-Oxley suggests that mandated compliance costs should not be under-estimated (see Basilo 2007). From a marketing perspective, one of the fears of measuring everything is a fear of loss of creativity. Einstein is reputed to have said *"You can't count everything that counts and everything you can count doesn't count"*. Warming to this theme, Stirtz (2006) counsels against trying to measure all marketing outputs (and certainly not its intermediate products, as would be required for comprehensive intangible value reporting).

Personally, we are optimistic, and the source of this optimism stems from trends in both professions. Given the current emphasis of marketing and accounting illustrated in Figure 2, it is unsurprising that a joint purpose is not always clear and that conflicting objectives abound (arrow 1). However, trends in marketing to prove its value must be expressed in the language of accounting, leading to a much stronger

FIGURE 2 Current and future drivers of marketing - accounting coordination

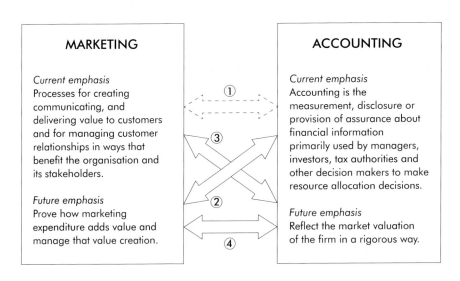

arrow 2. Similarly, trends in accounting towards more value relevance are going to force accountants to understand the future contribution that marketing is poised to make (in terms of its market based assets), arrow 3. However, as both functions move to support the idea of a value based firm, it will not be an intersection of self interest that unites them to work more closely together, but a confluence of mutual interest (arrow 4). This view is very much in keeping with the strategy mapping view of the firm advanced by Kaplan and Norton (2004) and obviously involves other functional groups, such as HR and R&D as well.

METHODS OF ADDRESSING THE GAPS

Given this somewhat rosy view of the future of marketing-accounting liaison, it behoves us to identify some steps as to where and how this might happen. We believe that a number of steps are necessary to further this process. We note that much can be learned from already established methods in the sphere of managerial accounting as well as from early efforts within the marketing discipline; we do this by drawing on appropriate examples in making our suggestions for going forward.

Inter-relation of uncertain information with financial statements

Consideration of a broader range of information does not have to mean 'recognition' in a financial accounting sense where accounting data have to pass the tests of relevance and reliability to be 'booked' through to the financial statements. Disclosure may well do. Inter-relation implies that those analysing company performance can understand how different pieces of information relate to each other and they get a consistent and complete view of the world. Many accounting scholars have pointed to the inconsistencies of current GAAP accounting practices. It is clearly inconsistent to recognise externally generated (purchased) intangible assets, but not internally generated ones; the argument for this is of course the relative 'reliability' (or more accurately, the 'verifiability') of the former and the relative uncertainties inherent in the latter. Penman (2007, p.640) acknowledges that *"financial statements contain estimates and estimates involve speculation"*. Rather than trying to ring fence the known and the unknown, we argue it makes much better sense to understand the probability distribution (or at least the variance) of each variable. Black and white. Known and unknown. This dichotomisation gains less meaning as the value of current assets in generating future cash flows moves uncomfortably into the middle of the spectrum between 0 and 1. By studying the distribution of intermediate productive factors, and understanding their relationships with other variables, we can then attempt to be more scientific about the distribution of likely earnings outcomes from different forms of intangible assets. Essentially, this is what financial analysts are doing now on an individual judgment-forming basis. Indeed, an early proponent of shareholder value analysis (Rappaport 1986) basically urges just such an approach in a more recent paper calling for disclosure of payoff estimates with confidence levels and also providing investors with confidence levels for various accounting accruals made in the computation of revenue and expense items (Rappaport 2006).

Better reporting of intermediate constructs

Ambler and Roberts (2006 a, b) argue strongly against the use of a silver metric; a single set of financial measures of future performance without a set of intermediate measures behind them, on which they are based, and a causal link that leads between the two. It is interesting that Nagar and Rajan (2005) find empirical support for this position. They report *"we find that metrics do not individually predict future earnings, but gain significance in a collective setting, increasing the predictive power substantially"*.

With respect to intermediate measures, the need is there, but not the performance. Eccles et al. (2001, p. 133) show that while many of these measures are seen as important to managers, the current information gap is perceived to be substantial. Customer turnover rates, new product success rates, customer acquisition costs, brand equity, and segment performance are just some of the intermediate marketing variables where analysts and investors in their survey identified a large or very large gap.

We believe that intermediate marketing measures will not be accepted by the financial community unless they are based on a sound business model (value chain analysis) and collected by objective, reliable and valid methods. Penman (2007, p.8) has a point in one of his criticisms when he says of the dot com crash,

> *analysts relied heavily on non-financial metrics like page views, usage metrics, customer reach, and capacity utilization. These metrics may give some indication of profitability but they don't guarantee it. The onus is on the analyst to show how these indicators translate into future profits.*

All management disciplines, including managerial accounting, are developing good techniques to map such processes (e.g., Kaplan and Norton 2004) and to calibrate such maps. Again, performance does not match the desire. Ittner and Larcker (2003) note that most respondents in their survey of 157 companies do not trace causality between their measures. Of the 23% that do, they had a 2.95% higher ROA and a 5.14% higher ROE than other respondents. Doyle (2000, Figure 2.1) has a nice diagram in which he depicts organisation value drivers being harnessed by marketing value drivers to create financial value drivers. This linking provides a valuable way in which marketing can be thought of as harnessing the distinctive competences of the firm to meet customer needs and thus generate economic rents for it. It coincides reasonably closely with Kaplan and Norton's (2004, Figure 7-1) strategic mapping process.

Start with objectives

O'Halloran and Mosher (2004) point out that the identification of objectives is a prerequisite to the specification of appropriate measures and they provide a useful beginning. Ambler (2003, p. 5) also observes that what we measure should be dictated by the decisions that are going to be based on that measurement. Lev (2003a) provides a nice framework of what that might look like from an accounting perspective, while Srivastava et al. (1998) show what it might look like from a marketing one. An obvious place to search for synergy between accounting and marketing is in the common elements of these two approaches.

Quantify risk and uncertainty

One of the problems accountants have with recognising intangibles is the uncertainty of the future returns that arise from them. Methodology for corporate risk assessment is now well-developed. The statistical models that sophisticated marketers such as General Mills use provide confidence limits to their estimates. We need to refine and then incorporate measures of uncertainty. A probabilistic view of the world will allow appropriate associated discount rates to be identified. To undertake this, firms need to identify sources of threat (to calculate the distribution of the persistence of current earnings) and growth (to estimate the opportunity to generate new ones). While there are certainly imponderables in the environment, any valuation is going to implicitly take these into account. How much better off would we be if we were to undertake that exercise systematically and explicitly. Such risk assessment (Eccles et al. (2001, p. 154) identifying various types of market, credit, operational, and accounting risks is good business practice and a precursor to taking action to prevent negative outcomes.

Acceptability to all parties

If joint (or at least co-ordinated) measurement, reporting and monitoring methods are to be successful, they must be acceptable to all players.

Accountants

In order to be accepted by accountants joint monitoring and measurement systems must be objective and transparent. Ambler (2003, p. 8) suggests that perceived objectivity for the marketing department may be achieved by turning the market research responsibility over to the CFO. We remain agnostic about this idea, but endorse the need for both actual and perceived objectivity and transparency.

Where many measures do not pass the reliability criterion, there is a strong argument for disclosure rather than recognition. Disclosure provides the information and then the market can decide on its value. From an industry perspective, Gross (2001), for example, argues for disclosure, rather than recognition of brand values. Disclosure brings with it a strong signal. Eccles et al. (2001, p. 144) quote findings from a laboratory simulation, which finds that "Explicit disclosures" (of risk) *"lead to more efficient market reactions, even when the same information can be inferred from the financial statements"*. Meanwhile, Luft and Shields (2003) show in an experimental setting that individuals are not totally efficient in assimilating information on intangibles.

This joint and coordinated reporting does not marginalise accounting, but rather establishes its relevance and context. Lev (2000, p. 14) says that he does not want to throw the baby out with the bath water (even if he does not use those terms). He says *"GAAP accounting, however, is highly relevant as a feedback system against which the extensive array of expectations forming the basis of both internal and external decisions are continually evaluated and revised"*.

Marketers

Marketers need information that will help them to focus marketing activity. They know that some forms of marketing activity (e.g., price promotions) have more substantial short term effects, while others (e.g., mass media advertising) if they are to be effective will be relatively more so in the longer term. Any coordination with better accounting information must better inform those trade offs (including uncertainty and time value of money differences).

Marketers need to undertake both market sensing and market facing activities. The rules of value establishment for the firm can also be applied to the customer. This is happening extensively in business to business marketing in terms of the calculation of economic value to the customer. However, as the concept of the networked organisation evolves, the use of accounting disciplines to assess (and distribute) value will also need to be applicable to customers, consumers and collaborators.

Shareholder value analysts

From a financial analyst perspective, intermediate constructs must be related to value downstream and marketing activity upstream. This is also already beginning to happen. Brands (what marketers build) have been shown to be associated with the market value of the firm, which signals the generation of future benefits (e.g., Barth et al. 1998 and Ambler 2003, p.72). Superior customer management (those for whom marketers build brands) has also been shown to be a leading indicator of market value and earnings growth (e.g., Fornell et al. 2006). Hand (2003) shows a 24 cent net present value for each dollar spent on advertising. It shows increasing returns to scale, suggesting that it can represent a barrier to entry and that under-investment carries with it a double penalty.

Barriers must be overcome

While many of the actions above aim to leverage drivers to a closer accounting-marketing relationship, we must also address barriers in order for it to be successful. For example, one prerequisite to success is that capable internal systems must precede external reporting (European Commission 2003). The credibility of these must be established. For example, Gray (2004) suggests that marketing information is not valued because the linkages to financial outcomes are hard and have not been proven in many organisations. Legacy systems make such migration difficult, but moves to enterprise software promote the potential for integrated and internally consistent reporting.

For information to be credible, systems must be in place to ensure against manipulation and address moral hazard and adverse selection problems. Penman (2007, Table 17.1) identifies possible sources of manipulation. And we are likely to see new forms of audit of performance, somewhat akin to the due diligence processes undertaken in acquisition activity. In this area accountants have well-developed skills.

Of course there can be a tension between the value of the more detailed information to the investor and proprietary costs of such disclosure to the firm. Such a tension can act as a (strong) potential barrier to such disclosures (Verrecchia, 1983). For example, the loss of commercially sensitive information to competitors and trade partners has been identified as a threat (McLannahan 2003). This to some extent is offset by the ability to benchmark performance on a much wider and more diagnostic set of variables. Some firms are addressing this problem by the use of indices to disguise sensitive data.

By-products of cooperation

Closer cooperation between marketers and accountants is likely to lead to a skills interchange. Accountants can teach marketers a number of business disciplines that may well increase their efficiency. For example, the use of variance analysis in managerial accounting to analyse where actual performance deviated from budgeted performance can lead to a learning organisation. Reporting Standards recommended or mandated by FASB and scorecards and tools such as a DuPont analysis developed within the spheres of managerial accounting and analysis can help marketing on its road to increased professionalism and accountability. Similarly, marketers can teach accountants a number of techniques. Marketers have quite sophisticated models about the sales trajectories of new products (the diffusion of innovations). The details of marketing (income generating) activities are likely to give accountants a comprehensive view of the health of the firm and its future ability to generate free cash flows.

Effects on other stakeholders

Other groups are likely to benefit from (and become involved in) this more integrated view of the firm. This includes other stakeholders within the firm such as other functional groups. The European Commission (2003) has identified the need for a more holistic view of the firm. CEOs and Boards will find decision making easier when differences between the marketing view of the world and that of the accounting department have been reconciled, leading to more objective decision making. External to the firm, shareholders will be better informed. Amir et al. (2003) studied whether financial analysts were filling the information gap left by firms failing to report on the marketing (and other) assets. While they found that this was somewhat the case, analysts only made up for a small part of the information gap. Government and regulatory bodies also have a lot to gain. Governments have a policy role in the provision of infrastructure and regulation to maximise competitiveness. The British Minster for Trade and Industry, Patricia Hewitt, sees better information on firms as one means for governments to undertake this function more effectively (Department of Trade and Industry 2004). To quote the European Commission (2003) *"The hidden productive economy demands new measurement tools"*. We have provided some ideas as to how this might be done. Some of the steps involved in the process are summarised in Figure 3. Different variables and different measures may be used for different purposes by different stakeholders but what is required are what

FIGURE 3 Some steps required to bring about marketing – accounting information coordination

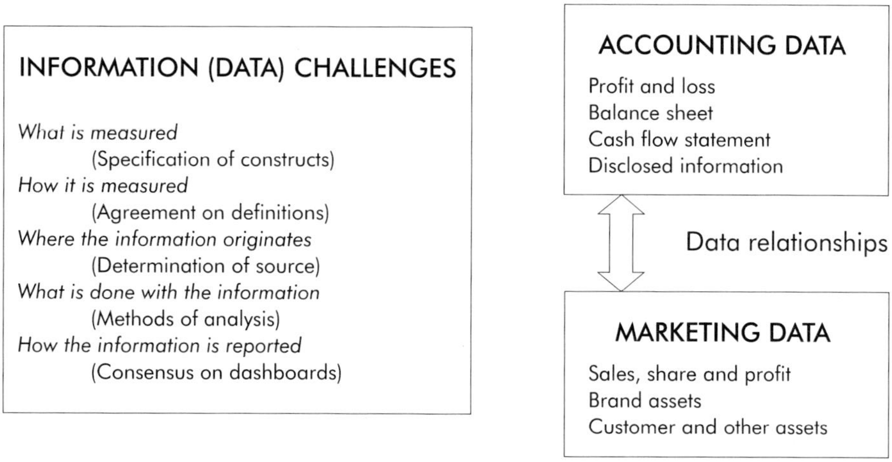

INFORMATION (DATA) CHALLENGES

What is measured
       (Specification of constructs)
How it is measured
       (Agreement on definitions)
Where the information originates
       (Determination of source)
What is done with the information
       (Methods of analysis)
How the information is reported
       (Consensus on dashboards)

ACCOUNTING DATA
Profit and loss
Balance sheet
Cash flow statement
Disclosed information

Data relationships

MARKETING DATA
Sales, share and profit
Brand assets
Customer and other assets

sociologists would call bridge points between shared nodes (variables) and agreed relationships (common links). That is, we need shared definitions in each language and translations between them. Obviously, it is very important that such initiatives are not only supported by government (as is happening in Denmark and France), but also by industry bodies and professional and standards associations.

SUMMARY AND CONCLUSIONS

We have argued that both accounting and marketing face challenges to their respective roles of reporting and generating firm performance through customer facing activities. While both groups must understand the market imperative to relate their activities to a modern understanding of the value of the firm (shareholder value analysis), there needs to be a morphological relationship between them. Neither profession has to surrender what they do. They just have to relate it to the value created in the long term for the firm. We also believe that what might previously have been seen as odd bedfellows can have considerable synergy in facing this challenge together. Marketing can gain financial discipline and credibility from accountants, while accountants can gain a deeper understanding of the nature of the assets they are describing and a richer view as to how the firm is performing in harnessing them from marketers. Shareholder Value Analysis provides a powerful mechanism by which both groups can find a common ground. Again, neither side needs to stop doing what they have been doing. What each does need to do is to draw a link to the approaches and objectives of the other. To some extent this is already happening as evidenced in Rappaport (2006). All stakeholders are likely to benefit as it happens further, as long as it is pursued in a careful and rigorous way. We are optimistic because trends in both disciplines call for a wider view of their role in the value creation and measurement process.

REFERENCES

Ambler, T. (2003), *Marketing and the Bottom Line*, 2nd Ed., London: Prentice Hall.

Ambler, T. and Roberts, J. (2006a), "Beware the Silver Metric: Marketing Performance Measurement has to be Multidimensional", In: T. Ambler and J. Roberts, *Report 06-113*, Cambridge: Marketing Science Institute.

Ambler, T. and Roberts, J. (2006b), "A Word of Warning Clarified: Reactions to Peppers and Rogers Response", In: T. Ambler and J. Roberts, *Report 06-115*, Cambridge: Marketing Science Institute.

Amir, E., Lev, B. and Sougiannis, T. (2003), "Do Financial Analysts Get Intangibles?", *European Accounting Review*, Vol. 12, No. 4, pp. 635-659.

Balachandran, S. and Mohanram, P. (2006), "Conservatism and the Value Relevance of Accounting Information", *Working Paper*, Columbia Business School, New York.

Barth, M., Clement, M., Foster, G. and Kazsnik, R. (1998), "Brand Values and Market Capitalization", *Review of Accounting Studies*, Vol. 3, No. 1-2, pp. 41-68.

Basilo, T. (2007), "Reducing Sarbanes-Oxley Compliance Costs", *The CPA Journal*, Vol. 77, No. 1, pp. 6-8.

Department of Trade and Industry (2004), *Creating Value from Your Intangibles*, London: Department of Trade and Industry.

Doyle, Peter (2000), *Value-Based Marketing*, Chichester: John Wiley.

Eccles, R., Herz, R., Keegan, M. and Phillips, D. (2001), *The Value Reporting Revolution: Moving Beyond the Earnings Game*, New York: John Wiley.

European Commission (2003), *The PRISM Report European Commission Information Technologies Programme*, October, Report Series 2.

Financial Accounting Standards Board (2008, as amended), *Statement of Financial Accounting Concepts No. 1 – Objectives of Financial Reporting by Business Enterprises.*

Fornell, C., Mithas, S., Morgeson, F., and Krishnan, M.S. (2006), "Customer Satisfaction and Stock Prices: High Returns, Low Risk", *Journal of Marketing*, Vol. 70, No. 1, pp. 3-14.

Gray, D. (2004), "A Report on the Costs and Benefits of Measuring Intellectual Capital Assets", *Working Paper*, Cranfield University School of Management.

Gross, N. (2001), "Commentary: Valuing Intangibles is a Tough Job, but it Has to be Done", Cover story, *Business Week* (August 6).

Hand, J. (2003), "The Increasing Returns to Scale of Intangibles". In: Hand, J. and Lev, B., (eds.), *Intangible Assets: Values Measures, and Risks,* Oxford: Oxford University Press, pp. 303-331.

Ittner, C. and Larcker, D. (2003), "Coming Up Short on Non financial Performance Measurement", *Harvard Business Review*, Vol. 81, No. 11, (November), pp. 88-96.

Kanodia, C., Sapra, H. and Venugopalan, R. (2004), "Should Intangibles be Measured: What are the Economic Trade-Offs?", *Journal of Accounting Research*, Vol. 42, No. 1, pp. 89-120.

Kaplan, R. and Atkinson, A. (1989), *Advanced Management Accounting*, 2nd Edition Englewood Cliffs: Prentice Hall.

Kaplan, R. and Norton, D. (2004), *Strategy Maps*, Boston: HBS Press.

Kotler, P. and Keller, K. (2006), *Marketing Management*, 12th Edition, Upper Saddle River, NJ: Prentice Hall.

Kumar, N. (2004), *Marketing as Strategy*, Boston: HBS Press.Lev, B. (2000), "New Accounting for the New Economy", May, *Working paper*, Stern School of Business, New York University.

Lev, B. (2000), "New Accounting for the New Economy", May, *Working paper*, Stern School of Business, New York University.

Lev, B. (2001), *Intangibles*, Washington: Brookings Institution Press.

Lev, B. (2003a), "Remarks on the Measurement, Valuation and Reporting of Intangible Assets", *Economic Policy Review* (September), Federal Reserve Bank of New York, pp. 17-22.

Lev, B. (2003b), "What then must we do?", In: Hand, J. and Lev, B. (eds.), *Intangible Assets: Values Measures, and Risks,* Oxford: Oxford University Press, pp. 511-525.

Lev, B. (2004), "Sharpening the Intangibles Edge", *Harvard Business Review*, (June) pp. 109-116.

Luft, J. and Shields, M. (2003), "Why Does Fixation Persist? Experimental Evidence on the Judgment Performance Effects of Expensing Intangibles", In: Hand, J. and Lev, B. (eds.), *Intangible Assets: Values Measures, and Risks*, Oxford: Oxford University Press, pp. 414-446.

McLannahan, B. (2003), "Hidden Treasures", cfo.com (December 30). Available at: http://www.cfo.com/article.cfm/3011043?f=related, [Accessed 22nd June 2008].

Nagar, V. and Rajan, M. (2005), "Measuring Customer Relationships: The Case of the Retail Banking Industry", *Management Science*, Vol. 51, No. 6, pp. 904-919.

O'Halloran, P. and Mosher, P. (2004), "Marketing: Underrated, Undervalued and Unimportant", Accenture Access Newsletter. Available at: http://www.accenture.com/Global/Services/By_Industry/Communications/Access_Newsletter/Article_Index/MarketingUnimportant.htm, [Accessed 22nd June 2008].

Penman, S. (2007), *Financial Statement Analysis and Security Valuation*, 3rd Edition Boston: McGraw Hill.

Rappaport, Alfred (1986), *Creating Shareholder Value*, 1st Edition New York: The Free Press.

Rappaport, A. (2006), "Ten Ways to Create Shareholder Value", *Harvard Business Review*, Vol. 84, No. 9, (September), pp 66-77.

Srivastava, R., Shervani, T. and Fahey, L. (1998), "Market-Based Assets and Shareholder Value: A Framework for Analysis", *Journal of Marketing*, Vol. 62, No. 1, (Jan), pp. 1-14.

Srivastava, R., Shervani, T. and Fahey, L. (1999), "Marketing, Business Processes, and Shareholder Value: An Organizationally Embedded View of Marketing Activities and the Discipline of Marketing", *Journal of Marketing*, Vol. 63, (Special Issue), pp. 168-79.

Stirtz, K. (2006), "You Can't Measure Everything. So Don't Even Try", *Small Business*. Available at: http://www.allbusiness.com/marketing-advertising/strategic-marketing/3875202-1.html [Accessed 22nd June 2008].

Urban, G. and Hauser, J. (1993), *Design and Marketing of New Products*, 2nd Edition Englewood Cliffs: Prentice Hall.

Verrecchia, R. (1983), "Discretionary Disclosure", *Journal of Accounting and Economics*, Vol. 5, pp. 179-194.

Exploring accounting and market orientation: an interfunctional case study

Robert M. Inglis, *School of Accounting and Law, RMIT University, Australia*

Abstract Over the past two decades, the cognate disciplines of marketing and management accounting have embraced a wider strategic conceptualisation in which customers, customer value and competitive positioning have become common research themes. The market orientation concept exemplifies the extant research within the marketing literature in which a firm's interfunctionally coordinated resources are focused on understanding and competitively responding to customers' needs. Within the management accounting literature, a range of similarly focused techniques, interpreted in this study as market-oriented accounting (MOA), have evolved in which information for decision-making is fashioned by the firm's customers and competitors. The findings of an interfunctional case study highlight a number of factors which potentially moderate the adoption of MOA and reveal a space in conceptual linkages between market orientation and contemporary management accounting techniques. Brand, reliability and informality in information and communication protocols emerge as strong interfunctional themes signalling the potential for future research of interdisciplinary cooperation.

INTRODUCTION

The aim of this paper is to contribute to the interdisciplinary research literature on marketing and management accounting. It is motivated by calls for the development of a greater understanding of how marketing and accounting interrelate in both theory and practice. The seminal work of Narver and Slater (1990) on market orientation is taken as the point of departure for considering the conceptual interface with management accounting. More particularly, consideration is given to a range of management accounting techniques (e.g. attribute costing and whole-life costing) concerned with providing information about a firm's costs of meeting customer needs and competitors' costs to satisfy the same customer needs. These techniques are characterised in this study as market-oriented accounting (MOA) and embrace an organisation-wide view of costs incurred in the process of creating value for customers. Value, in this instance, is reflected in product attributes – features, benefits or characteristics – from which customers derive utility and are prepared to pay a price.

This paper then reports the findings of a case study which was designed to describe and explore the market-oriented accounting practices across a range of organisational functions and the context within which they were conducted. Research across functions was regarded as critical in keeping with the organisation-wide emphasis prevalent in conceptions of market orientation (Narver and Slater 1990; Narver, Slater and Tietje 1998) while providing the opportunity to identify the presence of MOA in functions other than accounting (Anderson 2007).

Contextually, the case findings provide an insight into changes in competitive positioning and an organisational focus on brand, motivations for the content of accounting information and informality in competitor analysis. While varying degrees of detail of customer needs and competitor positions were apparent, there was little evidence across functions of market-oriented accounting techniques.

The paper is structured as follows. In Section two, a conceptual framework is developed in which the points of interface between market orientation and management accounting are identified. A synthesis of the market orientation literature is presented with a particular focus on Narver and Slater's (1990) conception of market orientation and linkages to accounting content. The management accounting discipline is then examined and a range of accounting techniques and approaches consistent with a market-oriented emphasis on customers and competitors are identified and locate management accounting in a broader market orientation framework. In Section three, details of the research design are presented together with an overview of the case study organisation. Section four presents the findings of a cross-functional analysis of the market-oriented accounting practices of a large Australian manufacturing organisation. The paper concludes with a discussion of the main findings and suggestions for future research.

THEORETICAL FRAMEWORK

Market orientation

The work of Narver and Slater (1990) and Kohli and Jaworski (1990) has spawned much of the research and debate into market orientation over the last two decades (see, for example, Morgan and Strong 1998; Gray, Matear, Boshoff and Matheson

1998; Harris 2000; Gonzalez-Benito and Gonzalez-Benito 2005). Research persists into the market orientation - business performance link (Hult, Ketchen and Slater 2005) with an increasing number of studies from Asia and Europe reporting consistent findings of a positive relationship between market orientation and organisational performance (see Gonzalez-Benito and Gonzalez-Benito 2005, for a review of published studies in the 1990-2003 period). Investigation of the market orientation – innovation link continues to develop (see, for example, Santos-Vijande et al. 2005) while more recent attention has been given to the market orientation and customer relationship interface (Helfert, Ritter and Walter 2002; Javalgi, Martin and Young 2006) and interrelated notions of customer value (Clark, 2001; Berghman, Matthyssens and Vandenbempt, 2006; Anderson, Narus and van Rossum 2006), customer profitability (Ryals 2005) and customer equity (Bauer and Hammerschmidt 2005). Increased interest in the accounting and marketing information interface is also evident at both firm and product levels with particular emphasis on customers (Goebel, Marshall and Locander 1998; Zeithaml, Rust, and Lemon 2001; Helgesen 2007) vis-à-vis competitors.

The market orientation concept has been described as one that defies easy definition and use at an operational level but one in which several key features are apparent (Uncles 2000). Many of these features develop from the Narver and Slater (1990) conceptualisation of market orientation, which has tended to be the most preferred research approach (Gray and Hooley 2002; Morgan and Strong 1998; Gray et al. 1998) and has been adopted as the conceptual framework in this study.

Narver and Slater (1990) conceptualise market orientation as comprising three, equally important, interrelated components – customer, competitor and interfunctional coordination. In describing these three components (or "*orientations*"), Narver and Slater emphasise the requisite organisational behaviours - activities and processes - involved in obtaining and sharing information about customers and competitively responding to customer needs.

Narver and Slater (1990) also describe two "*decision criteria*" – long-term and profit focus. The former reflects a view that a market orientation is implicitly linked with the competitive survival of the firm and a long-run decision perspective is unavoidable (p 22). The latter decision criterion – profit – is tied to a rational economic view of the firm as one which seeks to generate wealth for its owners. For organisations to maximise long-term profitability requires having a sustainable competitive advantage which develops from the creation of competitively superior value for customers (Porter 1985; Aaker 1992). This notion of competitive advantage underpins a customer orientation which is defined by Narver and Slater (1990, p. 21) as

...the sufficient understanding of one's target buyers to be able to create superior value for them continuously (or, per Levitt 1980, to create continuously an "augmented product").

Narver and Slater (1990) maintain that value is created for customers through the provision of product attributes (features, functions, benefits) that better satisfy their needs and/or reduce customer acquisition costs and costs in using the product (Porter 1985, p. 135-137; Forbis and Mehta 1981; Anderson and Narus 1999; Kotler 2000). Founded upon economic theories about consumer behaviour, customers' purchase decisions are influenced by the attributes of a product/service rather than the product per se (Lancaster 1966; Stokmans 1991; Myers and Shocker 1981). Products encompass both tangible, more objectively measurable attributes such as physical product components and intangible, more subjectively measurable attributes, for example, brand, taste, prestige.

Providing the composition of attributes required by the customer will also affect the supplier's product costs (Lindgreen and Wynstra 2005) and profit potential (Ulaga and Chacour 2001). Conceptually, the interaction between product-attributes, customer-value creation, costs and profits reflects a point of interface between marketing orientation and accounting information. This said, there remains a lack of research into these interactive constituents (Lindgreen and Wynstra 2005; Wouters, Anderson and Wynstra, 2005).

A competitor orientation, as the second of the three behavioural components of a market orientation, is closely linked with the customer component of a market orientation in its product attribute emphasis. Following Porter (1985), Narver and Slater maintain that in order to provide superior value to customers the seller requires knowledge of competitor capabilities and costs to provide comparable product attributes (see also, Day and Wensley 1988; Day 1990; Aaker 1992). The extent of "how much" information and understanding is sufficient to allow informed decision-making about competitive product planning is not considered in detail in the literature (Gray et al. 1998; Morgan and Strong 1998) and is an aspect given relatively less attention (than customers) within the market orientation literature.

The third behavioural component - interfunctional coordination - is linked closely to both the customer and competitor components of a market orientation and involves the coordinated utilisation of organisational resources in creating superior value for buyers (Narver and Slater 1990). Lafferty and Hult (2001) view interfunctional coordination as a *"unifying principle"* in which information about customers and competitors is accessed and disseminated throughout the organisation through the concerted efforts of all functions. Kumar, Subramanian and Yauger (1998) consider that the extent of a firm's market orientation is dependent upon successful interfunctional coordination. The interfunctional sharing of information is a critical component of a market orientation; however, relatively limited research evidence is available on the functional composition of organisations (Uncles 2000) and the acquisition, content and communication of marketing and accounting information across all functions.

In sum, a central tenet of market orientation is the creation of customer value through the offering by the supplier of a range of product attributes (benefits, features, characteristics). To do so profitably and competitively, the supplier requires an understanding of the costs of the "value-creating" attributes and competitor costs of providing comparable attributes. Despite the product attribute/customer value creation focus of a market orientation, research into profit (as a decision criterion) associated with a market orientation has tended to focus on outcome metrics of business-unit level performance.

Management accounting

Literature within the discipline describes management accounting as the process of identification, measurement, analysis and communication of information which is used by management for organisational planning and decision-making (see, for example, Horngren, Foster and Datar 2006; Drury 2008). In this sense, management accounting can be conceived as a "rational" model for objectively quantifying and analysing organisational activities and one that provides a language for discourse and interpretation (Boland and Pondy 1983).

Taking Narver and Slater's conceptualisation of market orientation, in this study management accounting information relates to the costing of product attributes that create value for the customers and which potentially yield a profit to the firm. A number of market-oriented accounting techniques (MOA) have developed over the past two decades in response to criticism of the management accounting discipline as providing information which is out-dated and somewhat simplistic (Johnson and Kaplan 1987; Kaplan 1984; Cooper and Kaplan 1987), too focussed on internal historical cost information (Howell and Soucy 1987) and lacking in strategic direction (Shank and Govindarajan 1988). Roslender (1995) and Roslender and Hart (2002, 2003) characterise a range of these techniques in a strategic context in which integrated marketing and accounting information is used as a "*generic approach*" to strategic positioning.

In looking at the customer component of a market orientation, Guilding and McManus (2002) identify a number of market-oriented accounting practices: individual customer profit analysis; customer segment profit analysis; lifetime customer profit analysis and; valuations of customers as assets. An increased research emphasis on these practices is apparent in both the management accounting and marketing disciplines (see, for example, Helgesen 2007; Ryals and Cox 2005; Van Raaji 2005; Andon, Baxter and Bradley 2001).

The extant accounting literature on customer costing and profit analysis advocates the use of an activity-based approach in identifying and costing those non-physical product activities that relate to a particular customer or customer group (O'Guin and Rebischke 1995; Smith and Dikolli 1995; Kaplan and Narayanan 2001). In this approach, the cost "object" is the customer, with the costing and tracing of the physical products undertaken separately from other customer-activity costs. For detailed management information about customer costs, the use of a hierarchy on four main levels - order, customer, channel and market level costs - is advocated (O'Guin and Rebischke 1995; Petty and Goodman 1996) which reflects the different cost behaviour of activities at each level. A number of potential benefits of the activity-based approach have been identified. These include providing detailed information on sources of profitable business (Connolly and Ashworth 1994; Helgesen 2007), marketing and pricing strategies (Booth 1994; Van Raaij 2005) and for resource allocation (Petty and Goodman 1996). Notwithstanding these benefits, there may be substantial economic costs in its implementation and operation (Innes, Mitchell and Cobb 1992; Bromwich and Bhimani 1994) and/or wider managerial costs in the loss of future value added through developments in functions such as marketing (e.g. in terms of creativity and innovation) and human resource management (Armstrong 2002) where the outputs are difficult, if not impossible, to calculate.

While customer oriented, the practices identified by Guilding and McManus (2002) do not make explicit the detail of the attributes of a product which create value for customers (Bromwich and Bhimani 1994; McNair and Polutnik 2001).

Inglis (2005) identifies a number of "*customer-oriented*" accounting practices/ techniques that provide information on or about customers' product-attribute needs. Target costing (TC) (Kato, 1993) and function cost analysis (FCA) (Yoshikawa, Innes and Mitchell 1995) are noted as particular approaches to costing product attributes. Target costing is informed by value analysis (VA) and value engineering (VE) techniques (see Miles 1961) in which interdisciplinary teams (including marketing and accounting participants) play an integral role in identifying and detailing customer needs and the firm's costs of product functions designed to meet these needs (see Shillito and De Marle 1992, p.252-256).

As a derivative of VA/VE, FCA seeks to facilitate the cost-effective design of products by costing the various items, parts and activities involved and provide a view of what the product offers the customer and *"in a way which ensures that it still reflects customer needs"* (Yoshikawa, Innes and Mitchell 1995, p.416). The determination of whether product functions are redundant or are too costly is made by reference to market intelligence about the monetary value to customers of each product function. A dual emphasis is placed on increasing value for customers while reducing the life-cycle costs of the supplier.

Similarly, whole-life costing (WLC) considers costs from a customer point of view by highlighting both the acquisition (e.g. purchase price and installation costs) and ownership costs (e.g., repairs, maintenance, environmental and disposal costs) of the customer (Shields and Young, 1991), the latter reflecting an important "product" attribute in customer purchase decisions (Artto, 1994).

However, the practice most in keeping with a customer orientation is the attribute-based costing (AC) approach advanced by Bromwich (1990, 1991, 1992). Taking an economic perspective, Bromwich (1990, p.28, 30) draws upon the work of Lancaster (1979) in emphasising the value provided to the consumer in a range of attributes that comprise the product. Bromwich emphasises the connection between product attributes and cost information and outlines a model for the matching of product attributes (or "benefits" as they are more often described) with organisational costs (Bromwich 1991; see also, Bromwich and Bhimani 1994). Customer-defined product attributes in this model are categorised in terms of physical product attributes, attributes (benefits) that are derived from the point of sale (outlet), and other attributes (benefits).

Building on Bromwich's work, Partridge and Perren (1994) develop a model to illustrate the allocation of attribute costs for a car supplier with an integrated distributor network. Walker (1991, 1992), proposes the use of an activity-based costing approach in assigning overhead costs to product attributes. Conjoint analysis is used to determine customer preferences for, or utility of, particular attributes which are then matched to the relevant operating activities. Despite its market-oriented focus, AC has received minimal attention within the accounting literature and application in practice (Cravens and Guilding 2001).

In turning to the competitor component of a market orientation, Bromwich's attribute-based costing presents as the one most closely aligned with Narver and Slater's position. Bromwich (1990) views cost information about product attributes over time as crucial to a firm's sustainability of product strategies. Sustainability in this context revolves around whether the product, in the form of a "bundle of attributes", offered by a firm at a given price, is viewed more favourably by customers than competitors' products. Customer preferences for a variation in product attributes provide a basis for competitive differentiation (Lancaster 1979).

Target costing (TC) incorporates a form of competitor product-attribute costing (see, for example, Cooper and Chew 1996; Kato, Boer and Chow 1995). Research into TC practices undertaken by Tani, Okano, Shimizu, Iwabuchi, Fukuda and Cooray (1994, p.74.) found that competitors' costs is the most important factor in setting target costs. Fisher (1995, p.54) locates the need for competitor information at the attribute level through advocating the use of quality function deployment (QFD) - an approach for identifying customer-prioritised product characteristics - in analysing competitors to determine "best in class". He suggests the use of product reverse engineering - the "tear down" of a product to analyse design and production processes - a procedure which is generally accepted as facilitating the establishment of competitor product costs (Kato et al.1995; Aalbregste 1993; Cooper and Slagmulder 2004).

The third component of market orientation (Narver and Slater 1990), and arguably the most critical to its implementation, is interfunctional coordination. A number of management accounting techniques identify information sharing and activity coordination as a central element in the process of establishing attribute costs and competitive position. Target costing, whole-life costing and attribute costing all emphasise interdisciplinary cooperation in the process of creating value for customers, reflecting a common theme found in the work of Porter (1985) when discussing value-chain analysis and strategic competitive advantage. The organisation-wide interfunctional emphasis of market-oriented accounting can be contrasted with the early literature on marketing accounting which sought to extend the financial dimensions of accounting to the marketing function (Wilson 1981; Ratnatunga 1988; Ratnatunga, Pike and Hooley 1988).

Notwithstanding the conceptual linkages between a range of management accounting techniques and the three behavioural components of a market orientation, there has been relatively little advancement of these techniques reported within the management accounting literature (McNair, Polutnik and Silvi 2001; Langfield-Smith 2007). A notable exception is the field work by Roslender and Hart (2003, p.258) who observe the absence of research into the operationalisation of the attribute costing technique. Moreover, despite increased interest in TC and WLC in the 1990's, research into customer and competitor accounting remains very much a "*fledgling literature*" (Guilding 1999; Guilding and McManus 2002; Ansari, Bell and Okano 2007).

Organisational research on the adoption of "*advanced management accounting techniques*" has identified a number of barriers leading to the relatively slow uptake of market-oriented techniques such as target costing (Adler, Everett and Waldron 2000). According to Waldron (2005), major barriers include resource costs and time to implement new techniques, concerns with the usefulness of the "new" accounting information, a lack of understanding of the management accounting practices and a perceived reluctance of other functions to cooperate. Vaivio (1999), in looking at an organisation's effort to systematically "*quantify customers*" in terms of non-financial metrics, describes the complexity of the process, the manifestation of functional resistance and "*rival knowledge*" as influencing the process of quantifying customer knowledge.

In this study, we take the conceptual position that management accounting techniques provide a source of information input for sharing across all functions within an organisation. In a rational process, these techniques seek to quantify the costs associated with those product attributes that create value for the customer and provide information for objectively making decisions considering the firm's competitive and profit position. In this sense, market-oriented accounting is underpinned by economic theories of consumer behaviour in which utility (value) for the customer and costs of the supplier are derived from product attributes (Lancaster 1966, 1971; Grunert 1989; Stokmans 1991). While locating this study in a particular conception of market-oriented accounting, we are also concerned with exploring and describing the broader organisational context and practice in which marketing and accounting information resides, is used and conceived.

RESEARCH DESIGN

With a view to building theory about the marketing and accounting interface, the primary aim of this study was to describe and explore market-oriented accounting in an organisational setting. A case study was chosen as it is a valuable strategy where research and theory are in their formative stages (Eisenhardt, 1989; Yin, 1994; Benbasat, Goldstein and Mead, 1987). While there is a substantial body of literature dealing separately with market orientation and management accounting techniques, there is little organisational research evidence with respect to the market orientation and accounting interface at product-attribute level. A broad conceptual framework has been described in this paper; however, there remains a need to develop theory informed by reference to "real world" events (Gummesson 1991; McNair et al. 2001). Contextual conditions are considered highly pertinent given the external – customer and competitor – focus of market orientation.

A single case study was also considered best suited to provide a rich account of interfunctional communication and processes across a broad range of organisational functions (Gummesson 1991) and obtain access to potentially sensitive and confidential (competitive) information, details of which are difficult to elicit in other forms of data collection (Coad 1996).

The conduct of the case-study followed the relatively more formal, systematic process as described by Yin (1994) and Perry (1998) and included the development of a detailed case study protocol. Semi-structured interviews were to be conducted across a range of organisation functions, documentary evidence was to be reviewed and observations recorded of daily operational activities and processes. Multiple data sources and respondents' review of transcribed interviews strengthen construct validity and data reliability (Bonoma 1985; Stake 1995).

Conceptions of the interface of management accounting with customer, competitor and interfunctional components of a market orientation were to provide a degree of structure to the data collection and analytical process (Yin 1994; Perry 1998; Miles and Huberman 1994). The three components provided "thematic guides" around which broad questions for each organisation function about marketing and accounting information were developed. A number of "over-arching questions" were also designed to develop a "picture" of the organisational context and the structure, processes and people involved in product decisions and to capture the perceptions of the respondents' experiences related to the research (Perry 1998). Interview transcripts relating to each over-arching question and market orientation component were highlighted and coded based on a *provisional 'start list' of codes*" (Miles and Huberman 1994, p.58). For example, for the customer-orientation component, the code CU1 was used to analyse data about "customer product attributes".

In keeping with suggestions by Miles and Huberman (1994) and Perry (1998), each organisational function description was to conclude with a descriptive summary and details of key issues. These summaries and key issues would provide a basis for further analysis and description of the customer, competitor and interfunctional coordination components and market-oriented accounting practices across functions and allow common issues, patterns and themes to be identified. In analysing the data, the respondent's comments, observational and documentary evidence were to be reviewed for confirmatory or contradictory elements or any particular points of emphasis (Bonoma 1985).

Case organisation - NP

The case organisation, NP, was a large, well-established business unit that was a subsidiary of a publicly listed Australian company. Its primary activity was the manufacture and sales of heating and cooling products, composed of 19 product groups and 517 models, to customers in what were commonly referred to as the retail and specialist markets. The specialist market, which was the subject of examination in this study, encompassed the sale of whole-of-home "ducted" heating and cooling "systems" to specialist retailers (dealers), i.e., small-medium sized firms that provided advice to home-owners (end consumer) on, and installation of, heating and cooling systems. NP had an annual sales turnover in excess of AUD$60,000,000 and employed 250 management and staff (see Appendix 1 for additional company details). As a large organisation, it was considered that NP would be more likely to adopt contemporary - market-oriented - accounting techniques (Adler et al. 2000; Baird, Harrison and Reeve 2004).

The case study took place in NP's head office at which production facilities were also located. Data were collected over one week and involved in-depth interviews, observation and a review of organisational documents. Audio-taped interviews were conducted with the general manager (GM), national sales and marketing manager (NSMM), business manager (BM), commercial manager (accounting) (CM), product development manager (PDM), manufacturing and quality assurance manager (QAM). Multiple interviews were conducted with several of the managers over the course of the week in seeking additional details or clarification of previous discussions.

To ensure "triangulation" of data, a collection and review of internally and externally generated documents was undertaken as was observation of operations and meetings. Documentary evidence included consultant's market research reports, accounting reports, production documents, product costing sheets, sales reports, marketing literature, product review reports, warranty reports, and product pricing and profit estimates. Observatory data included a "walk through" of production and product development activities and attendance at a weekly management meeting. Being located in an office at NP's headquarters also provided the researcher with an opportunity for less formal observation and discussion with managers, details of which were later diarised. One month subsequent to the study, the researcher discussed the findings and data interpretations at a management meeting at NP's head office, a process which served to strengthen construct validity and reliability of the data.

FINDINGS

Organisational context

NP was in a period of strategic change. The General Manager (GM) and National Sales and Marketing Manager (NSMM) both reflected on how price competition (from overseas suppliers) in the retail market had meant that many of their retail products were *"selling at a loss"*. Combined *"with a lack of loyalty from retail customers"*, costly distribution and sale or exchange policies, NP had developed and recently implemented a more focussed strategy of competing in the "specialist installed" market and had withdrawn from the retail side of business.

In the Australian market, our products and the way we install them in the specialist field tend to be very much Australian orientated. If we are going to stay in manufacturing, ... then the least amount of risk is for us to pursue ducted product – ducted gas central heating because the market share, the size of the market, our brand name, very, very, powerful brand name. The control we have over the channels of distribution with specialists is a hundred times more than the control we have over a retailer

(NSMM)

Related to the shift in product-market positioning was the need to improve the financial position of the firm – recent NP financial reports indicated losses before interest and tax. The specialist market was one in which NP considered it would have substantially more "power" over customers and one which would provide sales and profit growth in the next five years. However, the withdrawal from the retail market had left NP with "idle" production capacity with associated high levels of fixed costs.

We have an infrastructure in place that could support much higher revenue than we currently have without spending an extra dollar on overhead

(GM)

It became apparent in interviews with the GM that there was an immediate need for NP to increase sales revenue and reduce product costs. Varying emphases on strategy, sales and costs themes emerged in the way in which the various functional managers responded to discussion about customers, competitors, interfunctional coordination and accounting information. For example, the discussion with the GM was more centred on increasing NP profit through strategic repositioning and a focus on "brand" as a basis for differentiating NP products. Discussions with the NSMM and BM were similarly focussed on "brand" and the development of relationships with specialist customers to build sales. Discussions with, and activities undertaken by, the QAM, PDM and CM were more focussed on product cost savings. A particular emphasis was placed on the reduction of product warranty costs which were considered to be too high.

Adding to the organisation context was the relatively recent (within the last 2 months) appointment of the CM (Accountant), the absence of a permanent production manager (the position was yet to be filled after three months of vacancy) and the recent appointment of the QA manager (who was also acting as production manager).

Customer orientation

Cross-functional data analysis revealed an understanding of seven key product attributes which were perceived as creating value for specialist-customers and are summarised in Appendix 2.

Information about specialist customers' needs was developed from two sources: first, sales representatives met with customers and provided feedback; second, customers completed customer satisfaction surveys, the parameters of which were developed from sales representatives' feedback. A review of the customer surveys revealed four main product attribute categories – product (including features, design, reliability and availability) competitiveness (including response to market demands, understanding of specialist customer needs, brochures and materials) customer service and support (including meeting delivery dates, product availability) and after sales service (including resolving complaints quickly, and availability of spare parts).

Product "reliability" was perceived by all functions to be a key product attribute for the specialist customer. Reliability was conceived as relating to delivery, spare parts and services (from NP) and in the operating capability of the physical (heating and/or cooling) product. Reliability was also frequently associated with the notion of establishing a "brand" on which the company could sustain a competitive advantage. A strong brand was perceived as an attribute of value to the specialist customer in that it was a platform on which products could be sold.

> *If you've got a good product, a good reliable product, a good brand and you get reliable business partnership ....If all this happens, it happens easily then they (specialist customers) will enjoy doing business with you*
>
> (BM)

> *...a good quality name that's going to give them long service. It gives them an association that they will be provided with a good after-sales service*
>
> (GM)

> *...delivery on time. The reliability of the product being installed. The reliability of the perception of the brand, you know it is a brand that they (specialist customers) can just portray from their businesses' point of view that this is a very reliable brand. That there are spare parts to back it up, there's a service division that is there to ensure the reliability of why this product is good*
>
> (NSMM)

Another theme that emerged from the cross-functional analysis was "Pre-sales support" (PSS). This reflects the product attributes associated with providing the specialist customer with a range of products and product "innovations" (product features such as remote controls, different colours, reduced product operating costs), supported by NP advertising and promotions, which facilitate the product sales of the specialists.

> *I guess from a dealer's perspective they're looking for - for a range of products to be able to support their business. And good gross contribution that they can achieve. Lack of - lack of a need for follow up warranty work and deliveries on time, basically*
>
> (CM)

> *The installation and time to install it and so on and so on, the product is not just the physical object any more it's a hell of a lot more. ...we are basically responsible for building their (specialists) business...responsible for getting customers through their door through advertising*
>
> (BM)

A cost reduction theme was also apparent across all functions with particular emphasis on improving aspects of "reliability" which, in turn, was perceived as a means to reduce the specialist customers' costs of doing business with NP (for example, less costs in dealing with customer warranty related matters) and, in turn, increasing the specialists' profits.

Providing attributes of reliability, brand, pre-sales support, and cost reductions can be viewed as contributing to the attribute of "easy to do business with" and in many ways serves to highlight the interrelated nature of the product attributes. Across functions, reliability (and its various aspects/components) was the product attribute that was central to product decisions and perhaps reflects the impact and importance of this attribute for the brand, the (potential) sales and costs of specialist customers and the profits of NP.

Competitor orientation

Data analysis across functions evidenced both formal (documented) and informal approaches to acquiring and using competitor intelligence. NP managers maintained knowledge of competitors' capabilities and activities, for example, in terms of producing quality products, pricing policies, management expertise, physical size (production capacity) and relative business-unit cost position. This knowledge had been acquired in an informal manner in a variety of ways including word-of-mouth within the industry, conversation at trade meetings, observation of competitors' advertising materials and competitors' production facilities (providing NP with an idea of competitors' capacity).

The firm also maintained formal reports of market volume and market share (based upon trade data) which was used to monitor competition at a product-group level. The GM and NSMM discussion of competitors was generally couched in terms of NP's strategic product-market positioning.

> *We are not driving to be nor do I believe we can be or have been a real low cost manufacturer. So what we have to do is use the value in our brand name. And if we can maintain the value in our brand name then that will enable us to always play in the market on the high end*
>
> (GM)

> *"X" is our number one competitor, (and) is a privately owned family business. I guess one of his (the owner of "X") key strengths is that all they do is ducted gas central heating and ducted evaporative cooling and their infrastructure and their manufacturing operation what-have-you is purely geared towards just doing those two things. So they do a pretty reliable job*
>
> (NSMM)

> *"X" would have a much smaller infrastructure than both competitor "Y" and ourselves. A few of our competitors spend a lot of money, more money than we do, on just brand image*
>
> (GM)

At a product level, competitors' price and product range lists were obtained "*each season*" from specialist customers and were a main source of information when planning price levels, product ranges and rebate deals with specialists.

> *...going into a season we say 'Okay, well what do we anticipate that they (competitors) will do with their pricing structure this year?' We know that their (competitors) rebate arrangements are essentially 3½%. ...don't be under any illusion that competitors don't have ours as well*
>
> (NSMM)

In terms of product attributes, there was no formal (documented and/or regular) recording of competitors' positions. One notable exception observed by the researcher was the reengineering of a competitor's product to identify its physical components and establish benchmarks for the (re) development of NP products. The product development manager (PDM) and quality assurance manager (QAM) indicated this initiative had been motivated by the high rate of product warranty claims and the organisation-wide emphasis on cost reduction.

Despite the absence of formal competitor intelligence, in the course of interviews and a "tour" of production operations, the QAM and PDM both identified aspects of competitors' (physical) products and production operations that suggested that an informal mechanism existed for acquiring competitor information. Both were aware of competitors' product development expertise, the use by the main competitor of "industrial design consultants", and production technologies.

> (Our biggest competitor have) a bloody good product – injection moulded and low cost. They are also almost vertically integrated. They make everything .... We are really an assembly shop

(PDM)

In terms of competing, the PDM considered NP were not cost competitive but that "we (NP) are big and we've got a (brand) name".

Interfunctional coordination

Across all functions the predominant theme for interfunctional coordination was the participation in the regular weekly business team meetings, a forum within which each manager would discuss various aspects of their function's activities. Accounting reports, particularly sales and warranty reports were a standard "agenda" item for each meeting but discussion was not restricted only to financial matters. As a relatively new initiative of the GM, there was a consensus among functional managers that the meetings were valuable in terms of developing an understanding of what was taking place across the various areas of the firm.

> At least it gives you an idea of what else is happening around the place and you can have a bit of input. And we can share problems and hopefully resolve them

(PDM)

> So we're all involved from the commercial manager to myself, to the GM. We tend to do ... we are very much crossed functioned - I need to know what's going on in finance, I need to know what's going on in quality. Prior to the GM coming on board, we didn't ever have those meetings

(NSMM)

Similarly, the QAM considered the meeting as a way in which the different views of managers could be combined to resolve problems and discuss ideas noting "you have got three or four different philosophies coming together".

While all functions shared the view that warranty costs were a major concern for the business which affected profitability and perceptions of the firm's product reliability, there was evidence to suggest that functions may not fully coordinate activities, communicate information and share a common view.

A cross-functional analysis reveals a variation in each function's conception of customer product-attribute needs (see Appendix 2). For example, the GM, NSMM and BM had an awareness of a broad range of customer needs while the PD and QA had a narrower conception of the range of customer product-attribute needs. There was also a variation across functions in their focus (strategic versus operational) and depth of understanding of competitor information. Three functions - QAM, PDM and CM – shared a view on the likely ("*inappropriate*") behaviour of the

Sales and Marketing function to reduce product selling prices in response to any reported reduction in standard product costs. Reduced selling prices in this case were considered to be inconsistent with the notion of high quality branded products. There were also a variety of understandings across functions of competitors and informal ways in which information which been acquired.

Market-oriented accounting

Although all functions, to varying degrees, maintained knowledge of those attributes of value to the customer and that NP was clearly targeting a particular customer market, i.e., specialists, there was an absence of market-oriented accounting. There was no deliberate linking of product attributes to accounting information when making product decisions, i.e., product attribute costing. The reduction of the specialist customers' costs was identified as an attribute of value to the specialist customers; however, no formal accounting information (e.g., whole-life costing) regarding these costs was used at NP.

Having not adopted attribute-based costing or related attribute techniques such as whole-life and target costing, not unexpectedly, NP did not undertake formal or regular competitor cost analysis at the product-attribute level. However, consistent with suggestions by Fisher (1995), two functions had sought to reengineer a competitor's product in seeking to identify potential cost reductions. Competitor information was maintained in terms of market share, competitors' sales volume data and pricing information, reflecting a similar approach to accounting for competitors advanced by Simmonds (1981, 1982, 1986). Other competitor information was more non-financial and descriptive in nature.

A number of accounting themes emerged in cross-functional analysis. First, there was a view that accounting information at NP was "traditional" with an emphasis on financial accounting - profit and loss (budget to actual performance) reports, standard product cost (material, labour and variable production overhead) information and warranty cost reports.

> *very traditional – financial information and this is ... very much the corporate standard (set by Head Office). (In my opinion) the accounting information did not provide the depth and extent of information required to make "informed management decisions"*
>
> (CM)

In confirming the commercial manager's view of accounting information, the GM expressed the view *"that no management under traditional costing systems knows what their true costs are"*. The GM also noted corporate policy and limited resources as factors which made the adoption of contemporary approaches to product costing, such as activity-based costing (ABC), highly unlikely.

> *It would conflict with our corporate reporting requirements. ...what it would do is generate more work for the accounting function to translate one set of ABC type accounts to the more traditional fully absorbed costing so there's a conflict there that would not be easy to resolve.*
>
> *...we'd need two or three people as an extra resource to give us that (ABC) information. I've no doubt that it would pay for itself because you would make better quality decisions. In the short-term who is going to wear the extra cost of those two or three people?*

The national sales and marketing manager considered that the adoption of contemporary approaches to customer and product costing and profit analysis may be counter productive in terms of providing "too much" information for decision-making.

> *it would be unproductive to give that level of information (to sales representatives)... sit down in their car for a couple of days and make sure what this (information) is all about..*

The second theme was a common view amongst managers that accounting information was not accurate and that more accurate product cost data were needed, particularly in the analysis and allocation of fixed overhead costs. Confirming the GM's view, the PDM queried the firm's understanding of "*overheads*" and its "*real cost structure*".

The QAM also considered that the actual and standard cost information in accounting reports was something that "*we don't measure very well*" with incorrect apportionment of (high) overhead costs to products.

The CM indicated that "*a lot of business decisions that are being made with less than ideal information*" and that he had an immediate focus on establishing more accurate information that users could understand and that was perceived by them as useful for decision-making.

The third theme that developed from the managers' concerns with cost information was a decision emphasis, particularly in the sales and marketing function, on maximising sales turnover and contribution margins (sales less variable product and selling costs) to ensure the high fixed costs of the business (associated with the previous retail business) were exceeded.

> *(I have) encouraged people to stop thinking about margin that in any way included an overhead cost. So you know, the old thing, it's contribution towards overhead and profit. Think about the business in a traditional way and we've got a good chance then of turning it around.*

(GM)

Of interest was the view of the PDM to the accounting information reviewed in the weekly and monthly management meetings.

> *I've never had any accounting training and I don't understand some of the monthly results and so forth but I don't think I really need to so I don't bother.*

DISCUSSION AND CONCLUSION

In undertaking this case study, management accounting techniques were located within a market orientation framework composed of three interrelated components – customer, competitor and interfunctional coordination – and two decision criteria – long-term and profit focus. Interpreted as market-oriented accounting, these techniques were viewed conceptually as a mechanism for quantifying the costs of product attributes from which customers derived value and the seller derived profit. This conceptual position was underpinned by economic theories of consumer behaviour and rational, structured organisational decision-making.

NP managers had an understanding of a range of interrelated product attributes developed from a predominantly "*market-back*" approach (Day 1990). These findings are consistent with those identified by Ulaga (2003) regarding "benefits" that create customer value. There was a shared recognition at NP of "brand" as a key attribute of value for specialist customers and a shared focus of organisational activities on a number of attributes which were perceived as being interconnected with brand (such as "reliability").

However, the notable absence of market-oriented accounting techniques prompts questions about conceptual linkages and the underlying theory and motivation for their adoption. A number of factors – financial immediacy, cost structure, accounting credence, informality in information protocols and resource constraints – emerge from the organisational context and case analysis which provide some insight into why this might be.

The immediate issue at NP was one of prioritisation of management actions to improve financial performance through reducing manufacturing costs, in particular, warranty costs. This was combined with a perceived need to increase sales turnover and utilise the idle production capacity and the associated high levels of fixed costs. Consistent with this priority, NP had sought to improve product performance (reliability) through the reengineering of physical product functions and operational process improvements.

This finding suggests that where immediate (short-term) organisational priorities emphasise cost reduction and process improvements, there is a reduced impetus for the development and implementation of MOA. This proposition is consistent with the work of Schonberger (1996, 2001) who supports an emphasis on process improvements vis-à-vis the adoption of accounting techniques to provide improved cost data for decision-making, particularly when faced with competitive pressure. Recent findings by Baird et al. (2004) also provide indications that firms may be less likely to adopt activity-based costing techniques where their objectives emphasise increased efficiency and effectiveness of operational processes.

Potentially moderating the motivation to adopt MOA is the assessment by NP managers of the firms competitive cost position. Consistent with the model developed by Day (1990, p. 158), NP managers formed a view that the high level of structural costs placed the firm at a cost disadvantage relative to competitors, a factor that had influenced the firm's competitive positioning on aspects of brand. In these circumstances, there may be decreased benefits for product decision-making of undertaking competitor cost analysis at a product attribute level – a central component of MOA – as the structural (business-unit level) cost differential between the firm and its competitors increases.

The absence of MOA might also be connected to "accounting credence". This term is used here to reflect the general lack of belief and confidence of managers at NP in the reliability (accuracy), relevance (usefulness) and behavioural implications of accounting, particularly cost, information for decision-making. Despite the GM's view on the potential of activity-based costing to "pay for itself", accounting for decision-making at NP focused on what might be termed "more trustworthy" (and less complex) conventional management accounting techniques of "break-even analysis" in maximising sales volumes of high margin products to meet business-unit level fixed costs. In this sense, accounting and creating customer value were separate events (Brock 1984; Armstrong 2002) with the latter managed at NP by a cross-functional focus on seven key product attributes. Product attributes and product costs, in this case, were not so *deeply intertwined* as envisaged by Bromwich and Bhimani (1994, p. 140) in describing their attribute costing technique.

A degree of informality also existed in the way in which product attribute and competitor information was acquired and shared across functions at NP. A less precise process of identification and specification of product attributes would seem inconsistent with (and may potentially moderate) the development and implementation of MOA underpinned by rational economic theories which seek to objectively and formally quantify the costs associated with product attributes.

This said, the informality in the acquisition and dissemination of information at NP may reflect a starting point in the process of developing more formal links between functions. The recent introduction of the weekly management meetings provided a means for this progression. Within these meetings, traditional accounting reports (e.g. profit and loss and warranty reports) also provided a foundation upon which a dialogue between functional areas was developed and ways in which future initiatives in product reliability and brand development might be undertaken with a view to improving firm performance.

Consistent with previous studies (Waldron 2005; Nielson et al. 2000) financial and human resource constraints and information system requirements were identified as "barriers" to the adoption of new accounting techniques. Interestingly, these barriers may be interpreted as influencing the less formal acquisition and communication between functions noted above while enabling greater interfunctional cooperation.

In concluding this paper, an examination across a wide range of organisational functions offered the potential to uncover examples of MOA. It would appear, however, that there remains a substantial space between the theoretical and conceptual linkages of market orientation and management accounting. The case findings suggest that MOA plays a less significant role in market orientation and a number of factors are revealed that might bear on this situation. When financial immediacy, cost structure, accounting credence, informality in information protocols and resource constraints are considered in conjunction, the motivation for the adoption of MOA would appear to be substantially reduced. In this context, a more pertinent question may be asked as to why firms would invest in MOA rather than other techniques, approaches or resources that might provide decision-relevant information such as value-based management, as was found in case studies by Roslender and Hart (2003) or, in the case of NP, brand-related or production improvement initiatives.

An alternative view is that the extent of MOA at NP may reflect its particular organisational setting at a point in time (Narver and Slater 1990; Kohli and Jaworski 1990) as it shifts its competitive positioning to emphasise brand as one of a number of value-creating attributes.

This raises the question as to whether, with the effluxion of time, there has been consideration or development at NP of market-oriented accounting techniques or endeavours to account for brands. To pursue this line of enquiry, future research might seek to explore the context of change in accounting practices in organisations over time. Action-based research designs (Coad 1996) provide the opportunity to explore patterns of interfunctional coordination and cooperation and gain insights into how the introduction of market-oriented accounting practices might better inform marketing decisions.

Notwithstanding the potential value of market-oriented accounting techniques described in this paper, consideration must be given to their relatively limited adoption over the past 25 years (Langfield-Smith 2007). Future research might therefore embrace alternative theoretical frameworks to investigate the interface between market orientation and management accounting which are not based upon, as was this study, economic theories of consumer behaviour and rational organisational decision-making. This is not to say that we should ignore the contribution of accounting in measuring economic performance, rather, it is that in wider and varied organisational contexts, customers, competitors and interfunctional coordination may be conceived, managed and interpreted in different, less prescribed, rational and economic, ways.

ACKNOWLEDGEMENTS

The author gratefully acknowledges the helpful comments of Professor Kosmas Symrnios, Alan Broadbent and the three JMM anonymous reviewers.

REFERENCES

Aaker, D.A. (1995), *Strategic Market Management,* New York: John Wiley and Sons.

Adler, R., Everett, A. and Waldron, M. (2000), "Advanced Management Accounting Techniques in Manufacturing: Utilization, Benefits and Barriers to Implementation", *Accounting Forum*, Vol. 24, No. 2, pp. 131-150.

Aalbregste, R.J., *Target Costing.* In: Brinker, B. (1993), *Handbook of Cost Management*, New York: Warren, Gorham and Lamont.

Anderson, J. C. and Narus, J. A. (1999), *Business Market Management: Understanding, Creating and Delivering Value,* NJ: Prentice-Hall

Anderson, J. C., Narus, J. A. and van Rossum W. (2006), "Customer Value Propositions in Business Markets", *Harvard Business Review*, Vol. 84, No. 3, March, pp. 91-99.

Anderson, S. W. (2007), "Managing Costs and Cost Structure Throughout the Value Chain: Research on Strategic Cost Management". In: Chapman, C. S., Hopwood, A. G. and Shields, M. D. (eds.), *Handbook of Management Accounting Research,* Vol. 2, Oxford: Elsevier, pp. 481-506.

Andon, P., Baxter, J. and Bradley, G. (2001), "Calculating the Economic Value of Customers to an Organisation", *Australian Accounting Review*, Vol. 11, No. 1, pp. 62-72.

Ansari, S. L., Bell, J. F. and Okano, H. (2007), "Target Costing: Uncharted Research Territory", In: Chapman, C. S., Hopwood, A. G. and Shields, M. D. (eds.), *Handbook of Management Accounting Research,* Vol. 2, Oxford: Elsevier, pp. 507-530.

Artto, K. A. (1994), "Life Cycle Cost Concepts and Methodologies", *Journal of Cost Management*, Vol. 8, No. 3, Fall, pp. 28-32.

Baird, K. M., Harrison, G. L. and Reeve, R.C. (2004), "Adoption of Activity Management Practices: A Note on the Extent of Adoption and the Influences of Organizational and Cultural factors", *Management Accounting Research*, Vol. 15, No. 4, pp. 383-399.

Bauer, H. H., Hammerschmidt, M. (2005), "Customer-based Corporate Valuation: Integrating the Concepts of Customer Equity and Shareholder Value", *Management Decision*, Vol. 43, No. 3, pp. 331-348

Benbasat, I., Goldstein, D. K. and Mead, M. (1987), "The Case Research Strategy in Studies of Information Systems", *MIS Quarterly*, Vol. 11, No. 3, pp. 369-386.

Berghman, L., Matthyssens, P. and Vandenbempt, K. (2006), "Building Competences for New Customer Value Creation: An Exploratory Study", *Industrial Marketing Management*, Vol. 35, No. 8, pp. 961-973.

Boland, R. J. and Pondy, L. R. (1983), "Accounting in Organizations: A Union of Natural and Rational Perspectives", *Accounting, Organizations and Society,* Vol. 8, No. 2/3, pp. 223-234.

Bonoma, T. V. (1985), "Case Research in Marketing: Opportunities, Problems, and a Process", *Journal of Marketing Research*, Vol. 22, No. 2, May, pp. 199-208.

Brock, J. J. (1984), "Competitor Analysis: Some Practical Approaches", *Industrial Marketing Management*, Vol. 13, No. 4, pp. 225-231.

Bromwich, M. (1990), "The Case for Strategic Management Accounting: The Role of Accounting Information for Strategy in Competitive Markets", *Accounting, Organizations and Society*, Vol. **15**, No. 1/2, pp. 27-46.

Bromwich, M. (1991), "Accounting Information for Strategic Excellence". In: *Okonomistyring OG Strategic-Nyeideer Nye erfarinjer,* (in English), Denmark: Systime.

Bromwich, M. (1992), "Strategic Management Accounting". In: Drury, C. (ed.), *Management Accounting Handbook*, Oxford, UK: Butterworth-Heinemann, pp. 128-153

Bromwich, M. and Bhimani, A. (1994), *Management Accounting Pathways to Progress,* UK: The Chartered Institute of Management Accountants.

Coad, A. (1996), "Smart Work and Hard Work: Explicating a Learning Orientation in Strategic Management Accounting", *Management Accounting Research*, Vol. **7**, No. 4, pp. 387-408.

Cooper, R. and Chew, W. B. (1996), "Control Tomorrow's Cost Through Today's Designs", *Harvard Business Review*, Vol. **74**, No. 1, January-February, pp. 88-97.

Cooper, R. and Kaplan, R. S. (1988), "How Cost Accounting Distorts Product Costs", *Management Accounting*, Vol. **69**, No. 10, April, pp. 20-27.

Cooper, R. and Slagmulder, R. (2004), "Cost Analysis Outside the Organization", *Cost Management,* May/June, pp. 44-46.

Clark, B. H. (2001), "A Summary of Thinking on Measuring the Value of Marketing", *Journal of Targeting, Measurement and Analysis for Marketing*, Vol. **9**, No. 4, pp. 357-369.

Cravens, K. S. and Guilding, C. (2001), "An Empirical Study of the Application of Strategic Management Accounting Techniques", *Advances in Management Accounting*, Vol. **10**, pp. 95-124.

Day, G. S. (1990), *Market Driven Strategy: Processes for Creating Value*, New York: The Free Press.

Day, G. S. (1994), The Capabilities of Market-Driven Organisations, *Journal of Marketing*, Vol. **58**, No. 4, October, pp. 37-52.

Day, G .S. and Wensley, R. (1988), "Assessing Advantage: A Framework for Diagnosing Competitive Superiority", *Journal of Marketing*, Vol. **52**, No. 2, April, pp. 1-20.

Drury, J. C. (2008), *Management and Cost Accounting,* London: Cengage Learning EMEA.

Eisenhardt, K. M. (1989), "Building Theories from Case Study Research", *The Academy of Management Review*, Vol. **14**, No. 4, pp. 532-550.

Fisher, J. (1995), "Implementing Target Costing", *Journal of Cost Management,* Vol. **9**, No. 1, pp. 50-59.

Forbis, J. L. and Mehta, N. T. (1981), "Value-Based Strategies for Industrial Products", *Business Horizons*, Vol. **24**, No. 3, pp. 32-42.

Foster, G. and Gupta, M. (1994), "Marketing, Cost Management and Management Accounting", *Journal of Management Accounting Research*, Vol. **6**, Fall, pp. 43-77.

Goebel, D., Marshall, G. W., and Locander, W. B. (1998), "Activity-Based Costing - Accounting for a Market Orientation", *Industrial Marketing Management*, Vol. **27**, No. 6, pp. 497-510.

Gonzalez-Benito, O. and Gonzalez-Benito, J. (2005), "Cultural vs. Operational Market Orientation and Objective vs. Subjective Performance: Perspective of Production and Operations", *Industrial Marketing Management*, Vol. **34**, No. 8, pp. 797-829.

Gray, B., Matear, S., Boshoff, C. and Matheson, P. (1998), "Developing a Better Measure of Market Orientation", *European Journal of Marketing*, Vol. **32**, No. 9/10, pp. 884-903.

Gray, B. J. and Hooley, G. J. (2002), "Market Orientation and Service Firm Performance - A Research Agenda", *European Journal of Marketing*, Vol. **36**, No. 9/10, pp. 980-988.

Grunfert, K. G. (1989), "Attributes, Attribute Value and their Characteristics: A Unifying Approach Involving a Complex Household Investment", *Journal of Economic Psychology*, Vol. **10**, No. 2, pp. 229-251

Guilding, C. (1999), "Competitor-focused Accounting: An Exploratory Note", *Accounting, Organizations and Society*, Vol. **24**, No. 7, pp. 583-595.

Guilding, C. and McManus, L. (2002), "The Incidence, Perceived Merit and Antecedents of Customer Accounting: An Exploratory Note", *Accounting, Organizations and Society*, Vol. **27**, No. 1-2, pp. 45-59.

Guilding, C. and Moorhouse, M. (1992), "The Case for Brand Value Budgeting".In: Drury, C. (ed.), *Management Accounting Handbook,* London: Butterworth-Heinemann.

Gummesson, E. (1991), *Qualitative Methods in Management Research,* CA: Sage,

Harris, L. (2000), "The Organizational Barriers to Developing Market Orientation", *European Journal of Marketing,* Vol. 5, No. 6, pp. 598-624.

Helfert, G., Ritter, T. and Walter, A. (2002), "Refining Market Orientation From a Relationship Perspective", *European Journal of Marketing, Vol.* 36, No. 9/10, pp. 1119-1139.

Helgessen, O. (2007) "Customer Accounting and Customer profitability Analysis for the Order Handling Industry – A Managerial Accounting Approach", *Industrial Marketing Management*, Vol. 36, No. 6, pp. 757-769.

Horngren, C. T., Foster, G. and Datar, S. M. (2006), *Cost Accounting: A Managerial Emphasis,* Upper Saddle River, New Jersey; Pearson Prentice-Hall.

Howell, R. A. and Soucy, S. R. (1990), "Customer Profitability: As Critical as Product Profitability", *Management Accounting (USA),* Vol. 72, No. 4, October, pp. 43-47.

Hult, G., Ketchen, D. and Slater, S. (2005), "Market Orientation and Performance: An Integration of Disparate Approaches", *Strategic Management Journal,* Vol. 26, No. 12, pp. 1173-1181.

Inglis, R. (2005), *Market Orientation and Accounting Information: A Product-level Study*, Unpublished MPhil, University of Stirling, Scotland.

Innes, J., Mitchell, F. and Cobb, I. (1992) *Activity-based Costing: Problems in Practice.* London: CIMA

Javalgi, R, Martin, C. and Young, C. (2006), "Marketing Research, Market Orientation and Customer Relationship Management: A Framework and Implications for Service Providers", *Journal of Services Marketing,* Vol. 20, No. 1, pp. 12- 23.

Johnson, H. T. and Kaplan, R. S. (1987), *"Relevance Lost - The Rise and Fall of Management Accounting",* Boston, Mass: Harvard Business School Press.

Kaplan, R.S. (1984), "Yesterday's Accounting Undermines Production", *Harvard Business Review,* Vol. 62, No. 4, July-August, pp. 95-101.

Kato, Y. (1993), "Target Costing Support Systems: Lessons from Leading Japanese Companies", *Management Accounting Research*, Vol. 4, No. 1, pp. 33-47.

Kato, Y., Boer, G. and Chow, C. W. (1995), "Target Costing: An Integrative Management Process", *Journal of Cost Management*, Vol. 9, No. 1, Spring, pp. 39-51.

Kohli, A. K. and Jaworski, B. J. (1990), "Market Orientation: The Construct, Research Propositions, and Managerial Implications", *Journal of Marketing,* Vol. 54, No. 2, April, pp. 1-18.

Kotler, P. (2000), *Marketing Management: The Millennium Edition,* NJ: Prentice-Hall,

Kumar, K., Subramanian, R. and Yauger, C. (1998), "Examining the Market Orientation-Performance Relationship: A Context-Specific Study", *Journal of Management,* Vol. 24, No. 2, pp. 201-234.

Lafferty, B.A. and Hult, G. T. (2001), "A Synthesis of Contemporary Market Orientation Perspect ives", *European Journal of Marketing,* Vol. 35, No. 1/2, pp. 92-109.

Lancaster, K. J. (1966), "A New Approach to Consumer Theory", *Journal of Political Economy,* Vol. 74, No. 2, pp. 132-157.

Lancaster, K. J. (1971), *"Consumer Demand: A New Approach",* New York: Columbia University Press.

Lancaster, K. (1979), *Variety, Equity and Efficiency: Product Variety in Industrial Society,* New York: Columbia University Press.

Langfield-Smith, K. (2007), "Strategic Management Accounting: How Far Have we Come in 25 Years?", *Accounting, Auditing and Accountability Journal*, Vol. 21, No. 2, pp. 204-228.

Lindgreen, A. and Wynstra, F. (2005), "Value in Business Markets: What do we Know? Where are we Going?", *Industrial Marketing Management,* Vol. 34, No. 7, pp. 732-748.

Maltz, E. and Kohli, A.K. (2000), "Reducing Marketing's Conflict With Other Functions: The Differential Effects of Integrating Mechanisms", *Journal of Academy of Marketing Science,* Vol. 28, No. 4, pp. 479-492.

Mason, K., Doyle, P. and Wong, V. (2006), "Market Orientation and Quasi-integration: Adding Value Through Relationships", *Industrial Marketing Management*, Vol. 35, No. 2, pp. 140-155.

McNair, C. J., Polutnik, L. and Silvi, R. (2001), "Cost Management and Value Creation: the Missing Link", *The European Accounting Review*, Vol. 10, No. 1, pp. 33-50.

Miles, L. D. (1961), *Techniques of Value Analysis and Engineering*, New York: McGraw-Hill.

Miles, M. and Huberman, M. (1994), *Qualitative Data Analysis*, CA: Sage.

Morgan, R. E. and Strong, C. A. (1998), "Market Orientation and Dimensions of Strategic Orientation", *European Journal of Marketing*, Vol. 32, No. 11/12, pp. 1051-1073.

Myers, J. H. and Shocker, A. D. (1981), "The Nature of Product Related Attributes", *Research in Marketing*, Vol. 5, pp. 211-236.

Narver, J. C. and Slater, S. F. (1990), "The Effect of a Market Orientation on Business Profitability", *Journal of Marketing*, Vol. 54, No. 4, October, pp. 20-35.

Narver, J. C. and Slater, S. F. and Tietje, B. (1998), "Creating a Market Orientation", *Journal of Market Focused Management*, Vol. 2, No. 1, pp. 241-255.

Nielsen, J., Bukh, P. and Mols, N. (2000), "Barriers to Customer-oriented Management Accounting in Financial Services", *International Journal of Service Industry Management*, Vol. 11, No. , pp. 269-286.

Partridge, M. and Perren, L. 1994, "Cost Analysis of the Value Chain: Another Strategic Role for Strategic Management Accounting", *Management Accounting (UK)*, Vol. 72, No. 7, July/August, pp.22-26.

Perry, C. (1998), "Processes of a Case Study Methodology for Postgraduate Research in Marketing", *European Journal of Marketing*, Vol. 32, No. 9/10, pp. 785-802.

Porter, M. E. (1985), *Competitive Advantage*, New York: The Free Press.

Reinartz, W. and Kumar, V. (2000), "On the Profitability of Long-life Customers in a Noncontractual Setting: An Empirical Investigation and Implications for Marketing", *Journal of Marketing*, Vol. 64, No. 4, pp. 17-35.

Ratnatunga, J. (1988) *Accounting for Competitive Marketing*, London: CIMA Publications.

Ratnatunga, J, Pike, R. and Hooley, G. (1988), "The Application of Management Accounting Techniques to Marketing", *Accounting and Business Research*, Vol. 18, No. 72, pp. 363-370.

Roslender, R. (1995), "Accounting for Strategic Positioning: Responding to the Crisis in Management Accounting", *British Journal of Management*, Vol. 6, No. 1, pp. 45-47.

Roslender, R. and Hart, S. J. (2002), "Integrating Management Accounting and Marketing in the Pursuit of Competitive Advantage: The Case for Strategic Management Accounting", *Critical Perspectives on Accounting*, Vol. 13, No. 2, pp. 255-277.

Roslender, R. and Hart, S.J. (2003), "In Search of Strategic Management Accounting: Theoretical and Field Study Perspectives", *Management Accounting Research*, Vol. 14, No. 3, pp. 255-279.

Ryals, L. (2005), "Making Customer Relationship Management Work: The Measurement and Profitable Management of Customer Relationships", *Journal of Marketing*, Vol. 69, No. 4, pp. 252- 261.

Ryals, L. and Knox, S. (2005), "Measuring Risk-adjusted Customer Lifetime Value and its Impact on Relationship Marketing Strategies and Shareholder Value", *European Journal of Marketing*, Vol. 39, No. 5/6, pp. 456-472.

Santos-Vijande, M. L., Sanzo-Perez, M J., Alvarez-Gonzalez, L. I. and Vazquez-Casielles, R. (2005), "Organizational Learning and Market Orientation: Interface and Effects on Performance", *Industrial Marketing Management*, Vol. 34, No. 3, pp. 187-202.

Schonberger, R. J. (1996), *World Class Manufacturing: The Next Decade*, New York: The Free Press.

Schonberger, R. J. (2001), *Let's Fix it, Overcoming the Crisis in Management*, New York: The Free Press.

Shank, J. K. and Govindarajan, V. (1988), "Making Strategy Explicit in Cost Analysis: A Case Study", *Sloan Management Review*, Vol. 29, No. 3, pp. 19-30

Shields, M.D. and Young, S.M. (1991), "Managing Product Life Cycle Costs: An Organizational Model", *Journal of Cost Management,* Vol. 5, Fall, pp. 39-52.

Shillito, M.L. and De Marle, D.J. (1992), *Value: Its Measurement, Design and Management,* USA: John Wiley and Sons, Inc.

Simmonds, K. (1981), "Strategic Management Accounting", *Management Accounting (UK),* Vol. 59, No. 4, April, pp. 26-29.

Simmonds, K. (1982), "Strategic Management Accounting for Pricing: A Case Study", *Accounting and Business Research,* Vol. 47, No. 12, pp. 206-214.

Simmonds, K. (1986), "The Accounting Assessment of Competitive Position", *European Journal of Marketing,* Vol. 20, No. 1, pp. 16-31.

Slater, S. F. and Narver, J. C. (2000), "The Positive Effect of a Market Orientation on Business Profitability: A Balanced Replication", *Journal of Business Research,* Vol. 48, No. 1, pp. 69-73.

Stake, R. E. (1995), *The Art of Case Study Research,* CA: Sage.

Stokmans, M. J. W. (1991), *The Relative Importance of Product Attributes: Consumer Decision Theories in New-product Development,* The Netherlands Delft University Press,

Tani, T. Okano, H., Shimizu, N., Iwabuchi, I., Fukuda, J. and Cooray, S. (1994), "Target Cost Management in Japanese Companies: Current State of the Art", *Management Accounting Research,* Vol. 5, No. 1, pp. 67-81.

Ulaga, W. and Chacour, S. (2001), "Measuring Customer Perceived Value in Business Markets: A Prerequisite for Marketing Strategy Development and Implementation", *Industrial Marketing Management,* Vol. 30, No. 6, pp. 525-540.

Ulaga, W. (2003), "Capturing Value Creation in Business Relationships: A Customer Perspective", *Industrial Marketing Management,* Vol. 32, No. 8, pp. 677-693.

Uncles, M. (2000), "Market Orientation", *Australian Journal of Management,* 25, 2, pp. i-ix.

Vaivio, J. (1999), "Examining 'The Quantified Customer'", *Accounting, Organizations, and Society,* Vol. 24, No. 8, pp .689-715.

Van Raaij, E. M. (2005), "The Strategic Value of Customer Profitability Analysis", *Market Intelligence and Planning,* Vol. 23, No. 4, pp. 372-381.

Walker, M. 1991, "ABC Using Product Attributes", *Management Accounting,* Vol. 69, No. 9, October, pp.34-35.

Walker, M. 1992, "Attribute Based Costing", *Australian Accountant,* Vol. 62, No. 2, March, pp.42-45.

Waldron, M. (2005), "Overcoming Barriers to Change in Management Accounting Systems", *The Journal of American Academy of Business,* Vol. 6, No. 2, March, pp. 244- 249.

Wilson, R. M. S. (1981), *Financial Dimensions of Marketing: a source book Vol 1.* London: Macmillan in association with the Institute of Cost and Management Accountants.

Wouters, M, Anderson, J.C. and Wynstra, F. (2005), "The Adoption of Total Cost of Ownership for Sourcing Decisions – A Structural Equations Analysis", *Accounting, Organizations and Society,* Vol. 30, No. 2, pp. 167-191.

Yin, R. K. (1994), *Case Study Research, Design and Methods,* , CA: Sage

Yoshikawa, T., Innes, J. and Mitchell, F. (1995), "A Japanese Case Study of Functional Cost Analysis", *Management Accounting Research,* Vol. 6, No. 4, pp. 415-432.

Zeithaml, V. A., Rust, R. T. and Lemon, K. N. (2001), "The Customer Pyramid: Creating and Serving Profitable Customers", *California Management Review,* Vol. 43, No. 4, pp. 118-142.

APPENDIX 1

NP Company and management profile

The company employed around 250 management and operational staff and was financially responsible for generating a return on investment. The functional management organisation structure is outlined below.

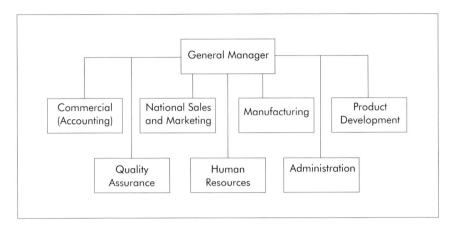

The Human Resources and Administration functions were not part of this case study. Brief profiles of those involved in this study follow:

General Manager (GM): aged in the mid 40's, MBA qualified with an engineering background and had been in this position for the past two years.

National Sales and Marketing Manager (NSMM): aged in the mid 40's, the NSMM had been in this management position for three years having had a general management position with a similar, but smaller, business in another country.

Business Manager (BM): aged in the mid 40's, the BM had been with the firm for one year, was MBA qualified and had previously worked in market research.

Product Development Manager (PDM): the PDM was an engineer aged in the late 40s and had worked with the firm for almost three years. Although the Product Development (PD) department was often referred to as "Research and Development", the activity emphasis, according to the PDM, was more on product development of existing lines than product research.

Quality Assurance Manager (QAM): the Quality Assurance manager (QAM) was an engineer with 20 years experience with a leading Japanese motor vehicle manufacturer before joining NP one year prior. Before taking up his role as the QA manager, he had been the manufacturing manager at NP while the position was temporarily vacant.

Commercial Manager (CM): the CM was a qualified certified practising accountant (CPA) aged in his mid 30's with engineering industry and chartered accounting experience. The CM, who had only been employed by NP for two months, was responsible for financial reporting and financial controls but more so providing "commercial advice to other members of the business team". These decisions included break-even analysis on products, the costs to "re-work" (re-design) existing products and financial analysis on entering new product markets.

APPENDIX 2

Product attribute cross-functional summary

Attribute	Brief description	Data source - evidence
Reducing the customers costs – increasing the customer's profit	Reducing the number of installers and the time required to install product – increasing the productivity of the specialists' installers. Reduced warranty claims. Provide training.	NSMM, BM, CM, PDM, QAM Warranty reports
Brand image	Perception of brand – whether can they portray the brand that from a business point of view is a reliable brand	NSMM, BM, GM, PDM, CM
***Reliable* delivery**	Stock availability to allow delivery on time and rapid response to customer demands for installation	NSMM/BM, CM, GM Inventory reports
After sales service	NP have a reliable spare parts and a service division	GM, NSMM, BM Meetings
Innovation of *"product"*	Provide innovation of product which could be used as a basis to influence customers to purchase (Specialist has something to sell)	GM, NSMM, BM, PDM Market research reports
Product range	Range of products that support the specialist business	CM Marketing documents
Easy to do business with	The specialist finds doing business with NP is easy and enjoyable	GM, NSMM, BM
Promotions assistance	Generate lead enquiries through media advertising and promotions	CM, NSMM, BM

The recognition and measurement of brand assets: an exploration of the accounting/marketing interface

Nevine El-Tawy, *Brunel University, UK*
Tony Tollington, *Brunel University, UK*

Abstract The asset recognition criteria presented in this paper break free from the narrow definitional and rule based perspective of accounting epistemology to offer an alternative view based on the recognition of artefacts and the related notion of separability. The purpose is to explore the nature of a trademarked brand "asset" currently excluded from disclosure in the accounting domain but included in the marketing domain usually as a constituent part of brand equity. That exclusion is based on the 'uniqueness' of a brand and an inability to separate brand assets from the other assets of a business. However, we show that it is actually 'additivity', or the lack thereof, which is the principle reason for the exclusion of brand assets from financial statements. Whilst the paper is inevitably accounting biased, the subject matter is nevertheless of interest to those marketers who view brands as assets.

INTRODUCTION

Unlike the marketing domain, the epistemological basis within the financial accounting domain is dominated by rules. Those rules are supposedly grounded on overarching conceptual frameworks (ASB 1999; FASB 1984 1985; IASB 2001) and the results of institutionally led external consultation processes (for example, ASB (1995x,y,z)) that legitimate the conceptual frameworks and rules, and the accounting regulatory bodies creating them, in the 'eyes' of society. However, the reality is somewhat different.

First, consider for example, that the definitions of an asset in most accounting conceptual frameworks (CF) specify that an asset should produce "*future economic benefits*" (ASB 1999, para4.7-23; FASB 1985, para6.25-33; IASB 2001, para 49, 53-59) without specifying how the benefits should be measured or, indeed, what should be measured? On this basis a brand would qualify to be disclosed as an asset in the financial statements (and have been previously – see Tollington 2002) but it is left to a specific accounting rule (IAS38) to nullify this qualification on different grounds, addressed later on, thus weakening the link between the CF and the accounting rules. Second, the respondents to an accounting rule-setting consultation process are typically those parties interested in the particular accounting rule being created or revised. It is therefore not surprising that the respondent constituency is narrowly drawn comprising, in the main, financial institutions, professional accounting practices, company finance directors, accounting academics as well as a minority of other interest groups. The tentative conclusion to be respectively drawn from these comments is that the accounting rule-based epistemology is inherently normative and self-referential in nature. In other words, as long as society accepts the rule-based social construction of financial statements as a faithful representation of financial reality, and uses it as such, then, de facto, those rules and the related financial statements are legitimate in the 'eyes of society' on the basis of their own normative merits (see Hines 1988; Searle 1995).

Of course, socially 'acceptable' representations of financial reality become entirely 'unacceptable' in the face of corporate collapses such as Enron and Worldcom. Whether the blame for such occurrences can be laid entirely at the door of accountants is a moot point but they do raise the ages-old accounting problem of a profession that wishes to disclose twenty-first century economic decision-relevant figures whilst retaining a tried and tested nineteenth century (and older), legalistic, transaction based system of accounting that tends to ignore non-transactions-based assets, notably, the internally-generated intangible ones (see Tollington 2001a). So, finally, we come to the purpose of this paper. The above IAS38 international accounting rule (IASB 1998), applicable in the UK from 2005, states that "*internally generated brands...shall not be recognised as intangible assets*" (IAS38, para 63) regardless of whether they are measured at cost (IAS38, para 21(b)) or at valuation and whether they are capable of creating future economic benefits (IAS38, para 21(a)) because they are "*unique*" (IAS38, para.78) and they "*...cannot be distinguished from the cost of developing the business as a whole*" (IAS38, para64). We seek to explore the nature of this rule, and more, by reference to asset recognition criteria. In particular, through the use of these criteria, we show that it is the aforementioned "*ages-old accounting problem*" rather than the IAS38 reference to "*uniqueness*" that lies at the heart of the decision not to include internally-generated or, indeed, most purchased brands (see Tollington 1998a) on the balance sheet. These criteria constitute a considerable development of work already given exposure in the marketing literature (Tollington 1998b) because they are now based on the new tripartite structure of Figure 1.

A problem, though, is that the criteria presented later on in this paper are equally self-referential and, therefore, can only be advanced on the subjective basis that they offer a 'better' basis on which to construct financial reality. That assertion would probably require some proof in the accounting domain (a problem perhaps if self referential?) if only because the ontological security blanket offered by the existing transactions-based accounting system is one that will not be relinquished or modified lightly. Indeed, in the accounting domain, the use of 'asset recognition criteria' have

FIGURE 1 The recognition boundary for assets: inside the circles using artefacts to establish a separable and physical identity for intangible assets

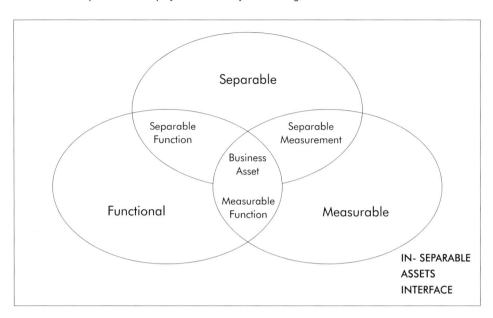

already been rejected by one regulatory body on the rather dubious grounds of "*introducing circularity*" (ASB 1999). However, that does not prevent their exposure in the marketing domain given that the above IAS38 rule indicates a worsening of the brand asset disclosure situation despite the rather dated, but still relevant, pleas of the Chartered Institute of Marketing (1993) that it should be otherwise:

> It is not the acceptance of brand equity which has been at the heart of the debate; it is whether accounting practices can adapt to a changing business environment in which 'worth' is typified by a set of intangible assets. This is an issue which our accounting colleagues show a persistent lack of commitment to resolve. And resolved it should be.

THE STRUCTURE OF THE PAPER AND THE CENTRALITY OF FIGURE 1 WITHIN IT

In the first section of the paper the difference between brand assets (accounting domain) and brand equity (marketing domain) is examined in order to ground the paper in the literature. Thereafter we look at the three circles in Figure 1, specifically, that an asset should be functional, separable and measurable. A definition of what is meant by 'separable' is given in appendix A. It is at the intersections between these three characteristics that the asset recognition criteria are developed and applied to brand assets in the subsequent three sections of the paper. Finally, there is a discussion about the contribution of these criteria to the literature.

The square boundary in Figure 1 encompasses all business assets[1] and within

---

[1] The term has to remain vague because what constitutes a 'business asset' is subject to the political policy choices of accounting regulators.

the three intersecting circles represents the business asset element for accounting purposes according to the related criteria presented later on. The space between the circles and the square boundary represents those inseparable assets the recognition and measurement of which are indeterminate for accounting purposes. This pictorial clarity between separable and inseparable assets in Figure 1 is not presently reflected in the accounting domain itself. We obviously think it should be. Why?

What we have at present in the accounting domain is a mixture of separable and inseparable assets, for example, a purchased patent and purchased goodwill, respectively - both transactions-based, both regarded as intangible assets on the balance sheet. However, unlike a separately purchased patent, no one in their right mind would purchase goodwill *separately* from the other assets of a business. And, unusually in the accounting domain, it has been practically possible in the past to extract and disclose a separable intangible asset, such as a brand asset, from an inseparable purchased goodwill 'asset' as evidenced historically in the accounts of companies like Cadbury Schweppes Plc and Diageo Plc (see Tollington 1998b). It begs the question: what other separable intangible assets are 'hiding' within purchased goodwill and should they even be connected to it? The point is that it is a muddled financial picture, for example, most companies leaving brand assets subsumed within an inseparable purchased goodwill 'asset' and others, like Cadbury's and Diageo, disclosing separable brand assets on the balance sheet. Figure 1, a product of our own invention, is intended to bring some clarity on what is a 'separable' and 'inseparable' intangible asset for accounting purposes through the use of asset recognition criteria. The example being used herein is in respect of brand assets but Figure 1 clearly has a wider application. Indeed, the issue of the separability of goodwill, and labour related 'assets' too, are already the subject of two more papers by the authors and more 'asset' types will follow as we progressively and subjectively assess the usefulness of the asset recognition criteria connected to Figure 1. Figure 1 and the related asset recognition criteria in Table 1 are therefore an appropriate contribution to the literature because we would argue that one is unlikely to investigate a more fundamental topic than the nature of an asset. We are grateful to the JMM editors/reviewers for publishing this thought provoking paper (to "...*stimulate much thought*" as one reviewer concluded) because we hope that others will develop what we have done into a more robust form over time.

COMPARING BRAND ASSETS TO BRAND EQUITY

To repeat, the key feature of Figure 1 is 'inseparable assets' together with their 'separable' counterparts, the issue being generally known as separability (see Napier and Power 1992). So, for example, a separability-related criterion, to be presented later on, is that an asset should be capable of transference and, therefore, not necessarily on the basis of an actual business transaction as would typically be the case in the accounting domain. It follows that a brand asset should be capable of transference too. However, there is a lack of clarity in the terms like 'brand assets' and 'brand equity' (see appendix B) and therefore in the nature of what is capable of being transferred. For example, Aaker (1991) refers to "*brand equity as a set of brand assets and liabilities linked to a brand...*" As such, a rather dubious source of finance, 'brand equity', is used interchangeably with the application of that finance to equally dubious 'brand assets', at least from an accounting perspective. The term 'equally dubious' is used here in the sense that the nature of fickle brand equity related "assets" (if they be so?), such as brand loyalty, name awareness, perceptions as to quality, brand associations, etc (see Aaker 1991, p16), means that transference cannot be shown to have occurred, or be capable of occurring, without empirical evidence to that effect. This would be costly and impracticable to perform on a routine basis certainly in comparison with existing accounting practices where such marketing-based "assets" are ignored.

The one remaining attribute of brand equity not referred to above (see Aaker 1991, p16 again) is *proprietary associations*" such as trademarks and patents. In contrast to the other brand equity attributes, above, a trademark is separable. So, for example, in the case of the separability-related transference criterion addressed previously, it is relatively easy to perform contractually in respect of a trademark, whereas, no one in their right mind would contract for name awareness, perceptions as to quality etc on their own. Nevertheless, with the transference of the trademark would pass the other four brand equity attributes or "assets" because Aaker (1991, p16) is clear in referring to a "*set of assets*". The conduit, though, is the trademark. What links the accounting and marketing domains in this regard is the legal formalism (McBarnett and Whelan 1991) that makes the 'unrecognisable/intangible' become 'recognisable/tangible' in terms of a surrogate artefact, in this case, trademark registration documents or a court order following a successful defence of a brand for the tortuous act of 'passing-off' (see Tollington 2001b).

The next three sections of the paper address this surrogate artefact approach within some asset recognition criteria, which in turn are grouped around the three circle intersections in Figure 1. The details of the criteria within those three groups are presented in summary in Table 1.

The three groups in Table 1 are repeated individually and in detail in Tables 2, 3, 4 in the next three sections of the paper.

TABLE 1 The application of the asset recognition criteria to trademarked brands

Criteria	Trademarked brand
Separable Function (see Figure 1, Table 2):	
a. Right to control	Yes
b. Right to future use	Yes
c. Right to security	Yes
d. Capability of transference	Yes
e. The absence of a duration	Yes
f. The prohibition of harmful use	Yes
g. The liability to execution	Yes
h. The right to a residuary character	Yes
Measurable Function (see Figure 1, Table 3):	
i. The right to capital	Yes
j. The right to discharge capital	Yes
k. The right to income	Yes
Separable Measurement (see Figure 1, Table 4):	
l. Additive measurement method	No
m. Observed measurements only	No
n. Bundles of assets disallowed	Yes

SEPARABLE FUNCTION OF AN ASSET (SEE FIGURE 1)

The legal view of separability is that of assets capable of being disposed of or discharged separately without disposing of a business of the undertaking (Companies Act 1985 Sch.4A,9(2)). There is no mention of measurement here, only a function: disposal or discharging. Clearly, one cannot perform this function where the asset in question is intangible unless, instead, there is some surrogate artefact that is disposed of or discharged as being representative of the intangible asset. In most cases the artefact will be documentary: an invoice, receipt, court order, patent letters, trademark registration, EU quota document, copyrighted document and so on (see Upton 2001, p69 for list of separable intangible assets, also, Seetharaman et al. 2004, p525 for a list of separable and inseparable intangible assets). The use of artefacts represents an expanded recognition boundary for accountants because they are not necessarily linked to a transaction but still a restrictive one to other interest groups (see Hall 1991 1992). Consider in this regard the marketing notion of "specific assets", that is, professional know how and skills, knowledge and working skills, specialist training and tailored deliver routines (Payan and Svensson 2007) non of which would be separately recognisable in the accounting domain. Indeed, the possible disclosure of such human based 'assets' was thoroughly debated in the 1970/80's under the banner of Human Resource Accounting (see Brummet, Flamholtz and Pyle 1968 1969ab; Hermansson 1964) and dismissed principally on the basis of a lack of empirical referents (see Scarpello and Theeke 1989). For example, as Lev (2001) points out, the specialist training investment by one company can easily be appropriated by another at no cost to them, thus highlighting the absence of an important criterion in respect of a separable function: control over use (see Table 2).

Table 2 shows the eight asset recognition criteria that are pertinent to the establishment of a separable function for a brand asset.

MEASURABLE FUNCTION OF AN ASSET (SEE FIGURE 1)

Assets per se are not measurable except in respect of their function, notably, their use in appropriating income – see appendix C. That income, though, may be part operating revenue and part capital holding gains. Also, just because an asset has apparently finished operating (a worked out gravel pit) does not mean that there are no operating gains (from a boating lake or rubbish dump, instead) or holding gains (from an increase in land prices) to be obtained. Much depends on how one wants to measure income and the related increase or decrease in the capital of a business: from an operating stance or from an operating and holding stance? This matters because if in the accounting domain the latter stance prevails (known as 'comprehensive income', see Bertoni and De Rosa 2005; Cauwenberge and De Beelde 2007; IASB 2003; Newberry 2003; Barker 2004) then, in principle, this should include income (if any) from holding an investment in brand 'equity' or brand 'capital'. In practice, though, no measurable function is recognised at all in the accounting domain – a source of concern to marketers (Oldroyd 1994). It follows, that if the capital investment in brand 'equity' is not recognised in the accounting domain, the operating revenue from that 'equity' is also not recognised, the two being linked on a 'chicken and egg' basis. The only exception in the past has been where an investment has been made in purchased goodwill from which the brand has then been extracted – a convoluted process (see Tollington 1998a).

TABLE 2 The separable function of a brand asset (see Figure 1)

Criteria	General Description – Intangible Assets	Application to Trademarked Brand Assets
a. Right to control an asset	Control exercised for a purpose: appropriation - usually income but not always. Consider, instead, lending without recompense or holding assets to prevent control by others. In the absence of an artefact there is little control over who may appropriate (Lev 2001, p52).	Control over its appropriating capabilities may be established through custom and practice and be accepted as such without challenge (no artefact). However, constructive control is over the legal property rights, which can be established by trademarking or by a successful action for the tort of 'passing-off' (both artefact based).
b. Right to future use	Not scarce resource: use by many at the same time eg. seawater or atmospheric nitrogen. Scarce resource: use is linked to restrictive controls (Ijiri 1975, p52). Scarcity is pertinent here.	'Use or lose it' clause to trademark registration (the legal artefact). Absence of an artefact does not prevent others from use, typically, by copying. Artefact deters copying but use cannot be prevented unless court sanctioned. Renewal of right to future use upon expiration of the trademark or franchise term.
c. Right to security	Security is in the expectation that appropriation will run in perpetuity unless determined otherwise, such as by statute. For example, a contract (the artefact) may secure for a lending institution access to future appropriations eg. royalty income from securitised assets, such as Robbie Williams music copyright.	Security in long-lived super-brands like Cadburys particularly where it is capable of being sold or franchised to other businesses, as with, for example, Cadburys cakes. Security is probably less likely in an obscure brand.
d. Capability of transference (including disposal)	Assumes the existence of an artefact so that the business entity acquiring the intangible asset can demonstrate that the right to control its use has passed to them. The capability is sufficient rather than actual transference.	Can occur contractually and may or may not be supported by transference of a trademark registration document – both artefacts. Transference can occur independently of the other assets to which it may have been originally tied, for instance, the 'Virgin' brand.
e. Absence of a duration	The interest of the user of a business asset is best served by a determinable time horizon for planning purposes where longer is usually more valuable than shorter. Where the function of an intangible asset can be separated from the human being and is vested in an artefact the duration is determined by social norms, notably legalistic ones.	The absence of visual awareness is no guarantee that the brand is 'dead' eg. Triumph motorcycles. And a trademark may be renewably long-lived even where exposure to the brand is minimal.

Cont'd...

Criteria	General Description – Intangible Assets	Application to Trademarked Brand Assets
f. Prohibition of harmful use	Asset usage can impose costs on others eg pollution costs. Because social norms, notably, statutory ones, indicate who must pay to have their interests protected against the costs imposed by another party, improper use of an asset is often prohibited. Consider, for example, the creation of 'carbon credits' (documented artefacts) where pollution quotas may be traded within and between countries, in the same manner as fishing quotas, in order to sustain life.	'Harmfulness' is a matter of social judgement. So, for example, a 'Auschwitz' brand would probably regarded as being harmful, at least to the Jewish community, whereas, the 'FCUK' brand might be regarded a being clever, rather than harmful, through its similarity to a sexual swearword.

Only a fool would deliberately set out to instigate a hostile response to a brand – a self-imposed prohibition. |
| **g. Liability to execution** | Comprehends a particular use: settling debt. This is dependent on the existence of an artefact and its sufficiency for the stated purpose, the latter being a matter of agreement between the parties. The artefact is important otherwise the intangible asset could potentially become a vehicle for defrauding creditors, and national income would suffer accordingly as those with liquid capital would be wary of lending it to those with assets lacking this proviso. | A high profile trademarked brand may well be accepted in settlement of a debt. Anyone with enough money can create a luxury car but there is only one Rolls Royce brand and it clearly had worth to BMW or they would not have bought it. A lender would know this too. |
| **h. Right to residuary character** | Refers to a situation where the rights to the artefact lapse. There must be social rules for deciding what to do, for whatever reason, where the pre-existing legal rights to an intangible asset are no longer present. For some intangible assets, though, there is no residuary character eg. patents. | The statutory expiration of a trademark unless renewed.
Brands may still be protected under the tort of passing off. |

In presenting the next three criteria in Table 3 we have to take a stance on the relationship between capital and income and we choose the comprehensive income approach. We do so because we seek to show that the capital invested in a business is not maintained (see Hicks 1939; Gynther 1970; Revsine 1981; Tweedie and Whittington 1984; Guttierrez and Whittington 1997; Arden 2005) or increased/decreased solely by operating it. Our prejudice, our normative positioning is therefore towards reflecting in the financial statements increases or decreases in the value of assets, including the intangible ones, between two balance sheet dates regardless of whether that was obtained through operating and/or holding an asset.

TABLE 3 The measurable function of a brand asset (see Figure 1)

Criteria	General Description – Intangible Assets	Application to Trademarked Brand Assets
i. Right to capital	Fisher (1906, p52) refers to capital as "*a stock of wealth existing at an instant in time*", Salvary (1997) refers instead to a "*stock of money*" expressed in nominal terms. In both cases *capital* may be interpreted in accounting terms as a positive difference of assets over liabilities at the year-end though the amount of that positive difference depends on ones view of capital maintenance, discussed above.	The constituent nature of brand equity (Aaker 1991, p16) is more broadly based than in respect of the artefact based focus of this paper. Wood (1995, p550), though, in referring to de Chernatony and McDonald (1992), adopts the "stock of wealth'"argument in that brands represent a source of "*added value*" (see also Wood 1996). However, where marketers and accountants differ would undoubtedly be in the recognition of the added value from such abstract sources as identified by Aaker (1991) - see Keller 1993 about the different motivations of accountants and marketers. From the accounting perspective the only physically verifiable brand equity attribute is in respect of the trademark.
j. Right to discharge capital	Comprehends the right to alienate an asset, or to consume it, or to destroy or waste it, or by any other means, discharge it and thereby deny oneself the right to appropriate, for example, the oil rich owners of a patent for a safe, cheap, compact and highly efficient source of generating electricity may, in their own interest, simply not use it. Thus it may exist as an artefact and it may have the potential to produce great wealth and yet, in practice, never do so. The action of discharging assumes a separable function from the other assets of a business unless this action occurs collectively. This right is the antithesis of a market-based view because the free movement of the capital typically associated with such assets is deliberately constrained by an entity-specific policy decision.	Brand capital or brand equity can be discharged inadvertently, for example, Gerald Ratner of Ratners Jewellers talking about his "*crap products*". However, previously damaged brand equity, like John West foods, can successfully reappear on retail shop shelves many years after they were first withdrawn. It is hard to establish a norm but that would not remove the right to eliminate a brand, and thereby any capital in it, simply by permanently removing it from public attention.
k. Right to income	The right to income is linked to the right to capital, as outlined previously in respect of capital maintenance (see, for example, Whittington 1974).	Refers to the premium income appropriated by the brand but separating it from the income attributable to product to which it is attached is difficult. However, it is entirely possible to reconstruct charts of accounts to one that is market and brand orientated, instead. So, prima facie, there can be a reasonable attempt to establish brand related net incomes if there was the political will to do so.

SEPARABLE MEASUREMENT OF AN ASSET (SEE FIGURE 1)

Any asset measurement should be both individual and additive so that, in principle, the measurement of 'the whole' disclosed picture of financial reality, however that is represented, is equal to the 'sum of its individual disclosed parts', whether aggregated or disaggregated. Consider the following related criteria in Table 4.

TABLE 4 The separable measurement of a brand asset (see Figure 1)

Criteria	General Description – Intangible Assets	Application to Trademarked Brand Assets
l. Measurement should be additive	Capital is measured on the basis of mixed measurement methods (ASB 1999, p79; IASB 2001, para.100) rather than a single method eg. Historic cost, realisable values etc. Comparability is undermined. The problem is compounded where monetary measurement occurs at different points in time, as with many valuation methods.	Various measurement methods are employed (price premium, royalty payments, P/E multipliers etc) and therefore they are not additive.
m. Measurement should be based on observation	The obvious problem of observing something that is intangible is obviated in this paper through the use of physical substitutes: artefacts, typically, documents. One can currently observe a transaction based cost or a readily ascertainable market value or an event such as a court order where the damages can be reasonably estimated from documents. The same cannot be said for many valuation based methods where the time frame is often future based and therefore not observable (see Aitken 1990, p229).	The observation process can be one of verifying regulatory compliance in the use of a 'selected valuation method' without material error in the way the measurement is conducted – a process of indirect verification. Of course, the unresolved problem is which method constitutes 'the best' measurement method in the first place – a process of direct verification (see IASB 2006b; Barth 2007, p14). See Arthur Andersen & Co. (1992) for political lobbying to this effect.
n. Measurement of bundles of assets should be avoided (wherever possible)	A separable measurement is tied to a single asset, rather than as a bundle, otherwise, it may be possible to inadvertently dispose of or discharge individual assets, *notably the intangible ones*, whilst leaving the measurement of the bundle intact. The danger, particularly in respect of intangible assets, is that one ends up disclosing the measurement of something that has little or no function let alone a separable function.	The most controversial criterion because, according to Aaker (1991), brand equity is a *"set of assets"* ie. bundled, and virtually impossible to un-bundle and measure separately. We do not try. Politically one must decide an appropriate lowest level of aggregation or, perhaps more appropriately, disaggregation at which to report assets (is it bricks and mortar or is it a building?). Our decision is based upon the trademark artefact. Whatever marketing "asset" that may or may not be attached thereto (eg. name awareness) is ignored in the accounting domain.

A DISCUSSION ABOUT THE CONTRIBUTION TO THE LITERATURE

What is not clear from the criteria presented in Tables 2, 3, 4 is whether all the boxes in the summary Table 1 have to be labelled 'Yes' for an asset to be confirmed. If that was the case then, in respect of trademarked brands, the challenge lies in respect of establishing an additive (criterion l, Table 1) and observed measurement (criterion m, Table 1). Let us address these two criteria next in reverse order.

The observation of compliance with a valuation method established by an accounting rule may well satisfy criterion m. However, as we saw earlier in respect of the IAS38 rule, brands should not be disclosed at all in the accounting domain because of their 'uniqueness'. Hence, there is no related accounting rule concerning measurement despite political lobbying to the contrary:

> [Arthur Andersen 1992, p11]...believes that it is possible to codify the valuation methodologies and improve the general understanding of the valuation process, such that users and preparers of accounts can have more confidence in the incorporation of intangible assets into financial statements. This view is supported by the considerable consensus within the business and professional community regarding valuation methodologies...

Yet, the content of Table 2 indicates that trademarked brands are no more 'unique' than some other assets. For example, comparatively, a trademark brand is no more unique than many uniquely built infrastructure assets that appear in published accounts and, as such, we would contend that the label of 'uniqueness' is a smokescreen for the real issue: establishing a reliable separable measurement from the other assets of a business. Clearly, where the measurement is transactions based cost (the brand is purchased separately) the observed measurement is easy to establish, reliably. The real issue here is the extent of the allowable use of valuation methods in accounting and, in particular, the observed reliability thereof. Notably, where these methods are applied to non-transactions-based, yet, visually recognisable intangible assets like trademarked brands. And that issue strikes at the very heart of accounting as a discipline, referred to previously as the 'ages-old' problem. So, what is preventing the accounting profession from regulating a brand valuation method into existence? We suspect the answer lies in criterion l: 'addivity', address next.

Whether one supports a multi-measurement-base stance to accounting (mixing historic cost, replacement cost, realisable value, economic values etc), or not, depends to some extent on the economic 'relevance' of the measurement methods being used vis-à-vis their comparative 'reliability' with, say, a pure transactions based cost approach. However, it is not as simple as that because even within a pure transactions-based cost approach there is a mixture of historical prices and current prices depending on when the transaction occurred (IASB 2006c), and, the cost may not always be readily identifiable where, for example, the asset is self-constructed or acquired as a bundle (see criterion n, again). Likewise, if one attempted to adopt a purely market based fair value approach, then, as Barth (2007, p12) rightly points out, the sum of the assets less liabilities is still unlikely to be equal to the market value of the equity because not every 'asset' is recognisable. We have seen that that is the case when we looked at the constituent nature of brand equity. So, the conclusion to be reached is that when time and money are mixed in any measurement basis it becomes inherently non-additive over time. In other words, the accounting profession cannot win in this regard and all it can do is to set boundaries that limit the subjectivity of the methods being used to those it regards as being 'more reliable'. In effect, since we have put up a reasonably convincing argument as to the 'assetness' of trademarked brands, what we have here at the accounting/marketing interface is really a dispute about political policy choices concerning 'appropriate' valuations-based methods – see appendix D. The same is applicable to the intellectual capital domain (see appendix E) and the finance domain (see appendix F) as regards "value-relevant" accounting expenses that nevertheless exhibit the revenue generating capabilities of assets from a market perspective (including finance orientated value-relevant articles from the marketing domain). It is clear from the sheer variety of valuation methods and value-relevant models 'on offer' (appendices D,E,F) that it would be a formidable task to select the 'most appropriate' one to use in the accounting domain. That said, any valuation bases which are future based (cashflow projections and future income streams) are inherently non-additive and that probably eliminates many methods if *all* the criteria (Table 1) are relevant to a decision about the asset status of brand assets and assets in general.

As we write the International Accounting Standards Board is reviewing its conceptual framework. As regards assets, the epistemological focus is upon revisions to the definition of an asset – largely semantics (se IASB 2006a). The criteria presented in this paper break free from this narrow perspective to offer an alternative view based on artefacts, mostly of a documentary nature. To many in the marketing community, though, this 'alternative' will still be too restrictive if only because of its central reliance on separability. And they would be correct to some extent because some intangibles may need to be bundled or teamed together in order to produce wealth – the opposite of controversial criterion n. However, the boundary line has to drawn somewhere (see Lev and Zarowin 1999), in this case, using artefacts, otherwise verification becomes a 'nightmare' to perform. Others may wish to draw this boundary line differently and we welcome that contribution.

REFERENCES

Aaker, D. and Jacobson, R. (1994), "The Financial Information Content of Perceived Quality", *Journal of Marketing Research*, Vol. **31**, No. 2 (Spring), pp. 191-201.

Aaker, D. A. (1991), *Managing Brand Equity*, New York: The Free Press, p.15.

Aaker, D. A. (1992), "The Value of Brand Equity", *Journal of Business Strategy*, Vol. **13**, No 4, July/Aug, pp.27-32.

Aaker, D. A. (1996), "Measuring Brand Equity Across Products and Markets", *California Market Review*, Vol. **38**, No.3, pp. 102-130.

Aitken, M. (1990), "A general theory of financial reporting: Is it possible?", *International Journal of Accounting*, Vol. **25**. No. 4, pp. 221-233.

Andriesson, D. (2005), "Implementing the KPMG Value Explorer: Critical success factors for applying IC measurement tools", *Journal of Intellectual Capital*, Vol. **6**, No. 4, pp. 474-488.

Arden, D. (2005), "An accounting history of capital maintenance: Legal precedents for managerial autonomy in the United Kingdom", *Accounting Historians Journal*, Vol. **32**, No. 1, pp. 1-25.

Arthur Andersen (1992), *The Valuation of Intangible Assets*, Special Report No p.254, Business International Ltd, January, pp. 1-104.

ASB (1995x,y,z) *Responses to the Public Hearings on Goodwill & Intangible Assets* held 26-28 September, Accounting Standards Board. (x, y, z = day one, day two, day three).

ASB (1999), *Revised Financial Reporting Exposure Draft: Statement of Principles for Financial Reporting*, Accounting Standards Board, March, pp.1-108.

Barker, R. (2004), "Reporting Financial Performance", *Accounting Horizons*, Vol. 18, No. 2, pp. 157-171.

Barth, M. E. (2000), "Valuation-based accounting research: Implications for financial reporting and opportunities for future research", *Accounting and Finance*, Vol. 40, No. 1, pp. 7-31.

Barth, M. E. (2007), "Standard-setting measurement issues and the relevance of research", *Accounting and Business Research*, Vol. 37, No. 2 (Special Issue: International Accounting Policy Forum), pp. 7-15.

Barth, M. E., Clement, M. B., Foster, G. and Kasznik. R. (1998), "Brand Values and Capital Market Valuation", *Review of Accounting Studies*, Vol. 3, No.1/2, pp. 41-68.

Barwise, P., Higson, C., Likierman, A. and Marsh, P. (1989), *Accounting for Brands*, London Business School/ The Institute of Chartered Accountants in England and Wales, pp.1-84.

Barwise, P., Higson, C., Likierman, A. and Marsh, P. (1990), "Brands as separable assets", *Business Strategy Review*, Vol. 1, No. 2 (Summer), pp. 43-59

Baxter, W. T. (1993), "Asset Values - Goodwill and Brand Names", *ACCA Occasional Research Report No. 14*, The Chartered Association of Certified Accountants, pp.1-35.

Bertoni, M. and De Rosa, B. (2005), "Comprehensive income, fair value, and conservatism: A conceptual framework for reporting financial performance", A paper for the 5th International Conference on European Integrations, Competition and Cooperation (Lovran, April 22-23 2005).

Biel, A. L. (1991), "The Brandscape: Converting Brand Image into Equity", *ADMAP*, Oct, pp.41-46.

Blackett, T. (1991), "The Valuation of Brands", *Marketing Intelligence and Planning*, Vol. 9, No 1, pp. 27-35.

Blackston, M. (1992), "Observations: Building Brand Equity by Managing the Brand's Relationships", *Journal of Advertising Research*, Vol. 32, No. 3, May/June, pp. 79-83.

Bontis, N. (2004), "National Intellectual Capital Index: A United Nations initiative for the Arab region", *Journal of Intellectual Capital*, Vol. 5, No. 1, pp.13-39.

Bounfour, A. (2003), "The IC-dVAL approach", *Journal of Intellectual Capital*, Vol. 4, No.3, pp. 396-413.

Broniarczyk, S. M. and Gershoff, A. (2003), "The Reciprocal Effects of Brand Equity and Trivial Attributes", *Journal of Marketing Research*, Vol. 40, No. 2 (May), pp.161-174.

Brummet, R. L., Flamholtz, E. G. and Pyle, W. C. (1968), "Human resource measurement - a challenge for accountants", *The Accounting Review*, Vol. 43, No. 2, Apr, pp. 217-24.

Brummet, R. L., Flamholtz, E. G. and Pyle, W. C. (1969a), "Human resource myopia", *Monthly Labour Review*, Jan, pp. 29-30.

Brummet, R. L., Flamholtz, E. G. and Pyle, W. C. (1969b), "Human resource accounting: A tool to increase managerial effectiveness". *Management Accounting*, Vol. 51, No. 2 (August), pp. 20-25.

Burgman, R., Roos, G., Ballow, J. and Thomas, R. (2005), "No longer "out of sight, out of mind": Intellectual capital approach in Asset Economics Inc. and Accenture LLP", *Journal of Intellectual Capital*, Vol. 6, No.4, pp. 588-614.

Caddy, I. (2000), "Intellectual capital: recognizing both assets and liabilities", *Journal of Intellectual Capital*, Vol. 1, No.2, pp. 129-146.

Carroll, R. and Tansey, R. (2000), "Intellectual capital in the new Internet economy - Its meaning, measurement and management for enhancing quality", *Journal of Intellectual Capital*, Vol. 1, No. 4, pp. 296-312.

Carson, E., Ranzijn, R., Winefield, A. and Marsden, H. (2004), "Intellectual capital: Mapping employee and work group attributes", *Journal of Intellectual Capital*, Vol. 5, No. 3, pp. 443-463.

Cauwenberge, P. V. and De Beelde, I. (2007), "On the IASB Comprehensive Income Project: An Analysis of the Case for Dual Income Display", *ABACUS*, Vol. 43, No. 1, pp. 1-26

Chartered Institute of Marketing (1993), "A View from the Institute", *Marketing Business*, HHL, Feb, p. 20.

Chen, M., Cheng, S. and Hwang, Y. (2005), "An empirical investigation of the relationship between intellectual capital and firms' market value and financial performance", *Journal of Intellectual Capital*, Vol. 6, No.2, pp. 159-176.

Crimmins, J. C. (1992), "Better Measurement and Management of Brand Value", *Journal of Advertising Research*, Vol. 32, No. 4, July/Aug, pp. 11-19.

de Chernatony, L. (1993), "Categorizing Brands: Evolutionary Processes Underpinned by Two Key Dimensions", *Journal of Marketing Management*, Vol. 9, No. 2, pp. 173-188.

de Chernatony, L. and McDonald, M. (1992), *Creating Powerful Brands*, Oxford: Butterworth Heinemann.

de Chernatony, L. and McWilliam, G. (1989), "The Strategic Implications of Clarifying How Marketers Interpret Brands", *Journal of Marketing Management*, Vol. 5, No 2, pp. 153-171.

Dowling, R. D. (1993), "Developing Your Company Image Into Corporate Asset", *Long Range Planning*, Vol. 26, No 2, pp. 101-109.

Drobis, D. (1993), "Building Brand Equity With Public Relations", *Management Review*, Vol. 82, No. 5, May, pp. 52-55.

Egan, C. and Guilding, C. (1994), "Dimensions of Brand Performance: Challenges for Marketing Management and Managerial Accountancy", *Journal of Marketing Management*, Vol. 10, No. 6, pp. 449-472.

Erdem, T. and Swait, J. (1998), "Brand Equity as a Signalling Phenomenon", *Journal of Consumer Psychology*, Vol.7, No.2, pp. 131-157.

Erdem, T., Swait, J., Broniarczyk, S., Chakravarti, D., Kapferer, J., Keane, M., Roberts, J., Steenkamp, J. E. M. and Zettelmeyer, F. (1999), "Brand Equity, Consumer Learning and Choice", *Marketing Letters*, Vol. 10, No. 3, pp. 301-318.

Farquhar, P. H. (1989), "Managing Brand Equity", *Marketing Research*, Vol. 1, No. 3, pp. 24-33.

FASB (1984), "Recognition and measurement in financial statements of business enterprises", Statement of Financial Accounting Concepts No.5, Financial Accounting Standards Board.

FASB (1985), "Elements of financial statements", Statement of Financial Accounting Concepts No.6, Financial Accounting Standards Board.

Guilding, C. and Pike, R. (1990), "Intangible Marketing Assets: A Managerial Accounting Perspective", *Accounting and Business Research*, Vol. 21, No 18, pp. 41-49.

Guttierrez, J. M. and Whittington, G. (1997), "Some formal properties of capital maintenance and revaluation systems in financial reporting", *The European Accounting Review*, Vol. 6, No. 3, pp. 439-464.

Gynther, R. S. (1970), "Capital maintenance, price changes and profit determination", *The Accounting Review*, Vol. 45, pp. 712-730.

Haigh, D. (1998), *Brand Valuation – Understanding, exploiting and communicating brand values*, London: FT - Retail and Consumer Publishing.

Hall, R. (1991), "The Contribution of Intangible Resources to Business Success", *Journal of General Management*, Vol.16, No.4, Summer, pp. 41-51.

Hall, R. (1992), "The Strategic Analysis of Intangible Resources", *Strategic Management Journal*, Vol. 13, No. 2, pp.135-144.

Hermansson, R. (1964), "Accounting For Human Assets", Michigan State University Occasional Paper No.14.

Hicks, J. R. (1939), *Value and capital*, Oxford, UK: Clarendon Press.

Hines, R. (1988), Financial Accounting: In Communicating Reality, We Construct Reality, *Accounting, Organizations and Society*, Vol. 13, No. 3, pp. 251-261.

Hirschey, M. and Weygandt, M. H. (1985), "Amortization Policy for Advertising and Research and Development Expenditures", *Journal of Accounting Research*, Vol. 23, No. 1, pp. 326-335.

Holthausen, R. W. and Watts, R. L. (2001), "The relevance of the value-relevance literature for financial accounting standard setting", *Journal of Accounting and Economics*, Vol. 31, No. 1-3, pp. 3-75.

Housel, T. and Nelson, S. (2005), "Knowledge valuation analysis: Applications for organizational intellectual capital", *Journal of Intellectual Capital*, Vol. 6, No. 4, pp.544-557.

Hunt, D. (2003), "The concept of knowledge and how to measure it", *Journal of Intellectual Capital*, Vol. 4, No.1, pp.100-113.

IASB (1998), "IAS38 Intangible Assets". In: *International Financial Reporting Standards 2004*, International Accounting Standards Board.

IASB (2001), "Framework for the Preparation and Presentation of Financial Statements". In: *International Financial Reporting Standards*, International Accounting Standards Board, April.

IASB (2003), *Reporting Comprehensive Income*, International Accounting Committee Foundation.

IASB (2005), Comment letters CL1 to CL82 on a discussion paper prepared by the Canadian Accounting Standards Board for the International Accounting Standards Board (IASB) on *Measurement Bases For Financial Accounting – Measurement On Initial Recognition*, obtained from IASB website http://www.iasb.org.

IASB (2006a), "World Standard Setters Meeting: Agenda Paper 1B", Conceptual Framework Project, International Accounting Standards Board, September, pp. 1-6.

IASB (2006b), *Preliminary Views on an Improved Conceptual Framework for Financial Reporting: The Objective of Financial Reporting and the Qualitative Characteristics of Decision-Useful Financial Reporting Information*, International Accounting Standards Board.

Ijiri, Y. (1975), *Theory of Accounting Measurement*, Evanston, Illinois: American Accounting Association.

Kallapur, S. and Kwan, S. Y. S. (2004), "The Value Relevance and Reliability of Brand Assets Recognized by UK Firms", *The Accounting Review*, Vol. 79, No. 1, pp. 151-172.

Kamakura, W. A. and Russell, G. J. (1993), "Measuring Brand Value with Scanner Data", *International Journal of Research in Marketing*, Vol. 10, No. 1, pp. 9-22.

Kapferer J. K. (1992), *Strategic Brand Management: New Approaches To Creating And Evaluating Brand Equity*, London: Kogan Page.

Kaplan, R. and Norton, D. (2006), "Response to S. Voelpel et al., The tyranny of the Balanced Scorecard in the innovation economy", *Journal of Intellectual Capital*, Vol. 7, No. 3, pp. 421-428.

Kato Communications (1993), *Accounting for Brands*, Financial Times Business Enterprises, pp. 1-147.

Keller, K. L. (1993), "Conceptualising, Measuring, and Managing Customer-Based Brand Equity", *Journal of Marketing*, Vol. 57, No. 1, Jan, pp.1-22.

Keller, K. L. and Lehmann D. R. (2003), "How do brands create value? "*Marketing Management*, Vol. 12, No. 3, pp. 26-31.

Kerin, R. A. and Sethuraman, R. (1998), "Exploring the brand value-shareholder value nexus for consumer goods companies", *Journal of the Academy of Marketing Science*, Vol. 26, No. 4, pp. 260-271.

King, A. M. and Cook, J. (1990), "Brand Names: The Invisible Assets", *Management Accounting (USA)*, November, pp. 41-45.

Lev, B. (2001), *Intangibles – Management, Measurement, and Reporting*, Washington: Brookings Institution Press, pp.1-213.

Lev, B. and Zarowin, P. (1999), "The Boundaries of Financial Reporting and How to Extend Them", *Journal of Accounting Research*, Institute of Professional Accounting, Vol.37, No.2, pp.353-385.

Li, S. K. (2002), "Aggregating Capacity-Limiting Separable Inputs", *Southern Economic Journal*, Vol. 69, No. 2, pp. 470-478.

Liebowitz, J. and Suen, C. (2000), "Developing Knowledge Management Metrics for Measuring Intellectual Capital", *Journal of Intellectual Capital*, Vol.1, No.1, pp.54-67.

Low, J. (2000), "The value creation index", *Journal of Intellectual Capital*, Vol. 1, No. 3, pp. 252-262.

Mather, P. R. and Peasnell, K. V. (1991), "An Examination of the Economic Circumstances Surrounding Decisions to Capitalize Brands", *British Journal of Management*, Vol. 2, No. 3, pp. 151-164.

McBarnet, D. and Whelan, C. (1991), "The elusive spirit of the law: Formalism and the struggle for legal control", *The Modern Law Review*, Vol. 54, No. 6 November, pp. 848-873.

McPherson, P. K. and Pike, S. (2001), "Accounting, empirical measurement and intellectual capital", *Journal of Intellectual Capital*, Vol. 2, No. 3, pp. 246-260.

Mizik, N. and Jacobson, R. (2003), "Trading off between value creation and value appropriation: the financial implications of shifts in strategic emphasis", *Journal of Marketing*, Vol. 67, No. 1 (Jan), pp.63-76.

Mullen, M. (1993), "How to Value Intangibles", *Accountancy*, November, pp. 92-94.

Mullen, M. and Mainz, A. (1989), "Brands, Bids and Balance Sheets", *Acquisitions Monthly*, April pp.24-27.

Napier, C., Power, M. (1992) "Professional Research, Lobbying and Intangibles: A Review Essay", *Accounting and Business Research*, Vol. 23, No. 89, pp. 85-95.

Newberry, S. (2003), "Reporting Performance: Comprehensive Income and its Proponents", *ABACUS*, Vol. 39, No. 3, pp. 325-339.

Oldroyd, D. (1994), "Accounting and Marketing Rationale: The Juxtaposition within Brands", *International Marketing Review*, Vol. 11, No 2, pp.33-46.

Oliver, J. and Porta, J. (2006), "How to measure IC in clusters: empirical evidence", *Journal of Intellectual Capital*, Vol. 7, No. 3, pp. 354-380.

Palacios-Marques, D. and Garrigos-Simon, F. (2003), "Validating and measuring IC in the biotechnology and telecommunication industries", *Journal of Intellectual Capital*, Vol. 4, No. 3, pp. 332-347.

Park, C. S., Srinivasan, V. S. (1994), "A Survey-Based Method for Measuring and Understanding Brand Equity and Extendibility", *Journal of Marketing Research*, Vol. 21, No. 2, pp. 271-288.

Payan, J. M. and Svensson, G., (2007), "Co-operation, coordination, and specific assets in inter-organisational relationships", *Journal of Marketing Management*, Vol. 23, No.7-8, pp.797-814.

Pike, S., Fernstrom, L. and Roos, G. (2005), "Intellectual capital: Management approach in ICS Ltd", *Journal of Intellectual Capital*, Vol. 6, No.4, pp.489-509.

Pike, S. and Roos, G. (2004), "Mathematics and modern business management", *Journal of Intellectual Capital*, Vol. 5, No. 2, pp. 243-256.

Power, M. (ed.) (1990), *Brand and Goodwill Accounting Strategies*, Cambridge: Woodhead-Faulkner.

Rangaswamy, A., Burke, R. R. and Oliva, T. O. (1993), "Brand Equity and the Extendibility of Brand Names", *International Journal of Research in Marketing*, Vol. 10, No. 1, pp. 61-75.

Revsine, L. (1981), "A capital maintenance approach to income measurement", *The Accounting Review*, Vol. 56, No. 2, pp. 383-389.

Rodov, I. and Leliaert, P., (2002), "FiMIAM: financial method of intangible assets measurement", *Journal of Intellectual Capital*, Vol. 3, No. 3, pp.323-336.

Rubinson, J. (1993), "Equity Based Management", *Marketing Research*, Vol. 5, No 3, pp.7-11.

Saunders, J. (1990), "Brands and Valuations", *International Journal of Advertising*, Vol. 9, No. 2, pp. 95-110.

Scarpello, V. and Theeke, H. A. (1989), "Human resource accounting: A measured critique", *Journal of Accounting Literature*, Vol.8, pp. 265-280.

Searle, L. (1995), *The Construction of Social Reality*, New York: Penguin Press.

Seetharaman, A., Low, K. L. T. and Saravanan, A.S., (2004), "Comparative justification on intellectual capital", *Journal of Intellectual Capital*, Vol. 5, No. 4, pp. 522-539.

Simon, C. J. and Sullivan, M. W. (1993), "The Measurement and Determinants of Brand Equity: a Financial Perspective", *Marketing Science*, Vol. 12, No. 1, pp. 28-52.

Sudersanam, S., Sorwar, G. and Marr, B. (2006), "Real options and the impact of intellectual capital on corporate value", *Journal of Intellectual Capital*, Vol. 7, No. 3, pp. 291-308.

Tobin, J. (1969), "A General Equilibrium Approach to Monetary Theory", *Journal of Money, Credit and Banking*, Vol. 1, No. 1, pp.15-29.

Tollington, T. (1998a), "Brands: The asset definition and recognition test", *Journal of Product and Brand Management*,Vol.7, No.5, pp.180-192.

Tollington, T. (1998b), "Separating the brand asset from the goodwill asset", *Journal of Product and Brand Management*,Vol.7, No.4, pp.291-304.

Tollington, T. (1999), "The Brand Accounting Sideshow", *Journal of Product and Brand Management*, Vol. 8, No. 3, pp.204-218.

Tollington, T. (2001a), "UK brand asset recognition beyond transactions or events", *International Journal of Strategic Management* (*Long Range Planning*), Vol.34, No.4, pp.463-488.

Tollington, T. (2001b), "The separable nature of brands as assets: The UK legal and accounting perspective", *European Intellectual Property Review*, Vol. 23, No.1, pp.1-13.

Tollington, T. (2002), *Brand Assets*, London: John Wiley & Son.

Tweedie, D. P. and Whittington, G. (1984), *Capital maintenance concepts: The choice*, London UK: Accounting Standards Committee.

Upton, S. (2001), "Business and Financial Reporting, Challenges from the New Economy", Financial Accounting Series Special Report No.219-A, Financial Accounting Standards Board, April, pp.1-135.

van Mesdag, M. (1993), "Brands on the Balance Sheet", *Marketing Business*, Feb, pp.18-20.

Voelpel, S., Leibold, M., Eckhoff, R. (2006), "The tyranny of the Balanced Scorecard in the innovation economy", *Journal of Intellectual Capital*, Vol. 7, No.1, pp.43-60.

Wentz, L., Martin, G. (1989), "How Experts Value Brands", *Advertising Age*, January 16, p.24.

Whittington, G. (1974), "Asset Valuation, Income Measurement and Accounting Income", *Accounting and Business Research*, Vol. 5, No. 1 (Spring), pp. 96-101.

Wood, L. (1995), "Brands: The Asset Test", *Journal of Marketing Management*, Vol. 11, No 6, Aug, pp. 547-570.

Wood, L. (1996), "Added Value: Marketing Basics?", *Journal of Marketing Management*, Vol. 12, No. 8, pp. 735-755.

APPENDIX A

'Separable' or Separability': All the individual assets of a business, whether intangible or not, are separable from each other when it is possible to aggregate or disaggregate them (Li 2002) without loss or gain in the recognition and measurement of those individual assets such that the sum of them would always be equal to the whole of the assets of the business (see also IASB 2005, CL8). The 'whole' in this case would only comprise those business assets possessing the features of the three circles in Figure 1.

APPENDIX B

Some of the existing accounting and marketing literature related to this paper may be grouped as follows:

- **Brand assets:** (de Chernatony and McWilliam 1989), (King and Cook 1990), (Guilding and Pike 1990), (Hall 1992), (de Chernatony 1993), (Dowling 1993), (Oldroyd 1994), (Wood 1995), (Barth, Clement, Foster and Kasznik 1998), (Tollington 2002), (Kallapur and Kwan 2004), (Payan and Svensson 2007)

- **Brand value/valuation:** (Mullen and Mainz 1989), (Barwise et al. 1989 1990), (Saunders 1990), (Power 1990), (Blackett 1991), (Mather and Peasnell 1991), (Arnold et al. 1992), (Arthur Andersen 1992), (Crimmins 1992), (Kato Communications 1993), (Baxter 1993), (Kamakura, Russell 1993), (Mullen 1993), (van Mesdag 1993), (Wood 1996), Kerin and Sethuraman 1998), (Keller and Lehmann 2003), (Mizik and Jocobson, (2003), (Chu and Keh 2006),

- **Brand equity:** (Farquhar 1989), (Biel 1991), (Blackston 1992), (Aaker 1991 1992 1996), (Kamakura and Russell 1993), (Drobis 1993), (Rangaswamy, Burke and Oliva 1993), (Rubinson 1993), (Simon and Sullivan 1993), (Keller 1993), (Park and Srinivasan 1994), (Egan and Guilding 1994), (Kapferer 1992), (Erdem and Swait 1998), (Erdem, Swait, Broniarczyk, Chakravarti, Kapferer, Keane, Roberts, Steenkamp and Zettelmeyer 1999), (Broniarczyk and Gershoff 2003)

APPENDIX C

One should not confuse a 'measurable function' based on the physical and visual recognition of an artefact with the subsequent 'separable measurement'. It is obviously possible to project cash flows from a brand related advertising campaign and capitalise them but in that case the measurement becomes the basis for asset recognition. We argue that asset recognition (recognition of a stock of wealth) is logically a-priori to the measurement of that wealth, assuming it also complies with the other criteria presented in this paper.

APPENDIX D

Brand asset valuation methods. Consider, for example, the variety of valuation methods from the marketing domain categorised as follows (see Tollington 1999):

(a) **The Price Premium method**, where the revenues of an unbranded competing product are deducted from the revenues of a comparable branded product to establish the excess or premium revenue of the brand. Using this as a baseline, assumptions are made with respect to market growth, market shares, inflation etc., so as to establish cash flows for discounting purposes. A number of problems exist with this method quite apart from the obvious problems of subjectivity in cashflow construction and selecting an appropriate discount rate. For example, there may be no unbranded product which is comparable to the branded product and the method, by concentrating solely upon price, ignores costs and other factors such as manufacturing economies of scale from a high volume brand. Other criticisms of the method refer to its uni-dimensional view of brand equity, its reliance on high-quality physical attributes and the exclusion of revenues from the brand name (see Simon and Sullivan 1993, p30)

(b) **The Earnings Valuation method**, where a prudent Price/Earnings (P/E) multiplier or similar multiplier is applied to a brand's profits after eliminating, firstly, the profits from unbranded goods such as own label products, which are often produced in parallel to the brand and, secondly, the profits from assets which do not contribute to the brand's strength. In the case of a P/E multiplier there is an underlying and perhaps, unjustified assumption that the brand profits can be valued in the same way as the business as a whole. Other multipliers often rely on an assessment of the brand's strength, that is, longevity, leadership, legal protection etc. using a point-scoring system with all the attendant subjectivity associated with such a mechanism (for example, the Interbrand method, Young & Rubicam's Brand Asset Valuator method and David Haigh's Brand Value Added method (see Wentz and Martin 1989; Haigh 1998)). Of course, multipliers are of limited value if there is difficulty in isolating the brand's profits in the first place. Also, it is possible that the year(s) from which the brand profits are selected may not be a representative baseline upon which to use a multiplier.

(c) **The Royalty Payments method**, which involves determining the royalty income from licensing out of a brand or trademark. This provides a sum upon which either a discounted cashflow or multiplier can be applied. Leaving aside the secondary question of the appropriateness of the selected multiplier or discount rate, the main unanswered question is whether royalties are an effective surrogate for brand premiums?

(d) **The Market Value method**, which is almost impossible to determine simply because the market for brands is, at best, thin and volatile. Where the brand is being acquired, it is usually valued by reference to the entry price or replacement costs involved in creating similar brand loyalty, consumer and trade awareness, and so on. However, Simon and Sullivan (1993) argue that this method provides no information about the current value of brand equity from existing products. Also, costs derived under this method are highly subjective. For example, there is no doubt that a replacement "Virgin" brand would be expensive, but until it is undertaken there is no way of calculating the amount of money involved.

(e) **The Original/Historic Cost method**, which involves the aggregation of purchase and/or marketing and R&D expenditure relating to a brand. An obvious problem here is the isolation of costs specific to the brand alone, which may require the capitalisation of costs incurred decades ago. However, from an accountant's viewpoint this would be inconsistent practice because historic cost-based balance sheets require that asset values should represent the aggregation of costs not yet charged to the profit and loss account rather than those which have already been expended. It is also inconsistent because there are brands, such as Rolls Royce, where the cost of marketing is negligible and yet the brand value is substantial.

APPENDIX E

Consider, also, the sheer variety of valuation methods from the intellectual capital domain categorised as follows (see Pike and Roos 2004):

a. Direct Intellectual Capital methods (DIC):

Measures the £-value of the investment in the intangible asset assuming its constituency can be identified. Most of the 'investment', though, in the accounting domain is actually expensed: training, salaries etc. Likewise in respect of marketing assets, such as advertising and marketing personnel costs. In the IC domain DIC methods encompass:

Study	Label
Caddy (2000)	Intellectual Capital Formula
McPhersen and Pike (2001)	Inclusive Valuation Methodology
Rodov and Leliaert (2002)	Financial Method of Intangible Assets Measurement
Carson et.al (2004)	No label - model to measure IC components.
Andriesson (2005)	Value Explorer
Housel and Nelson (2005)	Knowledge Valuation Analysis (KVA

b. Market Capitalisation Methods (MCM) :

The difference between a company's market capitalisation and its stockholders' equity

Study	Label
Housel and Nelson (2005)	Market or Value Based Approach
Sudersanam et.al (2006)	Real Option Models (ROM)

c. Return on Assets Methods (ROA):

Divide the average pre-tax earnings for a company for a period of time by the average tangible assets of the company. Then compare the resulted ROA with the company industry average. The difference between both of ROAs is multiplied by the company's average tangible assets to calculate the average annual earnings. Divide the average earnings by the company's average cost of capital to derive an estimate of the value of the company intangible assets.

Study	Label
Lev (2001)	Residual Income Model
Chen et.al (2005)	Value Added Intellectual Coefficient (VAIC)
Burgman et.al (2005)	Future Value Management Methodology (FVMT)

d. Scorecard Methods (SC):

Uses a mixture of financial and non-financial indices:

Study	Label
Liebowitz and Suen (2000)	Proposed Knowledge Management Metrics
Carroll and Tansey(2000)	Metrics to measure human capital and structural capital
Low (2000)	Value Creation Index-VCI
Hunt (2003)	Self-Assessment Computer Analysed testing (SACAT)
Bonfour (2003)	Dynamic Valuation of intellectual capital (IC-DVAL)
Palacious-Marques and Simon (2003	Intellectual Capital Scale
Bontis (2004)	National Intellectual Capital Index
Pike et.al (2005)	Conjoint Value Hierarchy (CVH)
Oliver and Porta (2006)	Intellectual Capital Cluster Index (ICCI)
Kaplan and Norton (2006)	Balanced Scorecard
Voelpel (2006)	Systematic Scorecard (SSC)

APPENDIX F

Consider, also, the literature that addresses the difference between accounting book values and market values (for example, Tobin 1969), known as the 'value-relevance' literature:

* from the finance domain (see summary articles: Barth (2000); Holthausen and Watts (2001)). The brand and marketing related aspects of this literature include: Hirschey and Weygandt 1985; Barth et al. 1998; Guilding and Pike (1990), Mather and Peasnell 1991.
* from the marketing domain but finance orientated. The brand related aspects of this literature include: Aaker and Jacobson 1994; Kerin and Sethuraman 1998; Simon and Sullivan 1993.

Assessing marketing performance: don't settle for a silver metric

Tim Ambler, *London Business School, UK*
John H. Roberts, *London Business School, UK*

Abstract This paper starts with the premise that marketing should be accountable, and considers by which measure or measures it should be held to account. "Marketing" for the purposes of this paper is defined as satisfying customers and thereby maximising net inward cash flow. This suggests that marketing performance can and should be evaluated financially, ideally with a single number, or "silver metric". The authors review the arguments for and against silver metrics in general and, in particular, three popular candidates: ROI, Discounted Cash Flow (DCF) and Return on Customer. So far as performance evaluation is concerned, six objections to the use of ROI, five to the use of DCF and four to Return on Customer are identified. Furthermore, the authors highlight the critical and potentially misleading role of forecasts as benchmarks for performance assessment. At the same time, the value of DCF techniques, such as customer equity and customer lifetime value, is recognis ed for planning purposes. A more satisfactory means for assessing marketing performance is net profit plus any enhancement of the marketing asset albeit that requires multiple metrics, taken together as a proxy for future cash flows.

Keywords Marketing, Performance, Measurement, Metrics, Brand Equity, ROI, DCF

INTRODUCTION

Marketing can be defined in many ways (Srivastava and Reibstein 2005). It can be seen as a function or department within the organisation (American Marketing Association

2006) or as defined according to specific types of expenditure, such as advertising, promotion, or market research, but this narrows "marketing" considerably, especially for firms that do not undertake those functions, e.g. business-to-business. For the purpose of this paper, we define "marketing" as *"meeting needs profitably"* (Kotler and Keller 2006:5). In other words "marketing" here refers to what the whole company does to satisfy customers and thereby create shareholder value.

We are not therefore concerned with departmental performance nor with the productivity of a particular marketing activity, e.g. advertising, but with the company's overall achievement in marketing terms. These narrower performance questions depend on what particular goals they were assigned. Those differ from company to company; whereas the need to generate net cash flow through meeting customer needs is universal, even for not-for-profit organisations.

The assessment of the contribution of marketing to firm performance in this broad sense has become a major issue (Bahadir and Tuli 2002; Bruno, Parthasarathi and Singh 2005; Debruyne and Hubbard 2000; Morgan, Clark and Gooner 2002; Rust, Lemon and Zeithaml 2004), but views are polarised. One extreme argues that the ultimate purpose of marketing is to improve shareholder value and that marketing performance should therefore be judged by some single financial indicator, which we call a "silver metric". If shareholder value itself is not feasible, because it is confounded by too many other factors, then discounted cash flow (DCF) or return on marketing investment (ROMI or ROI) should be used. Furthermore, if marketers seek more support from the Board, they should express performance in this financial language.

The other extreme argues that financial measures are inadequate for explaining marketing performance since they do not satisfactorily deal with the marketing asset (often called *"brand equity"* Aaker 1991). In this camp, Ambler (2003) argues that the bottom line for marketing performance should be the net profit or cash flow in the period attributable to marketing plus the improvement in brand equity.

This paper examines both extremes and concludes with practical advice for academics and practitioners looking for reliable means of performance assessment. En route, we first explore the financial measurement of marketing and, within that, three of the best known methodologies: Return on Investment (ROI), Discounted Cash Flow (DCF) and Return on Customer (ROC) (Peppers and Rogers 2005). DCF is regularly reinvented and re-presented variously as net present value (NPV), brand valuation (Perrier 1997), customer lifetime value (CLV, Venkatesan and Kumar 2004; Gupta and Lehmann 2005), and customer equity (Rust, Lemon and Zeithaml 2004). Rust, Lemon and Zeithaml (2004), for example, define customer equity as *"the total of the discounted lifetime values summed over all of the firm's current and potential customers"* (p. 110). In a single brand firm, the brand valuation approach sums the same discounted cash flows as customer equity and the two are thus mathematically equivalent (Ambler et al. 2002). We therefore refer to all these as "DCF metrics."

We then show that the multi-dimensional nature of brand equity demands multi-dimensional measures, i.e. not just financial. Furthermore, managers need to be able to relate short term measures with the long-term. There is already a strong trend to look at non-financial performance alongside financial (Elkington 1998; ASB 2007). We discuss methodologies for assessing changes in brand equity and conclude with areas for future research and recommendations for management.

THE FINANCIAL MEASUREMENT OF MARKETING PERFORMANCE

At its simplest, managers would like a single number, representing profit in some way, for each alternative ways of meeting customer needs. The plan selected would be the one with the highest number. And then they would like to assess performance by comparing the actual resulting number with the one predicted in the plan. We call this single number a "silver metric", and it is the common goal of a number of methodologies such as ROI or DCF.

The American Marketing Association defines marketing accountability as:

The responsibility for the systematic management of marketing resources and processes to achieve measurable gains in return on marketing investment and increased marketing efficiency, while maintaining quality and increasing the value of the corporation.

(American Marketing Association 2005:1)

The significant part of that definition is the duality of short-term gains and enhancing the quality and value of the corporation, i.e. the intangible asset we call brand equity (Aaker 1991). The meaning of "brand" or "brand equity" and whether this is all or part of the marketing asset which some prefer to see from the customer's perspective, are considered in the Appendix in order not to interrupt the flow here. Evaluating marketing performance requires both to be considered, i.e. the gain in short term profit or cash flow adjusted by any change in brand equity. Brand equity is thus a proxy for the future improvement in cash flows attributable to the marketing activities during the period under review. It follows that if both could be established as cash sums, then they could be added together to give a single financial performance total, i.e. a silver metric.

This is an attractive idea: it is easy for the Board to comprehend, convenient for comparisons between plan and actual results and comparable with other Board investment decisions.

Lehmann and Reibstein (2006), however, show that it is not that simple. Diagnostic metrics are needed to interpret evaluative measures, the long-term needs to be considered separately from the short-term and different levels of managers need different metrics. Nevertheless it is possible to conceive a structure of metrics building up to a silver metric at the apex. Lehmann and Reibstein's structure (p.9) has expenditure leading to "*marketing metrics (awareness, preference, loyalty, satisfaction, etc.)*", leading to "*market results (sales, market share, profits, ROI, cash flow etc.)*", leading to financial performance and ultimately the firm's financial value. They conclude by considering growth as the ultimate metric which they represent as the P/E multiple (i.e. share price divided by earnings).

If the stockmarket had perfect forecasting ability, then shareholder value (or the P/E multiple) would indeed reflect marketing performance although it would also reflect other factors such as market sentiment and the levels of interest rates. Shareholder value is therefore somewhat distant from marketing performance and we are driven back towards the profit contribution and any gain in asset values that can be attributed to marketing.

Perhaps the most traditional marketing indicator has been sales, whether expressed as volume or turnover, but this has been superseded by profits since volume sales did not take prices or costs into account. The PIMS project (Buzzell and Gale 1987) took a different route and proposed market share as their key metric since that appeared to drive profitability. Later research, e.g. Gale (1994), showed however that both share and profits were driven by quality, although the interaction between perceived and actual quality was problematic.

Thus the traditional "top line" performance indicators have been replaced by "bottom line" indicators and we now review three of the most widely canvassed, namely ROI, DCF and ROC, in terms of their suitability as silver metrics.

ROI

Return on investment (ROI) was devised for comparing capital projects where investments are made once and the returns flow during the following years. ROI is the net return divided by the investment or, more correctly, the incremental profit as a ratio of the incremental expenditure. ROI is a valuable tool for its original purpose: namely comparing alternative investments.

The first objection to ROI or return on marketing investment (ROMI) is that marketing expenditure is not an "investment" in the original sense and is certainly not treated that way in company accounts. For capital projects, because cash flows may be some years off, the cost is typically expensed over a period of time. While marketing expenditure may influence later periods, it is generally directed just to the current year. All of it is accounted for in the profit and loss account, not the balance sheet. The idea that marketing is an investment rather than maintenance creates another problem for marketers, namely the expectation that marketing will always create incremental sales and profits. In this view, marketing is an optional extra to be employed if the ROI on these extra profits is good enough. In reality most marketing is maintenance whose ROI is as difficult to calculate as, for example, the maintenance of the company's offices.

Srivastava and Reibstein (2005) drew attention to the second objection to ROI when they noted that it requires the profit to be divided by expenditure whereas all other bottom-line performance measures consider profit or cash flow after deducting expenditure. Division rather than subtraction creates a conflict between cash flow or profit (subtraction) and the ROI ratio (division). The profit or economic value added or increase in shareholder value from marketing all require the costs to be deducted from sales revenue along with the other costs. Accounting and finance texts suggest that as long as capital (I) is not constrained, residual income rather than ROI is a more appropriate measure (e.g. Peirson and Ramsay 1998). If the denominator of the ROI fraction is constant, then the ratio comparisons are valid but also unnecessary: the alternative returns could be considered alone.

The third objection to ROI is that its pursuit causes underperformance and suboptimal levels of activity. This arises from the law of diminishing returns. After the point of the profit response curve where ROI is maximised, further sales will typically still make profits but at a diminishing rate until the response curve crosses the line into incremental losses. Thus the point of maximum ROI is reached before the point of maximum profit. In calculus terms, ROI is maximised when the *slope* of the rate at which new revenue exceeds new costs is greatest, while profit is maximised when the *level* of the excess of new revenue over new costs is greatest.

There are exceptions but they are rare. For example, a seller of ice creams on a beach may find 30% of those present to be on no-ice-cream diets and the remaining 70% happy to buy one each but no more. If his marketing costs are low, then both profit and ROI are maximised at 70% penetration since a ceiling has been reached.

In general, there is a range of activity for which incremental profit exceeds the cost, so total profit continues to increase, but ROI progressively reduces.

The fourth objection to ROI is that the incremental measures required for the R and I require the baseline figures, i.e. what would have happened without the expenditure. Apart from direct marketing where matching cells can be left as controls, baselines are hard to determine, likely to be subjective, and able to be manipulated by the marketer. A brand that is regularly promoted will have sub-normal, i.e. sub-baseline, sales in the non-promotional periods as retailers and consumers adjust their inventories and buying habits.

The fifth objection is that ROI has become a fashionable term for marketing productivity and used to describe any type of profit arising from marketing activities. As the director general of the (U.K.) Institute of Public Relations observed, *"Ask 10 PRs to define ROI and you'll get 10 different answers"* (Farrington 2004:15). The American Marketing Association White Paper (American Marketing Association 2005:8) on marketing accountability identifies six "ROI Measures Currently Used" (Figure 8):

- Incremental sales revenue
- Ratio of cost to revenue
- Cost per sale generated
- Changes of financial value of sales generated
- Cost of new customer (sic)
- Cost of old customer retention

Not one of these six is actually ROI, and thus the fifth objection is that marketers rarely mean ROI when they say "ROI." Of course this is a problem with usage rather than the ratio itself but if usage is so confused that the metric has no consistent meaning, then the adoption of the metric, ROI in this case, is not just meaningless, it can be downright dangerous.

The sixth and possibly most serious objection is that it usually ignores the effect on the marketing asset (brand equity) and the longer term (which we take to be the same issue). In theory it does not have to, but estimating brand equity valuations into the future is not usual ROI practice. If marketing activities have generated a million dollars in extra profit, after marketing costs of half a million, ROI enthusiasts would applaud, especially if no other "investment would have paid back so handsomely." If, however, the marketing activities had reduced the value of the marketing asset by two million, the story is reversed. This example underlines the value, noted earlier, of separating measures assessing short- and long-term marketing performance. ROI tends to assess only the former.

The British car industry from 1950 – 1970 provides examples of brands being milked for ROI, with too much dependence on promotions and without regard for their underlying brand equities (Church 1995). Names like Morris, Austin, Rover and MG had high reputation following WWII but management had little concern with marketing and great concern with managing costs down to achieve an acceptable ROI. "Marketing" took the form of cash promotions and incentives. As a result, quality was impaired relative to competition and marketing and innovation were starved of support. The industry imploded.

In summary, ROI metrics promote underperformance and short-termism. For them to be used insightfully in marketing requires so much judgment and so many caveats, perhaps with the addition of other metrics, that their raison d'être as a silver metric is lost.

DCF

As noted earlier, Discounted Cash Flow is the basic methodology for a number of apparently different techniques: net present value (NPV), brand valuation (Perrier 1997), customer lifetime value (CLV, Venkatesan and Kumar 2004; Gupta and Lehmann 2005), customer equity (Rust, Lemon and Zeithaml 2004) and, usually, brand valuation (Ambler et al. 2002). Whilst there are some differences between these techniques, the issues below are common to them all.

DCF techniques have long been used for comparing alternative investments and also, since the 1960s, for regulating utility prices (Brigham and Crum 1978). The issue with the use of DCF techniques for performance evaluation has largely to do with time. Planning involves the comparison of alternative *future* scenarios; comparing their expected outcomes in terms of *future* cash flows is entirely logical and was their original rationale.

The suitability of any tool, be it a spade or a market metric, depends on its intended usage. A spade may be a good spade but it is not much use for raking gravel. The question in this section is whether DCF techniques, designed as they are for future analysis, are also useful for evaluating performance to date, i.e. the *past*.

When we are looking forward to determine which marketing strategy will perform best, estimating the likely consequential cash flow, and risks, of each strategy is surely good practice. Discounting those cash flows back to NPV, whether in the guise of CLV, customer equity, or brand valuation, aids comparison. Furthermore, the contextual variables such as interest rates or economic growth can be standardised across the alternative strategies to highlight the differences arising from the managerial variables.

Comparing DCFs for the same period but where the calculations are made a year, say, apart, is more problematic than comparing forecasts for the same period and made at the same date with the same assumptions. Variances between the two need to be analysed in terms of contextual and managerial factors, and also their interaction, i.e. where changes in the environment caused the managers to change their actions. In theory this can be done and for the period where the cash flow is known, i.e. the year just completed, no real difficulty should be encountered. The problem lies with the unknowns, namely the old and new forecasts of future cash flows and the extent to which changes in those forecasts can be included as part of the prior year's performance.

We see five difficulties with using DCF techniques for performance evaluation:

- The lack of independence between the forecasters and the managers whose performance is being judged.
- The lack of certainty that forecasts are correct.
- Confounding forecasting error with performance variance.
- Reconciling multiple forecasts.
- Taking credit today for marketing activities in the future.

Taking these in turn, the opportunities for gaming are apparent. Negotiating a low DCF for the out years (after the first) in the previous year followed by a high one at the end of the period will appear as high performance whatever the reality. Putting forecasting in the hands of others, e.g. the finance department, is little better as they have less idea of what the marketers have in mind or the likely outcomes.

Secondly, independence would not guarantee that the forecasts were accurate. Assume that a characteristic of poor, or at least inexperienced, marketers is that they have inflated expectations of the results of their marketing. In this case, poor marketers will present higher DCFs than their more talented and experienced peers. So their performance will look better than it is, at least in the short term. This demonstrates at a bare minimum the need for some objective standards in judging the reliability of such estimates, given the moral hazard associated with their generation. But that is only part of the difficulty. These forecasts require judgements about future economic conditions, interest rates and risk none of which bear on the performance to date.

Thirdly, a forecast is not a benchmark and it is therefore not a useful basis for performance assessment. A forecast is not what should happen but what is expected to happen. If performance is exactly in line with forecast, it may be good or bad or middling. All we know is that the forecast was accurate. If there is a major variance between forecast and performance, we need other information, e.g. performance last year or the state of the market or the plan and how well it was prepared, to determine performance. It may just have been a poor forecast. Marketers, it is said, always perform well: either results are excellent and above forecast or the forecast was wrong.

The fourth problem area concerns which DCF forecasts should be used for comparison. Most firms have only one formal plan each year but forecasts are generated many times a year and each can be used for DCF purposes. This is because top management are pressing for no surprises, i.e. to know ahead of time what the result will be. Management is pressing to minimise any variance between forecast and performance. This is a related point to the one above but the additional point here is that apparent performance will depend on which forecast (DCF) is used as the comparator.

The final problem area is that using future DCF for to-date evaluation means taking credit for future marketing activities. And there is an infinite number of possible futures. We cannot know which one should be selected. Clearly a DCF which assumes higher marketing performance in the out years should not be used alongside a more pessimistic one for the purposes of assessing performance to-date. And yet the whole idea of using DCF is to take account of improved future performance arising from marketing activities in the year to-date.

In other words, one cannot separate future improvements due to *future* activities from future improvements due to *past* activities. The custom is just to take the future forecasts as being as accurate as possible thereby confounding the results from past and future activities.

There is, however, an opposing school of thought which should be considered and for which we have some sympathy. Whatever the theory, managers do, and probably should, try to combine past and future measures when making marketing decisions. The (relatively) known cash flow of the past (which cannot be influenced) differs from the more uncertain and only partially controllable cash flows of the future. Both are important and real. A typical problem is "Is past underperformance best addressed by sacking the manager, or should we retain the existing team to better use the experience?" In looking back and forward we need common metrics or at least a transformation between the past and the future. If the past and future were on the same track, it would be easier to identify progress toward the goal.

Our definition of marketing, namely the sourcing and harvesting of cash flow, leads to the impression that cash flow should be used as the silver metric for marketing performance. Ultimately, that is right: how much money was harvested? But we are never at "ultimately" and therefore we have to combine cash made to-date with some proxy for cash in future years. If a firm had 20-20 foresight, then the best proxy would be the long-term improvement in DCF, with suitable controls for the consistency of out-year variables, including future marketing activities. We do not consider that to be realistic and will consider, after reviewing the Return on Customer sophistication of DCF, whether multiple measures of brand equity provide a better proxy.

RETURN ON CUSTOMER

The third silver metric reviewed here is that proposed by Peppers and Rogers (2005), namely, Return on Customer. They claim that maximising ROC, Return on Customer, also maximises both current period and future profits. Larry Kudlow, Host of CNBC's "Kudlow and Company," has offered highest praise for ROC:

> *Finally! A business metric that can drive better management and a higher stock price. I predict soon you'll be hard pressed to find a company that isn't tracking ROC[sm].*

> (Kudlow 2005)

The Peppers and Rogers' definition of Return on Customer is:

> *ROC equals a firm's current-period [net] cash flow from its customers plus any changes in the underlying customer equity, divided by the total customer equity at the beginning of the period*

> (2005:16)

Considering both the change in short-term cash flow and the change in the marketing asset is valid and corresponds with our own view of performance measurement. Care must be taken when adding them together because the metrics represent different things. The questions therefore become how the change in the marketing asset is measured and whether ROC provides the assessment of marketing we are seeking.

Customer equity is, in line with Rust, Lemon and Zeithaml (2004), taken to be the NPV of future cash flows, or DCF. Of course, one practical problem is to know who all the future customers will be, and then what cash flows will be contributed in response to the infinite permutation of marketing activities that the firm may undertake in future.

The major problem, already noted for DCF, with using this silver metric to evaluate performance is "crystal-balling" the immeasurable future. As Peppers and Rogers themselves concede in a slightly different context and with a splendid confusion of tenses:

> *No one really knows what any company's discounted cash flow is going to be in the future*

> (2005:19)

Peppers and Rogers have defined ROC in various but equivalent ways and one is (Peppers 2005, slide 42):

$$ROC_i = \frac{\pi_i + \Delta CE_i}{CE_{i-1}}$$

where π_i is the cash flow for period i and CE is customer equity.

To understand what is really going on here, we need two time indices, one (τ) to represent the period for which cash flows are described and one (t) the time at which judgments are made. Thus, we can express ROC as:

$$ROC_t(\tau\text{-}1) = \frac{C_t(\tau\text{-}1) + CE_t(\tau) - CE_{t-1}(\tau\text{-}1)}{CE_{t-1}(\tau\text{-}1)}$$

where $C_t(\tau)$ is cash flow during the period from $\tau - 1$ to τ as estimated at time t, $CE_t(\tau)$ is customer equity at time τ as estimated at time t, and $ROC_t(t-1)$ is the Return on Customer between $\tau - 1$ and τ. τ relates to a time period of evaluation (usually in units of one year and taken as such here), whereas t stands for the moment at which the estimate is made. ROC looks at the cash flow for the period being evaluated and the customer equity looking forward.

Note that cash flows are in contemporary money:

$CE_{t-1}(\tau)$ is the same as $CEt(\tau)$ except the date of the forecast is a year earlier. Therefore $CE_{t-1}(\tau - 1) = C_t-1(\tau - 1) + CE_{t-1}(\tau)$. That is, the customer equity at time t−1 (estimated at time t) is the cash flow for period from $\tau - 1$ to τ plus the residual customer equity at the end of the period, t.

Substituting for $CE_{t-1}(\tau-1)$ in the ROC formula above gives

$$ROC_t(\tau\text{-}1) = \frac{\{C_t(\tau\text{-}1) - C_{t-1}(\tau\text{-}1)\} + \{CE_t(\tau) - CE_{t-1}(\tau)\}}{CE_{t-1}(\tau\text{-}1)}$$

In other words, ROC consists of two components or variances. The first is the degree to which short-term cash flow was greater than expected and the second the degree to which the year-end customer equity is greater than expected. If the prior forecast of the period's cash flow was accurate and the two estimates of customer equity consistent, ROC is zero, which is hardly the result Peppers and Rogers can have intended. If either component is greater than zero, we cannot distinguish poor forecasting from superior performance.

Thus, ROC does not measure return on the value of the marketing assets so much as the variance of the cash flow for the period just ended plus any change in forecast cash flows, both taken as a ratio of customer equity. This is directly analogous to abnormal earnings growth used to value performance changes in other equities (see Penman, 2004:201).

A difference is that this formula scales it by taking the ratio to incoming customer equity at time t −1, i.e. $CE_{t-1}(\tau - 1)$. Of course, doing so introduces many of the problems of ROI, not the least of which is that maximising ROC does not correspond to maximising the value of marketing to the firm. It assumes marketing is only about providing incremental profits rather than maintaining the business, as discussed under "ROI".

ROC is positive when the firm is doing better than was previously expected, but that information is available with less calculation. It does not indicate whether a high value for ROC is caused by inaccurate and inconsistent forecasting or marketing performance. There is something self-defeating about forecasting excellence since it should take into account the brilliance of the firm's marketing. For example, the ROC for a brilliant CMO, who is slightly unlucky, will be lower than that for a low-grade CMO who performs every bit as badly as expected. We see that ROC makes no allowances for environmental variables (such as unexpected competitive moves) which are beyond the control of the manager. Of course, whether it should depends totally on the purpose for which performance evaluation is being undertaken.

This relative performance aspect of ROC indicates that it will be particularly subject to "gaming", i.e., low budgeting and/or fattening short-term cash flow at the expense of the longer-term while maintaining the high forecasts for the out-years. This is a problem for all DCF techniques but especially for ROC.

Competitor performance or other forms of benchmarking would provide useful yardsticks, but they are not considered by ROC.

One final point that deserves note is that we also need to consider differences arising from the technical aspects of net present value techniques, like customer equity, rather than marketing performance. When we time-shift the forecast date, we usually also change the contextual or technical variables such as discount rates and market growth. As noted above, using DCF calculations simultaneously with the same technical variables is more reliable than comparing net present values calculated at different times. ROC shares this difficulty with other applications of DCF to performance measurement.

In summary, problems with ROC as a silver metric include:

- It confounds performance with forecast consistency. A higher forecast for the out-years will give the appearance, under ROC, of higher performance in the year to date, irrespective of the reality.

- Forecasts are inappropriate benchmarks since they seek to estimate what will happen, bad or good, not the level of performance which divides bad from good. Achieving forecast says nothing about performance quality.

- It treats discounted future cash as being identical with cash in hand. Any bank manager knows which is the more reliable.

- The forecasts for the same period, but made a year apart, will tend not to be comparable for reasons other than performance expectations.

THE METRICS NEEDED FOR ASSESSING MARKETING PERFORMANCE

The common ground in this debate is that performance should be assessed using a combination of short-term cash flow, or profit, compared with a valid benchmark, such as plan, and a proxy for the change in future cash expectations brought about by the marketing activities during the period under review. The area of debate is the nature of the proxy with one school seeking a single financial measure, or silver metric, and the other side arguing for a set of financial and non-financial measures of, in effect, brand equity. This paper makes the dichotomy more stark for the purpose of exposition: in practice, most advocates of the silver metric welcome additional measures and most advocates of the brand equity approach would find room for DCF methods alongside.

One argument for the former school is that marketers need to *"get real"* (Peppers and Rogers 2006:15) and talk to top management in purely financial terms because that is all they will listen to. Whilst the language of the Board is pre-eminently the language of money, no Board is too narrow to recognise the importance of other things such as customer relationships. There is a growing recognition of the need for non-financial performance indicators, especially where they predict future cash flow (Elkington 1998; ASB 2007). Sawhney and Zabin (2002) proposed that firms should take account, i.e. measure, not only customer relationships but also those with partners, suppliers and employees.

Evidence that top managements are now accepting the multiple metric approach comes from research into dashboards, e.g. Clark, Abela and Ambler (2006), which bring together the multiple measures seen by senior management into a clear, integrated and concise package. Thus, management needs simultaneously to see a range of metrics on a single page or screen giving an easy-to-read summary of key marketing metrics (McGovern, Court, Quelch, and Crawford 2004; Reibstein, Norton, Joshi and Farris 2005). They may not recognise these as measures of brand equity but an increasing number are using a panel of up to 20 metrics rather than being driven by a single number.

The portrayal of brand equity as the asset enhanced by good marketing and carried forward from period to period can be ascribed to Aaker (1991) and it is a crucial development in marketing theory. Consumers behave according to context and what is in their heads. Marketing therefore needs to be understood, and therefore measured, as a two-step process: creating demand and then converting that demand into sales. The first equates to intermediate effects of marketing (including the behavioural) and possible future platforms for cash (including psychological and relationship states of consumers and collaborators). Behavioural effects, such as sales volumes and the prices paid, can quickly be translated to financial equivalents but intermediate platform effects, such as intention to purchase or customer satisfaction, are another matter.

The importance of brand equity as a performance driver has been underlined by the quantitative analysis provided by Balasubramanian, Mathur and Thakur (2005). They found that greater intangible assets were linked with the creation of more shareholder value.

Perhaps the most surprising conclusion so far is the importance of understanding the difference between metrics for performance evaluation and planning. These activities are functionally different (though plans should yield the metrics to be used for performance assessment once the planned period is over and performance evaluation should inform future plans). We have made some specific criticisms of some specific silver metrics. However, even the best-targeted silver metric cannot provide an adequate report of either performance or plan.

Abandoning the search for a silver metric requires marketers to persuade their colleagues of a better way to assess the firm's marketing performance. The first step is to make the firm's long- and short-term goals explicit. For most large firms, this has more significance than may be obvious: by so doing, the CMO is serving notice that marketing contributes to the firm's corporate goals and the marketers wish to formalise that contribution. That is quite different from the convention of seeking a budget to fulfil separate goals set for "marketing" poorly defined, or the marketing department.

Once the goals are clarified and reduced to those where the market, or marketing, plays a major role, it is a short step to agreeing that at least one metric is needed to measure performance toward each goal.

The next stage requires some form of business model to show the linkages between inputs, including marketing actions, financial expenditure, competitive activities, and expected results.

One tool for business modelling is strategy mapping (Kaplan and Norton 2000). Some of these linkages would not be normally described as "marketing" but of the remainder, some are key steps toward the firm's goals. More conventionally, the chain of effects from inputs to intermediate variables such as awareness, attitudes, and intention to purchase, to behavioural variables and then financial metrics can be analysed to determine which measures appear to influence their consequential ones in a credible way (Lehmann and Reibstein 2006). Selecting metrics is ultimately a pragmatic matter of selecting those that work, in the sense of being consistently predictive. Some seem to have little predictive ability, possibly due to low variance, awareness for example, whereas others are too volatile to be reliable.

The flaws in the silver metric approach to performance evaluation both in theory and practice, drives us to side with the multiple metric approach. This may come as no surprise to most readers. However, we are being more specific: marketing performance can be assessed by comparing against a well formulated plan and/or prior performance using a combination of short-term net cash flow or profit and the change in brand equity. The change in brand equity can be measured with whichever metrics have previously predicted profit performance in later periods, adjusted by any more recent hard information.

In other words, the key is to see brand equity as a present asset which can be measured using past experience and current knowledge. Brand equity measurement, dashboard metrics and building the business model are different perspectives of the same solution, namely a set of metrics, ideally about 10 in number (Clark, Abela, Ambler 2006) which, taken together represent a proxy for future net cash flows.

LIMITATIONS AND FUTURE RESEARCH

This paper is at the theoretical level. Empirical research needs to examine the performance of metrics in the context both of evaluating marketing performance to date and planning. While we have argued for the use of multiple metrics generally and against specific silver metrics specifically, we cannot assess the loss of diagnosticity by operating at too summary a level without resorting to particular cases. What we can say, though, is that the more turbulent the environment; the higher the level of heterogeneity in terms of regions, product categories, and channels; and the lower the correlation between different objectives' achievement, the greater the damage that such simplification will cause.

We have considered performance evaluation but not planning nor the interaction between planning and performance assessment. We recognise that this may increase the number of metrics required with overlap between the two systems.

CONCLUSIONS

This paper has addressed the selection of metrics for the purpose of assessing marketing performance. Other purposes, for example, planning, may need other metrics. We discussed why any single silver metric is inadequate. We found six objections to the use of ROI in this context and can find no justification for using it or its variants.

The fact that NPV, customer lifetime value, brand valuation, and customer equity are all labels for the same discounted cash flow (DCF) technique may not be widely appreciated but it allowed us to consider them en bloc. DCF is useful for planning and may well be included in a set of performance metrics but none of the variants should be used as a silver metric in assessing performance.

Return on Customer seeks to bring together short- and long-term performance measured by cash flow for the period and the change in the marketing asset, proxied by customer equity.

That has merit but analysis reveals that the formula reduces to the short-term cash flow variance and the consistency of the longer-term cash flow forecasts. If reliable benchmark measures of performance were able to be calculated and used in place of expected values, it could have value, but any simplicity of the tool would be thereby lost.

Like it or not, firms have to accept that assessing marketing performance requires more than one variable. We attempted to provide a blueprint for assembling the minimum necessary measures for top management. The answer should be the same but this problem can be perceived in three ways: measuring the marketing asset (brand equity), designing a dashboard to help top management drive the business and creating the business model.

REFERENCES

Aaker, David A. (1991), *Managing Brand Equity*. New York: Free Press.

Aaker, David A. (1996), *Building Strong Brands*, New York: Free Press.

Ambler, Tim (2003), *Marketing and the Bottom Line*. 2nd edition. London: FT Prentice Hall.

Ambler, Tim, Bhattacharya, C. B., Edell, Julie, Keller, Kevin Lane, Lemon, Katherine N. and Mittal, Vitas (2002), "Relating Brand and Customer Perspectives on Marketing Management.", *Journal of Service Research*, Vol. 5, No. 1 (August), pp. 13–25.

American Marketing Association (2005), "Marketing Accountability Study: White Paper", Chicago, ILL.: American Marketing Association.

American Marketing Association (2006), "Marketing Definitions". Available at: http://www.marketingpower.com/content4620.php [Accessed June 29 2006].

ASB (2007), *A Review of Narrative Reporting by UK Listed Companies in 2006*, London, UK: Accounting Standards Board, January 2007.

Bahadir, Suleyman Cem, and Tuli, Kapil R. (2002), "Measuring Marketing Productivity: Linking Marketing to Financial Returns", Cambridge, Mass: Marketing Science Institute, Conference Summary Report No. 02-119.

Balasubramanian, Siva K., Mathur, Ike and Thakur, Ramendra (2005), "The Impact of High-Quality Firm Achievements on Shareholder Value: Focus on Malcolm Baldrige and J. D. Power and Associates Awards", *Journal of the Academy of Marketing Science*, Vol. 33, No. 4, pp. 413-422.

Blackett, Tom (1989), "The Nature of Brands". In: Murphy, J. (ed.), *Brand Valuation*, London: Hutchinson Business Books, pp. 1-11.

Brigham, Eugene F., and Crum, Roy L. (1978), "Reply to Comments on 'Use of the CAPM in Public Utility Rate Cases'", *Financial Management*, Vol. 7, No. 3 (Autumn), pp.72-76.

Bruno, Hernan A., Parthasarathi, Unmish and Singh, Nisha (2005), "Does Marketing Measure Up? Performance Metrics: Practices and Impacts", Cambridge, Mass: Marketing Science Institute, Conference Summary Report No. 05-301.

Buzzell, Robert D., and Gale, Bradley T. (1987), *The PIMS Principles: Linking Strategy to Performance*, New York, NY: Free Press.

Church, Roy A. (1995), *The Rise and Decline of the British Motor Industry*, Cambridge: Cambridge University Press.

Clark, Bruce, Abela, Andrew and Ambler, Tim (2006), "Behind the wheel", *Marketing Management,* Vol. 15, No. 3 (May/June), pp. 18-23.

Debruyne, Marion, and Hubbard, Katrina (2000), "Marketing Metrics", Cambridge, Mass: Marketing Science Institute, Conference Summary Report No. 00-119.

Elkington, John (1998), *The Triple Bottom Line of 21st Century Business.* Gabriola Is., British Columbia: New Society Publishers.

Farquhar, Peter H. (1990), "Managing Brand Equity", *Journal of Advertising Research*, Vol. 30, No. 4 (August/September), pp. 7-12.

Farrington, Colin (2004), "The Language Barrier", *FT Creative Business*, June 1st 2004, p. 15.

Franzen, G and Holzhauer, F. (1987), *Het merk I (tekens, namen en merken)*, The Netherlands: Kluwer Bedrijftswetenschappen B.V.

Gale, Bradley T. (1994), "The Importance of Market-Perceived Quality", In: Stobart P., (ed.), *Brand Power,* London and Basingstoke: Macmillan. pp. 65-84.

Gardner, Burleigh B. and Levy, Sidney J. (1955), "The Product and the Brand", *Harvard Business Review*, Vol. 33, No. 2 (March/April), pp. 33-39.

Gupta, Sunil, and Lehmann, Donald R. (2005), *Managing Customers as Investments,* Upper Saddle River, N.J.: Wharton School Press.

Kamakura, Wagner A. and Russell, Gary J. (1993), "Measuring Brand Value with Scanner Data", *International Journal of Research in Marketing*, Vol. 10, No. 1, pp. 9-22.

Kapferer, Jean Noel. (1992), *Strategic Brand Management: New Approaches to Creating and Evaluating Brand Equity*, London: Kogan Page..

Kaplan, Robert S., and Norton, David P. (2000), "Having Trouble with Your Strategy? Then Map It", *Harvard Business Review* Vol. 78, No. 5 (September-October), pp. 167–76.

Keller, Kevin Lane (1993), "Conceptualizing, Measuring and Managing Customer-Based Brand Equity", *Journal of Marketing*, Vol. 57, No. 1 (January), pp. 1-22.

King, Stephen (1973), *Developing New Brands,* London: Pitman.

Kotler, Philip (1994), *Marketing Management: Analysis, Planning and Control*, 8th edition, Englewood Cliffs, NJ: Prentice Hall.

Kotler. Philip, and Keller, Kevin Lane (2006), *Marketing Management,* 12th edition, Pearson Prentice Hall: Upper Saddle River, NJ.

Kudlow, Larry (2005), Available at: http://www.returnoncustomer.com/view.aspx?ItemID=28876 [Accessed 29th June 2006].

Lehmann, Donald R., and Reibstein, David J. (2006), *Marketing Metrics and Financial Performance*, Cambridge, Mass: Marketing Science Institute.

Leuthesser, Lance (1988), "Defining, Measuring, and Managing Brand Equity. Summary of Marketing Science Institute Conference", Report No. 88-104, Cambridge, MA: Marketing Science Institute.

McCarthy, Jerome E. (1960), *Basic Marketing: A Managerial Approach*, Homewood, ILL.: Richard D. Irwin.

McCarthy, Jerome E. and Perreault Jr., William D. (1991), *Basic Marketing: A Managerial Approach*, Homewood, ILL.: Richard D. Irwin.

McGovern Gail J, Court, David, Quelch, John and Crawford, Blair (2004), "Bringing Customers into the Boardroom", *Harvard Business Review*, Vol. 82, No. 11 (November) p. 70.

Morgan, Neil A., Clark, Bruce H. and Gooner, Rich (2002), "Marketing Productivity, Marketing Audits, and Systems for Marketing Performance Assessment: Integrating Multiple Perspectives", *Journal of Business Research*, Vol. **55**, No. 5, pp. 363–75.

Murphy, John M. (1990), *Brand Strategy*, Cambridge: Director Books (Fitzwilliam Publishing).

Park, Chan Su and Srinivasan, V. (1994), "A Survey-Based Method for Measuring and Understanding Brand   Equity and Its Extendibility", *Journal of Marketing Research*, Vol. **31**, No. 2 (May), pp. 271-288.

Pearson, Stewart (1996), *Building Brands Directly*, London: Macmillan.

Peirson, Graham, and Ramsay, Alan (1998), *Accounting*, 2nd edition. South Melbourne, Victoria, Australia: Addison Wesley Longman, p. 1050.

Peppers, Don (2005), "SPSS Predictive Analytics Summit: The Case for Real Time Marketing", March 3rd 2005, Copenhagen.

Peppers, Don, and Rogers, Martha (2005), *Return on Customer: Creating Maximum Value from Your Scarcest Resource*, Singapore Marshall Cavendish.

Peppers, Don, and Rogers, Martha (2006), "Response to Ambler and Roberts' Beware the Silver Metric", Cambridge, Mass: Marketing Science Working Paper 06-114.

Penman, Stephen H. (2004), *Financial Statement Analysis and Security Valuation*, 2nd edition, Boston, Mass.: McGraw Hill Irwin

Perrier, Raymond (ed.), (1997), *Brand Valuation*, 3rd edition, London, UK: Premier Books.

Reibstein, David, Norton, David, Joshi, Yogesh and Farris, Paul (2005), "Marketing Dashboards: A Decision Support System for Assessing Marketing Productivity", Philadelphia, PENN.: Wharton School Working Paper.

Riezebos, H.J. (1994) *Brand-Added Value: Theory and Empirical Research About the Value of Brands to Consumers*, Eburon Delft, PhD Series in General Management No. 9, Rotterdam School of Management.

Rust, Roland T., Lemon, Katherine N. and Zeithaml, Valarie A. (2004), "Return on Marketing: Using Customer Equity to Focus Marketing Strategy", *Journal of Marketing*, Vol. **68**, No. 1, pp.109–27.

Sawhney, Mohanbir, and Zabin, Jeff (2002), "Managing and Measuring Relational Equity in the Network Economy", *Journal of the Academy of Marketing Science*, Vol. **30**, No. 4, pp. 313-332.

Simon, Carol J. and Sullivan, Mary L. (1993), "The Measurement and Determinants of Brand Equity: A Financial Approach", *Marketing Science*, Vol. **12**, No. 1, pp. 28-52.

Srinivasan, V. (1979), "Network Models for Estimating Brand Specific Effects in Multi-Attribute Marketing Models", *Management Science*, Vol. **25**, No. 1 (January), pp. 11-21.

Srivastava, Rajendra K. and Reibstein, David J. (2005), "Metrics for Linking Marketing to Financial Performance", Cambridge, Mass: Marketing Science Institute, Special Report No. 05-200e.

Venkatesan, Rajkumar and Kumar, V. (2004), "A Customer Lifetime Value Framework for Customer Selection and Resource Allocation Strategy", *Journal of Marketing*, Vol. **68**, No. 4, pp.106–25.

APPENDIX

Defining the meaning of terms

The word "brand" can be interpreted to include or exclude the underlying product. Table 1 notes some sources for both understandings. Some authors use the word in both senses without, apparently, noticing the difference.

We prefer the inclusive use adopted in this paper because:

- Otherwise we would have to value the product asset as well as the brand asset in order to capture the marketing asset as a whole.

- Consumer experience of the unbranded product which would impact "product equity" also impacts the brand asset. Actual quality cannot be separated from perceived quality for very long. The quality of the ice cream itself is the whole foundation of the Haagen Dazs brand.

- Separating cash flows attributable to the unbranded product from those attributable to the branding is very difficult and not usually done in practice despite claims to the contrary, e.g. Murphy (1990). Kotler and Keller (2006, p.291) define brand and brand equity but then go on to endorse "one popular valuation method" which subtracts not the underlying product but the volume above "an average brand". And, under "managing brand equity" they attribute long-term brand leadership as due to "constantly striving to improve products, services and marketing". In other words, the underlying products and services are part of the brand.

- The treatment of packaging is ambiguous: it could be seen as part of the branding or as part of the product.

The inclusive use is also consistent with Ambler et al. (2002) who showed that the brand and customer approaches to the marketing asset are two perspectives of the same asset, not two separate assets. Furthermore, for a single brand company, the

TABLE 1 Alternative "Brand" Definitions

Excluding underlying product	Including underlying product
McCarthy, 1960	King, 1973
McCarthy and Perreault, 1991	Pearson, 1996
Kotler, 1994, but ->	Kotler, 1994 (p. 456)
Aaker, 1991, but ->	Aaker, 1996 (inside back cover)
Park and Srinivasan, 1994	Gardner and Levy, 1955
Farquhar, 1990	Murphy, 1990 (but not when it came to
Kamakura and Russell, 1993	brand valuation, p. 159)
Keller, 1993	Kapferer, 1992
Leuthesser, 1988	Franzen and Holzhauer, 1987
Simon and Sullivan, 1993	Blackett, 1989
Srinivasan, 1979	Riezebos, 1994

brand valuation and customer equity were, in principle, the same since they were both discounted company cash flows: same asset, same value. Of course, these two perspectives are important because they open the door to different analyses of the asset.

This asset, i.e. brand equity, consists, mostly, of what is in customer memories, conscious and unconscious, about the brand (Ambler 2003). There is an anomaly in that brand equity is owned by the brand owner even though it is largely in the heads of their customers.

Accordingly, while we use the term "brand equity" to refer to the whole marketing asset and "brand" to include the underlying product, we acknowledge that other papers use these terms differently.

Marketing/accounting synergy: a discussion of its potential and evidence in e-business planning

Paul Phillips, *University of Kent, UK*
Sue Vaux Halliday, *University of Surrey, UK*

Abstract Advances in technology create opportunities for new forms of arranging work, such as collapsing the boundaries between marketing and accounting. This makes it possible for management to identify the key attributes and processes required for a more integrated marketing/ accounting process.

This paper sheds light on how e-business planning is taking place and identifies the key areas that are, together, acting as barriers to aligning organisation design, structures and people in the digitised world. The study presents empirical evidence of *de facto* leadership being taken by the IT function, to the detriment of what might otherwise have been developed: a synergistic relationship between the marketing/accounting planning interface and business performance. We set this in the context of converging demands on the marketing and accounting professions and of the literature suggesting that complex marketing/accounting metrics need to be developed to enable effective performance management.

Results from our study in e-business planning and our discussion of the potential for increasing marketing/accounting synergy shed some initial light on how both marketing and accounting practices can perpetuate themselves by embracing and interacting with IT infrastructures and data on business performance. If accountants are to remain influential in the digital age, and marketers are to regain their seat at the top table, it is necessary to develop both a metrics dashboard and changes in organisational design. This will facilitate learning and flexibility to demonstrate credible planning processes and enable improved strategy implementation.

INTRODUCTION

The digitised world has radically altered the ways in which firms interact with their internal and external stakeholders. As organisations continue to embrace the Internet, one of the burning issues management face is that of getting people to adjust to new organisational processes. Organisations operating in digitised environments need to be continually enhancing a combination of inside-out and a range of competencies.

There has been significant managerial interest in the opportunities available to use e-business solutions to create competitive advantage. As stated by Swaminathan and Tayur, (2003) e-business can be defined as a business process that uses the Internet or other electronic medium as a conduit to fulfil business transactions. However, a critical assumption is that e-business encompasses e-commerce, and goes far beyond e-commerce to include the application of information technologies for internal business processes as well for the activities in which a company engages in commercial activity with suppliers and customers (Phillips 2003). These internal activities can include functional activities, such as marketing, accounting, human resource, and operations.

Deshmukh, (2006) notes that the effects of the Internet on accounting has given prominence to the term Extensible Business Reporting Language (XBRL). The flow of e-business velocity has highlighted the need for increased speed of available data for strategic decision-making. Consequently, applications such as XBRL have now evolved to enable business data to be made more readily available (Trites 2004). The role that XBRL can potentially play in enhancing internal and external communication of financial information suggests that this could revolutionise the entire accounting/marketing interface. To prepare the groundwork for further study in this potential, we discuss an exploratory piece of research that investigates the levels of formality, participation and thoroughness in e-business planning. For the purposes of this study, the focus is on the marketing/accounting interface: the thrust of this study is to make a preliminary, subjective assessment of whether an effective e-business planning process is associated with higher levels of business performance. If so, then a further, broader study into marketing/accounting synergy in the digitised environment is warranted.

We consider that marketers, who are keen to *regain a place at top table*" (Webster, Malter, and Ganesan 2003) would do well to recall that accountants have remained influential and survived within organisations due to their flexibility to readjust in two main ways (Ezzamel, Wilmott and Wilmott 1997). Over a significant period of time, accountants have taken advantage of IT to manage large databases, information sharing and networking. They have demonstrated the capacity to promote new ways of performing financial calculations. In addition, the history of how the concept of capitalism was invented is an illustration of the influence of accounting ideas on economies (Chiapello 2007). Accounting is a fundamental function within capitalism, but this alone does not fully explain the influence wielded by accountants in the UK. Marketing is a fundamental function that is nevertheless much less influential globally; as particularly researched in the US (Webster et al. 2003). Kotler is currently telling marketers that to have the influence that the function is due, they must respond to *"increasing pressure for financial accountability"* with *"smarter marketing"* (2006 p.17).

At the same time, the digital economy is now reshaping traditional work practices of the accountant and CEOs are now expecting accountants to be customer oriented with a broad understanding of the business. Processes and techniques that accountants could use to add value to the e-business planning process has not yet been explicated, so this paper seeks to partially address the lacuna in existing knowledge by exploring the broad areas where accountants can contribute. This convergence of concerns for marketing and accounting professionals lends urgency to addressing the marketing/accounting interface.

This paper, therefore, addresses three important gaps in knowledge regarding the marketing/accounting interface, that are, together, acting as barriers to aligning organisation design, structures and people in the digitised world. First, we examine the normative marketing/accounting literature from a performance perspective, and highlight the different focus of traditional marketing metrics (lead) and finance metrics (lag). Second, we propose that in a digitised world, and in ever changing markets, organisations should seek to develop a more integrated marketing/accounting planning process. Third, we present empirical evidence of the e-business planning process, including levels of participation by various functions, from which we draw a preliminary relationship between marketing/accounting planning and business performance. The study's design and methods and research model are described. Results, conclusions and implications for further research, more directly focussed upon the marketing/accounting interface are discussed.

LITERATURE REVIEW

Context

Relational assets are now seen to be central to a firm's success. Despite this the dot. com boom illustrates the temptation to ignore business fundamentals in pursuit of an immediate return on investment. It is worth musing, given hindsight, that the IT perspective dominated, at the expense both of building sustainable customer relationships and financial caution. So in the digitised age fundamental truths are reinforced rather than superseded. Our discussion of context sets the scene for focusing on the potential for increased marketing/accounting synergy in a digital world.

All marketers know that the key asset that a firm has is its customer base. Other assets are valuable largely inasmuch as they support this key asset. A key reason why relationships and partnerships have taken centre stage, as all acknowledge (c.f. Vargo and Lusch 2004 for an overview), is that it is generally cheaper to keep customers than to compete for new customers. Retaining customers is therefore the driving focus of relationship marketing, which necessitates, in turn, an emphasis on aligning internal relationship processes (Voima 2000). This internal focus will maximise marketing opportunities when it is re-organised around new IT capabilities in information processing. In this way, marketing in the digitised age, given that detailed, accessible data can be held even by mass marketers, can benefit from integrating its processes with accounting processes. New technologies have exploded the channel options and made identifying "*the levels of expenditure for each channel (given expected revenues from customers)*" much more urgent (Rust, Ambler, Carpenter, Gregory and Srivastava 2004 p.84).

Styles and Ambler (1994), when considering the antecedents of export performance, included a combination of external and internal resources of relationships and alliances, of long-term commitment and investment. It has been argued, as we show below, that it is more efficient to outsource skills and share them, even sometimes with competitors, than for each firm to have duplicate internal competence (Kay 1993). This suggests the potential synergy in the marketing/ accounting space in any firm. In the digitised world this also suggests that a complex set of processes need to have a multi-discipline, or multi-function set of performance metrics. Ambler and Roberts have since created a neat definition of marketing that takes it out of any marketing function, per se, and re-presents it as a core business process: *"what the whole firm does to source and harness cash flow"* (2006a p.3)

Two elements that come to the fore when considering this form of marketing are time and space. For it is over long periods that organisations build up a body of knowledge and skills through experience and learning-by-doing. This is a component of intellectual capital, the difference between book and market valuation in so many firms. The market valuation is not visible: it is not, therefore, straightforward to account for it. Marketing, and the market, deal with value creation and this is a potentiality for value to be derived. Roslender and Fincham (2004, in a discussion of how accountants might best account for intellectual capital note that value realization is the more accessible process for the accountant than putting a cash value to value creation, which has no attached cash flow. As they discuss the accountant's perspective on this they divide intellectual capital into three parts: *"human capital, customer or relational capital and organizational and structural capital"* (p.5). This presents new challenges for accountants, when measuring: human capital (intangible assets relating to employees), relational capital (non-financial performance measures linked with knowledge embedded in customers and suppliers) and structural (new ways of financial reporting, such as narrative reporting in company accounts).

Timing is an important element of each part. Although there is a future, potential dimension here, Kay (1993) suggests that the external linkages (perhaps akin to relational capital) that a company has developed over time and the investment in this network of relationships (generated from its past activities) form a distinctive competitive capability. Indeed, Kay argues that firms should outsource activities if carrying them out internally would require excessive investment to attain the lowest unit cost. Moreover, this can be transformed into competitive advantage when added to additional distinctive capabilities such as technological ability and marketing knowledge. When Ambler cites an example of successful marketing and development of useful metrics to hold it accountable, he uses Diageo. They use *"key metrics over time and across brands and countries, because showing its market places as they really builds trust – and trust is crucial to investment and improvement"* (2006 p.26). In other words, Diageo's metrics cover time and space.

To continue to set the scene for this paper promoting marketing/accounting synergy it is worthwhile noting that marketing competence in a firm will include a learning capability. Relationship marketing has shown interest in learning in relationships (Ballantyne 2003; Halliday 2005; Halliday and Cawley 2000) and learning has been seen as core to innovation in the new product development literature (Kok, Hillebrand and Biemans 2003; Toivonen 2004). Trusting relationships have been seen as vital for a firm to create value (Halliday 2004; Vargo and Lusch 2004). This applies externally and internally. Again, this embracing of new organisational process is complex. This has been partly modelled by Sinkula, Baker and Noorderwier 1997 (see Figure 1).

Their framework brings us back to our initial point for the paper: that for organisations operating in the digitised environment to succeed they need to be able to continually enhance their competencies. That is to say, they need to have processes in place for market-based learning.

FIGURE 1 A framework for market-based organisational learning

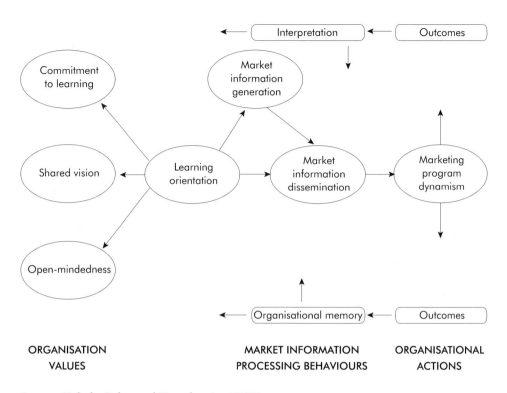

Source: Sinkula, Baker and Noorderwier (1997)

A final element to setting the context for this paper is to consider perceptions of how marketing has lost influence over the past ten to fifteen years. Webster et al. (2003) were commissioned by the Marketing Science Institute to review the period since Webster's seminal article predicting the future of marketing, published in 1992. Chief executives interviewed for this review stated unequivocally that financial pressures had eroded "*strategic thinking, customer focus and brand equity*" with a resulting "*negative impact on long-term business performance*" (p.34). To reverse this focus on the short-term some companies had altered their incentive schemes to incorporate evaluation of long-term performance and to punish individuals for short-term sales increases achieved at the expense of long-term margins. "*Others have strengthened the metrics they use to evaluate and reward marketing performance*" (p.39). However, the thrust of their research findings is that marketing is now less highly valued.

What are marketing metrics?

As we have just seen, Webster et al. (2003) have painstakingly researched the inability to quantify marketing's contributions to the firm (p.29). They concluded that "*the issue of measuring marketing productivity is the number one problem facing marketing management as it seeks to regain its seat at top table*" (p.49). This is of concern to accountants as much as to marketers in that it is in the marketing space that the firm creates value. It is a challenge for accountants as this is largely the puzzle of how to account for *"hidden value"* (Roslender and Fincham 2004 p.2). The significance of intellectual capital, of this hidden value, *"lies in the contribution these assets make to sustained value creation"* (p.1). As we noted earlier, Roslender and Fincham acknowledge that the accounting profession is not well placed to account for marketing's contribution, when it is seen as a subset of intellectual capital. In a study they carried out interviewing accountants specialising in intellectual capital they found little concerted effort to manage or account for it (Fincham and Roslender 2003). This is clearly disappointing, since Ambler summarised that *"for modern companies the creation of value increasingly depends on the control of intangibles such as brands, intellectual property, systems and data, human capital and market relationships"* (2002 p.47). So the challenge to quantify marketing's contribution is there to be met. From the marketing space Ambler proposed a set of metrics to indicate what is to be included in a working definition. He lists sales information, market share, marketing investment (into the brand), relevant end user satisfaction, relative price, perceived product quality, customer retention, sales to new customers, share of turnover of the previous three years' products launched, distribution, glossary of terminology (part of marketing management educating general management) and any particular measures chosen by the board (2002 p.49) Rust et al. (2004) concluded their review of the current field of measuring marketing productivity by noting

> The evaluation of marketing productivity ultimately involves projecting the differences in cash flows that will occur from implementation of a marketing action. In contrast, from an accounting standpoint, decomposition of marketing productivity into changes in financial assets and marketing assets of the firm as a result of marketing actions might be considered.

> p.86

This is a somewhat rudimentary understanding of metrics and the differences between marketing and accounting perspectives. Yet it provides us with a baseline for discussion of three issues in the marketing-accounting space in the firm, as identified below.

ISSUES IDENTIFIED IN DESIGNING PERFORMANCE METRICS FOR MARKETING

How to take a holistic view of the firm's performance?

Today marketing metrics are at the top of the research priorities identified by the Marketing Science Institute. And the *Journal of Marketing Management* is publishing this special edition which reviews the state of the field where marketing links with accounting to address marketing accountability. Yet, in 1999 Piercy discussed marketing and performance. He then defined marketing as *"an informational and cultural attribute of an organization, which describes essentially its market understanding and responsiveness to customer imperatives"* (p.638). As we have already noted, Ambler has since succinctly and sweepingly defined it as *"what the whole firm does to source and harness cash flow"*. Meanwhile the two key tasks for marketers are building and using brand equity (2006). The definition of performance has similarly evolved. What Piercy defined as *"the commonly desired achievements of the organization"* (p.624) at the outset of his paper was complicated by the research he carried out. For his key finding was that to achieve superior performance *"the internal marketing targets in such an approach would be better conceived as organizational systems development and inter-functional relationships*". Marketing, when linked to performance and accountability, has to be seen in the context of the whole firm – this does nothing to render the search for the 'silver metric' any easier. Most recently Phillips identified (2004 p.46) a key issue for marketing accountability as competing organisational silos. These are still preventing accounting from taking a holistic view. The challenge is the interpretation of multi-product, multi-functional information.

Bose (2006) identified that the key issue is to develop key performance indicators (KPIs) that provide a holistic and balanced view of the business. "*One potential approach is to think of individual KPIs not just as a singular metric, but as a balanced metric that incorporates several alternative dimensions*" (p.56). This very balance is derided by some, (Reichheld 2003; and Peppers and Rogers 2006). Peppers and Rogers recently proposed one 'silver' metric: return on customer. Another, currently welcome example, was introduced in December 2003, by Reichheld: a new loyalty metric, called net promoter. Reichheld states that the path to sustainable profit growth begins through the creation of more promoters and fewer detractors. The net promoter metric is the one number needed to successfully grow the firm. Reichheld (2006) later provides examples of how the single metric is sweeping corporate boardrooms, and reveals that some customer surveys only requires two questions: (1) How likely are you to recommend XYZ to a friend or colleague (0="not at all likely", and 10="extremely likely"), and (2) What is your primary reason for your rating in Question 1?

Although this is simplistic, it is clearly attractive to senior management. This may be partly due to the fact that it tackles the perception that with a range of metrics marketers are seen as ducking and diving between each different metric's implications, always suggesting a counterbalancing one, in order to evade hard questions being asked of marketing effectiveness. However, Ambler and Roberts (2006b) affirm that "*to believe that multiple measures are needed to describe multiple, partially independent and critical dimensions is not unreal*" (p.21).

What is to be measured?

Given the complexity of discerning what metrics are available and relevant, there is the issue of the content of the 'metrics dashboard'. Ambler has been cited as defining marketing metrics, but, as we have seen, the actual definition is still contested. Bose writes of a range of outcomes: "*to aid goal setting, monitor implications of organizational decisions, facilitate internal benchmarking, identify inefficiencies in core operations and identify cost saving and operations improvement opportunities*" (p.43). Voelpel, Leibold, Eckhoff, (2006) update the Balanced Scorecard approach having identified the danger of only counting that which is measurable. This concern, in turn, links to the issue of scope, for they noted that "*the properties of the parts are not intrinsic properties, but can be understood only within the context of the larger whole*" (p.47). They write of the context of "*an inter-connected and networked world*" (p.54). Bose (2006) suggests that subjective measures need to complement hard data. But how measurable are "*customer empathy or employee morale*" (p.50)? The search for the silver metric (or should this read, Holy Grail of the 21st century business planning bosses?) continues. Peppers and Rogers argue that they have found it: return on customer. However, Ambler and Roberts are clear in the debate fostered in the Marketing Science Institute working paper series, that this flatters to deceive.

How to combine perspectives on purpose and period under review?

Discounted cash flow calculations put all future options onto a level playing field. This is of great value when comparing across functional performance and different kinds of measurables. What it does not do is actually manipulate the real future. It again flatters to deceive. Any metrics need to align an organisation's activities with its strategic objectives (Swank 2003). If the two core tasks of marketing are building and then using brand or customer equity, innovation comes centre-stage with relationships. Taking advantage of opportunities as they present themselves is a necessary capability for continued market success. Nandone (2006) warns that a focus on past performance and understanding how it was caused leads to the danger of *"creating a culture devoid of risk taking, limited in vision and scared to reach for success"* (p.1). Voelpel et al. (2006) affirm that the 21st century is an innovation economy. This is a key challenge to the linear approach of the Balanced Scorecard metric, since, they argue, collaborative synergies can be harnessed from within, by innovation and partnering, by "co-*creating the business environment pro-actively*" (p.51). This surely is what is required in the age of digitisation of business processes. An important element of the innovation economy is that purpose then moves from the individual firm to the cash flows that could be created within networks of firms. Voelpel et al. are clear that shallow metrics such as a reliance on customer satisfaction are outmoded by the new emphasis, and ability of networks of firms to *"devote their energies to organizational fitness in creating and meeting customer need experiences"* (p.45). Indeed in developing their systemic scorecard they emphasise that *"the properties of the parts are not intrinsic properties, but can be understood only within the context of the larger whole"* (p.47)

What is sought is an aid to goal setting and identifying the financial implications of organisational decisions (Bose 2006). How can evaluation of the past most usefully drive good decisions for the unknown and contingent future? Phillips (2004) asked what business planning processes might take the place of accounting-based control processes? This question surfaces a really fundamental issue in that accounting deals with the past (lag) and decision making about marketing strategies and consequent verdicts on its performance is a forward looking process (lead).

SUMMARY

We have identified a key business challenge: getting people to adjust to new organisational processes in the digitised world. We see e-business as a challenge of organisation design in general and of collapsing boundaries between marketing and accounting processes in particular. We have seen that this collapse is part of the flexibility required to compete in the current innovation economy voiced by Voelpel et al. (2006). We have discovered that literature spanning the marketing-accounting space is embryonic. Encouraged by priorities set at the Marketing Science Institute (in turn set by practitioner demand) there has been a concern with marketing metrics – with providing accountability for marketing expenditure and with redefining marketing costs as investments. There is a welcome concern to increase marketing effectiveness as a contributor to business performance. Issues facing those designing new metrics across the marketing-accounting space have been identified in this as yet embryonic literature. We highlighted three: how to take a holistic rather than functionally fragmented view of the firm's performance; how to decide exactly what is to be measured and to what purpose and time frame. We therefore sought to deepen understanding of these issues by collecting primary data from practitioners currently involved in designing and evaluating their firm's performance metrics.

RESEARCH DESIGN AND METHODS

The research problem

We designed our study to build upon our understanding that, in a digitised world, and in ever changing markets, organisations should seek to develop a more integrated planning process. Therefore, our initial approach considers the relationship between an effective marketing/accounting planning process and perceptions of business performance. Our aim is not to address the marketing/accounting interface from both perspectives. Rather it is to expand the awareness from the accounting point of view. We restrict the focus as it provides a platform for ongoing work that will assess both perspectives of the marketing/accounting interface.

We wanted this exploratory piece of research to survey three elements of the e-planning process: formality, participation and thoroughness.

Hypotheses

The following hypotheses were proffered.

H1: *Level of e-business planning formality will be positively related to business performance.*

H2: *Level of e-business planning participation will be positively related to business performance.*

H3: *Level of e-business planning thoroughness will be positively related to business performance.*

Therefore we administered a questionnaire to participants at an accounting e-business conference. A key feature of the event was the need for accountants to work closer with their marketing departments. Since participants were mainly members of one of the leading professional accounting bodies and given the nature and focus of the conference, they were ideally placed to complete the questionnaires. The sample selected was not random, being drawn from the delegates at a conference. Demographic data relating to participants' organisational positions, industry type (service and manufacturing) and size of organisation (sales turnover and number of employees in an organisation) are detailed in Table 1.

Prior to the conference the instrument was pilot tested with groups of marketing managers, management accountants and academics to refine the design and focus the content. There was no evidence to indicate any misunderstanding of the survey items. The questionnaire was designed to preserve anonymity of participants, so they were not prenumbered for identification and participants did not have to reveal themselves or their company. The questionnaires were distributed at the conference and several reminders were made by the researcher and conference chairman for delegates to complete them. This resulted in 68 usable responses, which represented a response rate of 75%.

TABLE 1 Demographic data

Industry Type	
Service	53
Manufacturing	15
Total sample	68
Position of respondent	
Chief accountant/Controller	24
Financial Manager	13
Analyst	13
Project Accountant	9
IT	6
Other	3
Total sample	68
Size of organisation	
No. of employees	
0-10	5
11-50	10
51- 250	7
›250	46
Total sample	68
Sales turnover	
£0-£0.5m	4
£0.51m-£4.2m	8
£4.21-£24m	8
›£24m	48
Total sample	68

The research model

The multidimensional constructs of planning formality, participation and thoroughness have been operationalised in a variety of academic studies (Phillips, Davies and Moutinho 1999) and will be the core planning characteristics of the proposed framework. The marketing/accounting planning characteristics and business performance attributes were measured using a judgmental approach on 7-point Likert scales (1 to 7).

1. **Planning formality:** Formal strategic planning is an explicit and ongoing organisational process, Steiner (1979), with several components, including establishment of goals and generation and evaluation of strategies. However, as many earlier studies suffered from methodological deficiencies relating to the dichotomisation of planners into formal and informal, it was necessary to develop more rigorous methods for gauging the formality of the strategic planning process. Making use of Guttman scales, several researchers created a more sophisticated scaling procedure for the formality dimension. Pearce, Freeman and Robinson (1987) investigated the relationship between planning formality and financial performance. The formality construct being operationalised through the use of Guttman scales developed by (Wood and LaForge 1979), which was later endorsed by (Shrader, Taylor and Dalton 1984).

Key attributes for planning formality were:

- Setting explicit e-business goals
- Producing a written e-business plan
- Assigning implementation responsibilities to specified individuals/groups
- Seeking commitment to the e-business plan
- Developing plans by market segments
- Timely review of actual business performance against plan

2. **Planning participation:** Participation has been identified as a salient component of the planning process. Pearce, Freeman and Robinson (1987); McDonald (1982) concluded that it is essential for senior management to participate and be committed to planning, otherwise it will be impossible for the management team to initiate planning procedures and systems that can be used in a meaningful way. Piercy and Morgan (1989) argued that participation in planning from all management functions and at all levels is the only way to gain ownership and commitment to strategic plans.

   Key attributes for planning participation were the involvement of the following functions in e-business planning:

- Accounting
- Marketing
- IT
- Operations
- Personnel

3. **Planning thoroughness:** In today's tumultuous environment it seems logical that executives would benefit from obtaining guidelines or benchmarks associated with good strategic planning. By comparing such information with their own planning practices, they can incorporate good practices used by other organisations into their business unit. The identification and implementation of such key characteristics would cause an organisation to develop better strategic plans. These critical planning procedures can be evaluated by the measure of thoroughness.

   Key attributes for planning thoroughness were:

- We use knowledge and experience from different levels of staff
- We utilise marketing data from a number of different sources (e.g. consultants)
- We utilise sales and cost data relating to different e-business market segments
- This organisation provides adequate e-business training for staff
- This organisation uses a variety of motivational factors to encourage good e-business planning
- The time allowed for e-business planning is adequate

4. Performance: In today's competitive environment businesses are rightly concerned with confidentiality. This has always been a problem for researchers attempting to understand how to improve business performance. This study seeks to incorporate the important facet of business performance in terms of the ability of data being able to be pooled easily and electronically, and to mitigate the problem by not requiring participants to divulge sensitive financial or numerical information of any kind.

Respondents were asked *"how would you assess the overall business performance of your organisation relative to major competitors over the past year?"*

LIMITATIONS

Respondents were not equally shared across the functions in the firm that contribute to e-business planning; future studies into the marketing/accounting interface would most usefully pair responses to the survey instrument. Perceived business performance is a subjective measure based on perceptual, self-reported data. Despite, marketing research relying heavily on perceptual, including subjective performance measures (Haugland, Myrtveit, and Nygaard 2007), future studies should rely on objective measures (O'Sullivan and Abela 2007). For example, it would also be useful to pair perceptions of business performance with more objective indicators of business success. Not least to gain an idea of whether part of the synergy of the marketing/accounting interface might be in developing shared perspectives on performance that are more accurate when compared to objective results.

RESULTS

The descriptive statistics for e-business planning characteristics and business performance are shown in Table 2. Traditional planning thoroughness activities such as making use of knowledge and experience from different levels of staff (Mean = 5.04) and utilising marketing data from a number of different sources (4.57) had the first and second highest mean scores. Interestingly, the use of motivational factors scored the lowest mean score of 3.32.

Planning formality activities would appear not to be as mature as the other dimensions of the research model. The highest mean score was activities relating to assigning implementation responsibilities to specified individuals/groups (4.10), which was the lowest top score of planning: thoroughness (5.04), and participation (5.16). The variable with the lowest mean score was timely review of actual business performance against plan (3.12) is a timely reminder of the problems relating to the dot.com boom.

Planning participation was dominated by IT (5.16) and Marketing (4.88), whereas, personnel scored the lowest mean score of 2.37. These latter results highlight the reluctance of participants to involve personnel in the e-business strategy process. Interestingly the accounting function scored the second lowest mean of 3.91.

Business performance scored 3.74, which highlights the difficulties faced by the participants in the study. In order to conduct more in-depth tests for this study it was necessary to re-code data using percentile values of SPSS. Using aggregate scores for each planning characteristic the data were divided and recoded into three groups of low, medium and high as illustrated in Table 3.

TABLE 2 Descriptive Statistics (Likert Scale 1 to 7)

Variables	Mean	Std. Deviation
Planning thoroughness		
We use knowledge and experience from different levels of staff	5.04	1.77
We utilise marketing data from a number of different sources (e.g. consultants)	4.57	1.55
The time allowed for e-business planning is adequate	3.49	1.56
We utilise sales and cost data relating to different e-business market segments	3.44	1.71
This organisation provides adequate e-business training for staff	3.43	1.56
This organisation uses a variety of motivational factors to encourage good e-business planning	3.32	1.69
Planning formality		
Assigning implementation responsibilities to specified individuals/groups	4.10	1.90
Seeking commitment to the e-business plan	3.90	1.88
Setting explicit e-business goals	3.54	1.90
Developing plans by market segments	3.46	1.99
Producing a written e-business plan	3.34	1.88
Timely review of actual business performance against plan	3.12	1.74
Planning participation		
IT	5.16	1.81
Marketing	4.88	1.74
Operations	4.00	1.89
Accounting	3.91	2.01
Personnel	2.37	1.41
business performance	3.74	1.68

TABLE 3 Re-coding variables into quartiles

	Low	Medium	High
Variables			
Thoroughness	‹ 20	20-26	›26
Formality	‹18	18-26	›26
Participation	‹18	18-23	›23

Tables 4 to 6 provide the descriptive results for the relationships between each of the e-business planning characteristics and business performance. The one-way analysis of variance (ANOVA) results obtained from the testing the differences in business performance between planning levels are provided in Table 7.

The business performance mean scores and standard deviations were calculated for each e-business planning characteristic. The business performance scores for the planning formality levels for low, medium and high groups (Table 4) were 2.67 (N=27), 3.53(19) and 5.23 (22) respectively.

The business performance scores for the planning participation levels for low, medium and high groups (Table 5) were 3.09 (23), 3.88 (25) and 4.30 (20) respectively.

The business performance scores for the planning thoroughness levels for low, medium and high groups (Table 6) were 2.39 (23), 4.19 (27) and 4.78 (18) respectively.

TABLE 4 Descriptive results of planning formality and business performance

Level	Mean	N	Std. Deviation	Minimum	Maximum
Low	2.67	27	1.64	1	5
Medium	3.53	19	.84	2	5
High	5.23	22	1.11	3	7

TABLE 5 Descriptive results of planning participation and business performance

Level	Mean	N	Std. Deviation	Minimum	Maximum
Low	3.09	23	1.78	1	7
Medium	3.88	25	1.54	1	7
High	4.30	20	1.56	1	7

TABLE 6 Descriptive results of planning thoroughness and business performance

Level	Mean	N	Std. Deviation	Minimum	Maximum
Low	2.39	23	1.53	1	5
Medium	4.19	27	1.08	2	7
High	4.78	18	1.56	1	7

TABLE 7 Post Hoc ANOVA analyses for differences in business performance between planning levels

Planning	F	P	Test for significant paired differences
Formality	24.131	0.000	High› Low, Medium
Participation	3.119	0.051	High › Low
Thoroughness	17.638	0.000	High›Low, Medium

An ANOVA was undertaken to analyse relationships, as the objective was to assess the effect of a category variable (level of e-business planning) on a quantitative dependent variable (business performance). The reliability of the scale used to measure e-business planning was appraised using Cronbach's co-efficient alpha (Churchill 1979). The coefficient alphas for formality, participation and thoroughness were 0.9479, 0.7246 and 0.8317 respectively, which reflects the reliability of the scales. Table 7 presents the means and ANOVA summary results. It can be seen that all e-business planning characteristics were significant at a level $p < 0.05$. Overall, one may conclude that there is support for the hypothesised relationships.

To conclude the results, we note below that all three hypotheses were supported by the data collected.

H1: *Level of e-business planning formality will be positively related to business performance - An ANOVA was conducted with planning formality and business performance. The ANOVA procedure showed a statistically significant difference (F= 24.13, p<0.000) between high level and low level formal planners H1.*

H2: *Level of e-business planning participation will be positively related to business performance - The ANOVA procedure showed a statistically significant difference (F= 3.119, p<0.05) between high level and low level participative planners H2. These results therefore support H2.*

H3: *Level of e-business planning thoroughness will be positively related to business performance - The ANOVA procedure showed a statistically significant difference (F= 17.638, p<0.000) between high level and low level participative planners. These results therefore support H3.*

DISCUSSION

The results of this study suggest that planning formality and participation levels in the process are positively correlated with performance. In turn, the more detailed the planning, the more effective it is. And yet the accountants within our sample were not "strategically" influential in the e-business planning process. This is the case even though accounting has arguably been one of the most significant and pervasive forms of information processing within organisations. The study's results also show that personalised interaction and streamlined processes will deliver business results. And yet it appears that neither marketing nor accounting information is being used by those professionals. Rather, one of the salient issues identified in this study is the influence of the IT department vis-à-vis the accounting function during the e-business planning process. This confirms previous findings; whereas marketing strategy was once the driver of IT, it has now been replaced by IT driving businesses into the digital age (Venkatraman and Henderson 1998).

An interesting observation is that IT departments took a temporary lead in the e-business field, from accountants, in creating the early business models. Unfortunately, this led to the dot-com bubble, which eventually burst, so spectacularly. These earlier business models failed the number test, and fundamental financial rules were broken, such as net present value calculations, the cost to buy market share, and the medium and long term cost of serving the customer base.

Our findings also underline recommendation that accountants need to appreciate the fact that the Internet should be viewed as a disruptive technology (Phillips and Kirby 2002). It is therefore important for accountants and for marketers to understand the salient e-business strategy issues. Cooper (2002) also mentions the importance of accountants being well versed in IT.

Brouthers and Roozen (1999) assert that strategic accounting is a new, virtually unexplored area of strategic management. We consider that the synergy that could come from the marketing –accounting space being transformed into a genuine interface has the potential to provide the necessary information for much improved, strategic, decision-making. This interface, better understood and then implemented may be appropriate to help accountants and marketers improve the e-business planning characteristics of formality, participation and thoroughness. Strategic accounting could address some of the weak areas identified in this study. A good strategic accounting system, linked to marketing metrics capturing core relational assets should help e-businesses perform (i) environmental analysis, (ii) identify new e-business strategies, (iii) screen e-business strategy alternatives, (iv) formulate an e-business implementation, (v) implement the e-business strategic plan and (vi) control/evaluate the e-business planning process.

Margretta (2002) asserts that a business model is not the same thing as strategy, even though many people use the terms synonymously; business models only describe, as a system, how the pieces of a business fit together. They ignore two important dimensions – competition and organisational dynamics. A more contextual and dynamic approach is captured in the Systemic Scorecard (SSC). Voelpel et al. (2006) propose four foci to the SSC: to improve network shareholder value; to improve customer success and partnerships; the robustness and resilience of business-network processes, both competitive and collaborative and systemic knowledge management and innovation on each of four dimensions – financial, customer, business processes and learning and growth (p.55). To further the findings of this study we need to address questions such as: What are the characteristics of successful programmes for creating the marketing/accounting interface? For example, how should the firm emphasise cultural changes, change management processes, restructuring activities? It may be that this could now most usefully be explored by replicating Voelpel et al.'s study to other sectors and contexts to assess its contribution to the marketing and accounting interface.

CONCLUSION AND MANAGERIAL IMPLICATIONS

Despite the exploratory nature of the study and limitations of sample size, this study sheds light on how e-business planning is taking place. We conclude that a more systemic and multi-dimensional, holistic approach is needed to derive full benefits from the availability of tools such as XBRL and the transferability and accessibility of digitised data. If accountants are to remain influential in the digital age, and if marketers are to regain their seat at top table, we believe that it is necessary to develop a metrics dashboard. Also, there needs to be changes in organisational design that will facilitate learning and flexibility to demonstrate credible planning processes. If the lag and lead approaches can be combined synergistically at the accounting/marketing interface, the potential added value in enhancing the e-business planning process appears considerable. Traditional function or department based approaches to process improvement frequently have failed to deliver the required gains in overall performance. We are focussed on improving strategy implementation.

This paper reinforces the importance of the core e-business planning systems with emphasis on the planning characteristics of formality, participation and thoroughness. Naturally, practitioners at the marketing/accounting interface need to consider a wide variety of both environmental and organisational factors when designing, implementing, and improving e-business systems. A key to sustainable competitive advantage is having capabilities that are not easy to copy. The question remains, however, for researchers to identify those strategic marketing and accounting activities that are central in formulating strategy. Despite the recent calls for greater involvement by accountants in strategic planning, (Langfield-Smith 1997; Ittner and Larker 1997) there have been relatively few empirical papers. In the third millennium developing and implementing effective e-business systems should become a priority for accountants, working with others in the marketing-accounting space in firms.

Wang (2000) is of the opinion that e-business should be viewed less as a phenomenon of purely online business and more as a challenge of organisation redesign. Phillips (2003) asserts that organisations looking to implement an e-business strategy must align themselves internally with the demands that the dynamic environment imposes on strategic behaviour. We recommend investment in the design and execution of a further, broader study into metrics to create greater marketing/accounting synergy in the digitised environment.

REFERENCES

Ambler, Tim (2002), "Market metrics: what should we tell the shareholders?", *Balance Sheet*, Vol. 10, No. 1, pp. 47-50.

Ambler, Tim (2006), "Don't cave in to cave dwellers", *Marketing Management*, Vol. 15, No. 5, September/October, pp.25-29.

Ambler, Tim and Roberts, John (2006a), "Beware the silver metric: marketing performance measurement has to be multidimensional", *MSI Working paper series, Report No. 06-113*, pp 1-13.

Ambler, Tim and Roberts, John (2006b), "A word of warning clarified: reactions to Peppers and Rogers' response", *MSI Working paper series, Report No. 06-115*, pp. 19-21.

Ballantyne, David (2003), "A relationship-mediated theory of internal marketing", *European Journal of Marketing*, Vol. 37, No.9 pp. 1242-1260.

Bose, Ranjit, (2006), "Understanding management data systems for enterprise performance management", *Industrial Management and Data Systems*, Vol. 106, No. 1, pp. 43-59.

Brouthers, Keith, D. and Roozen, Frans, A. (1999), "Is it time to start thinking about strategic accounting", *Long Range Planning*, Vol. 32, No. 3, pp. 311-322.

Chiapello, Eve (2007), "Accounting and the birth of the notion of capitalism", *Critical Perspectives on Accounting*, Vol.18, No. 3, pp. 263-296.

Churchill, Jr. Gilbert, A (1979), "A paradigm for developing better measures of marketing constructs", *Journal of Marketing Research*, Vol. 16, pp. 64-73.

Cooper, Barry (2002), "The accountant of the future", *Accounting & Business*, April, ACCA, pp. 35-37

Deshmukh, Ashutosh (2006), *Digital Accounting: The Effects of the Internet and ERP on Accountants*, Hershey PA, IRM Press: Idea Group.

Ezzamel, Mahmoud, Lilley, Simon and Wilmott, Hugh (1997), "Accounting for management and managing accounting reflections on recent changes in the UK", *Journal of Management Studies*, Vol. 34, No.3, pp. 439-463.

Fincham, Robin and Roslender, Robin (2003), *The management of intellectual capital and its implications for business reporting*, report for the Institute of Chartered Accountants.

Greenyer, Andrew (2006), " Measurable marketing: a review of developments in marketing's measurability", *Journal of Business and Industrial Marketing,* Vol. **21**, No 4, pp. 239-243.

Halliday, Sue Vaux (2004), "Which trust? And when? Conceptualising trust in business relationships based on context and contingency", *International Review of Distribution, Retail and Consumer Research,* Vol.13, No. 4, pp.405-421.

Halliday, Sue Vaux (2005), "Making connections: the value of linking marketing knowledge and culture", *International Journal of Knowledge, Culture and Change Management,* Vol. **4**, pp.785-794.

Halliday, Sue Vaux and Cawley, Richard (2000), "Re-negotiating and re-affirming in cross-border marketing relationships: a learning-based conceptual model and research propositions", *Management Decision,* Vol. 38, No. 30, pp. 584-595.

Harris, Lloyd C.and Piercy, Nigel F. (1999), "A contingency approach to market orientation: distinguishing behaviours, systems, structures, strategies and performance characteristics", *Journal of Marketing Management,* Vol. **15**, pp. 615-646.

Haugland, Sven A., Myrtveit, Ingunn, Nygaard, Arne, (2007), "Market orientation and performance in the service industry: a data envelopment analysis", *Journal of Business Research,* Vol. **60**, p. 1191-1197.

Ittner, Christopher D and Larker, David F (1997), "Quality strategy, strategic control systems, and organisational performance", *Accounting, Organizations and Society,* Vol.22, No.3/4, pp. 293-314.

Kay, John. (1993), *Foundations of Corporate Success,* Oxford: Oxford University Press.

Kok, Robert A. W., Hillebrand, Bas and Biemans, Wim G. (2003), "What makes product development market oriented? Towards a conceptual framework", *International Journal of Innovation Management,* Vol. 7, No. 2, pp. 137-162.

Kotler, Philip (2006), "Re-engineering marketing", *The Marketer,* September, pp. 15-17.

Langfield-Smith, Kim. (1997), "Management control systems and strategy: a critical review", *Accounting, Organizations and Society,* Vol. **22**, No.2, pp. 207-232.

Margretta, Joan (2002), "Why business models matter", *Harvard Business Review,* Vol. **80**, No. 5, May, pp. 86-92.

McDonald, Malcolm, H. B. (1982), "International marketing planning: some new insights", *Journal of International Marketing,* Vol. 1, pp. 90-103.

Mizik, Natalie and Jacobson, Robert (2006), "Myopic marketing management: the phenomenon and its long-term impact on firm value", *MSI Working paper series,* Report no. 06-100, pp. 1-21.

Nandone, John (2006), "Free yourself from the tyranny of marketing metrics", *Advertising Age,* Vol. 77, Issue 47, pp. 1-3.

O'Sullivan, Don, and Abela, Andrew, W (2007), "Marketing performance measurement ability and firm performance", *Journal of Marketing,* Vol. 71, No. 2, pp. 79-93.

Pearce, John. A., Freeman, Elizabeth. B., and Robinson, Richard. B., (1987), "The tenuous link between formal strategic planning and financial performance", *Academy of Management Review,* Vol. 12, No. 4, pp. 658-675.

Peppers, Don and Rogers, Martha (2006), "Response to Ambler and Roberts' 'Beware the silver metric'", *MSI Working paper series* Report no. 06-114, pp. 15-18.

Phillips, Paul A. (2003), *E-business Strategy*: Text and Cases, Maidenhead: McGraw-Hill.

Phillips, Paul A. (2004), "The relationship between e-business planning and performance: an accounting perspective", *International Journal of Business Performance and Management,* Vol. 6, No. 1, pp 43-55.

Phillips, Paul A.; Davies, Fiona and Moutinho, Luiz (1999), "The interactive effects of strategic planning on hotel performance: a neural network analysis", *Management Decisions,* Vol. 37, No.3, pp.279-288.

Phillips, Paul A. and Kirby, David (2002), "The Impact of Electronic Business on Accountants: A Shareholder Value Perspective", *ACCA Research report no. 76*, London: Certified Accountants Educational Trust, ISBN 1 85908 377 3.

Piercy, Nigel, and Morgan, Neil A., (1989), "Strategic planning and the management accountant", *Management Accounting*, CIMA, November, pp.18-19.

Reichheld, Fred (2003), "The number one number you need to grow," *Harvard Business Review*, Vol. **81, No. 12** (December), pp.46-54.

Reichheld, Fred (2006), *The Ultimate Question: Driving Good Profits and True Growth*, Boston: Harvard Business School Press.

Rust, Roland, Ambler, Tim, Carpenter, Gregory S., Kumar, V. and Srivastava, Rajendra K (2004), "Measuring marketing productivity: current knowledge and future directions", *Journal of Marketing*, Vol. **68**, No. 4, (October), pp. 76-89.

Roslender, Robin and Fincham, Robin (2004), "Intellectual capital: who counts, controls?", *Accounting and the Public Interest*, Vol. **4**, No. 1, pp.1-23.

Shrader, Charles. B., Taylor, Lew, and Dalton, Dan. R., (1984), "Strategic planning and organisational performance: a critical appraisal", *Journal of Management*, Vol. **10**, No.2, pp.149-171.

Sinkula, James M., Baker, William E. and Noordewier, Thomas (1997), "A framework for market-based organizational learning: linking values, knowledge and behaviour", *Journal of the Academy of Marketing Science*, Vol. **25**, No. 4, pp. 305-318.

Steiner, George. A. (1979), *Strategic Planning: What Every Manager Must Know*, New York: Free Press.

Styles, Chris and Ambler, Tim (1994), "Successful export practice: the UK experience", *International Marketing Review*, Vol. **11**, No. 6, pp. 23-47.

Swaminathan, Jayashankar M and Tayur, Sridhar R (2003), "Models for supply chains in e-business, Management Science", Vol. **49**, No. 10, pp. 1387-1406.

Swank, Cynthia Karen (2003), "The lean service machine", *Harvard Business Review*, Vol. **81**, No. 10, October, pp. 123-129.

Toivonen, Marja (2004), "Foresight in services: possibilities and special challenges", *The Service Industries Journal*, Vol. **24**, No. 1, January 2004, pp. 79-98.

Trites, Gerald (2004), "Decline of the age of Pacioli: The impact of e-business on accounting and accounting education", *Canadian Accounting Perspectives*, Vol. **3**, No. 2, pp. 171-186.

Vargo, Stephen. L. and Lusch, Robert. F. (2004), "Evolving a new dominant logic for marketing", *Journal of Marketing*, Vol. **68**, No. 1, pp. 1-17.

Venkatraman, N. and Henderson, John. C. (1998), "Real strategies virtual organizing", *Sloan Management Review*, Vol. **40**, No. 1, pp. 33-48.

Voelpel, Sven C., Leibold, Marius and Eckhoff Robert A. (2006), "The tyranny of the balanced scorecard in the innovation economy", *Journal of Intellectual Capital*, Vol. **7**, No.1, pp. 43-60.

Voima, Paivi (2000), "Internal relationship management". In: Varey, Richard J. and Lewis Barbara R., (eds.), *Internal Marketing – directions for management*, London: Routledge.

Wang, Shouhong. (2000), "Managing the organisational aspects of electronic commerce", *Human Systems Management*, Vol. **19**, No. 1, pp. 49-59.

Webster, Frederick Jr., E. (1992), "The changing role of marketing in the corporation", *Journal of Marketing*, Vol. **56**, October, pp. 1-17.

Webster, Frederick Jr., E., Malter, Alan J. and Ganesan Shankar (2003), "How can marketing regain its seat at top table?", *Marketing Science Report no. 03003*, Working paper series Issue 3, pp. 29-47.

Wood, D.Robley., and LaForge, R. Lawrence. (1979), "The impact of comprehensive planning on financial performance", *Academy of Management Journal*, Vol. **23**, No. 3, pp. 516-526.

Exploring the potential of customer accounting: a synthesis of the accounting and marketing literatures

Lisa McManus, *Griffith University, Australia*
Chris Guilding, *Griffith University, Australia*

Abstract A review of the marketing and accounting literatures has revealed that to date no previous study has examined the intersection of the marketing and accounting literatures pertinent to Customer Accounting (CA). This paper provides a synthesis of these two literatures by exploring the potential of CA. It updates the recent achievements in the CA literature from an accounting perspective and explores the nature of marketing based measures pertaining to customer marketing and management. It appears there is considerable potential for accountants to draw on points of focus raised in the marketing literature to further advance customer focused accounting measures of performance.

INTRODUCTION

Customers constitute a fundamental tenet in generally accepted and applied marketing paradigms. This focus on customers appears to be somehow "lost in translation", however, for those managers aligned to the management accounting paradigm. Management accounting systems tend to be structured according to product, service or geographical territory and rarely according to customer groupings. Further, it appears as a non sequitur for an accounting ledger to recognise a customer or a group of customers as an asset. The disparate way in which customers are conceived of by these two organisational functions highlights the existence of a profound managerial schism. A schism is also in evidence when the findings of Foster and Young (1997) and Shields (1997) are compared. From their survey of American and Australian managers, Foster and Young (1997; p. 69) found that *"customer profitability/satisfaction"* was the *"the single most important current management priority"*. By way of contrast, in a review of the management accounting literature from 1990 to 1996, Shields (1997) failed to find a single study concerned with *"customer profitability/satisfaction"*.

While the extent of customer-focused research conducted from an accounting perspective still fails to rise above minimal attention, some consideration of the potential of accountants adopting a customer focus is now in evidence. Guilding and McManus (2002) conducted a study that stands in relative isolation as a survey concerned with appraising customer accounting (CA) adoption levels and the antecedents of CA adoption. Commentaries that provide an overview of the nature and potential of conducting customer profitability analysis include Cardinaels, Roodhooft and Warlop (2004); Chenhall (2003); Foster and Gupta (1994); Foster and Young (1997); and Luft and Shields (2003).

The marketing research concerned with customers appears as endless by comparison. Key points of focus in this literature include customer loyalty, customer retention, customer profitability, and customer satisfaction. Much of this literature provides some implicit dimensions of accountability that could be added to the management accountant's frame of reference. This paper overviews the accounting literature concerned with CA then addresses marketing perspectives most pertinent to CA by considering the marketing literature's achievements with respect to customer satisfaction, customer loyalty and customer profitability.

The paper's objective is to progress a synthesis of the accounting and marketing literatures concerned with CA. In so doing, it points towards techniques and constructs that management accountants might usefully consider in order to advance the way that CA is conceived and conducted (or not conducted). This signifies that the paper represents an attempt to broaden accountants' appreciation of the sphere of possible accountability constructs that can be monitored when determining the marketing function's achievements with respect to customer oriented performance. Although not explicitly addressed in this paper, it is interesting to conjecture the extent to which the conventional accounting mindset that has been characterised as historical and inwardly oriented (Guilding et al. 2000) represents a hindrance to accounting's capacity to view marketing constructs such as customer satisfaction and customer loyalty as important dimensions of performance worthy of incorporation in systems of accountability.

The remainder of the paper is structured as follows. The next section places CA in the broader context of strategic management accounting (SMA). In order to provide a stock take concerning the current state of the art with respect to customer accounting, and also our knowledge of customer accounting practices applied, the subsequent section attempts a comprehensive overview of the normative and empirical literatures concerning CA. The ensuing section describes the result of an examination of the marketing literature to determine themes most pertinent to CA. This examination has resulted in the distillation of three themes that lend themselves to accountability: customer satisfaction, customer loyalty and customer profitability. In reviewing these themes, prominence has been attached to any discussion relating to facets of performance measurement. The paper's final section provides a discussion and conclusion that explores how the insights provided by this study might be usefully built upon in subsequent research.

CUSTOMER ACCOUNTING – AN EXAMPLE OF STRATEGIC MANAGEMENT ACCOUNTING

Customer accounting represents a particular set of practices that can be seen to sit within an accounting subset that has been termed *"strategic management accounting"*. This factor is noteworthy as it appears that the beginnings of an accounting interest in CA, that was noted above, has occurred at a time of a growing appreciation of a need for management accounting to assume more of a strategic orientation.

It is more than two and a half decades since Simmonds (1981) first coined the term *"strategic management accounting"* (SMA), however there continues to be limited consensus on its exact meaning (Bhimani and Keshtvarz 1999; Coad 1996; Guilding, Cravens and Tayles 2000; Lord 1996; Nyamori et al. 2001; and Roslender and Hart 2003). In commenting on SMA's under-defined nature, Tomkins and Carr (1996) note it also lacks a general conceptual framework. Simmonds (1981) saw SMA as concerned with *"the provision and analysis of management accounting data about a business and its competitors for use in developing and monitoring the business strategy"*, (p. 26). Simmonds extolled management accountants to take more of a strategic perspective and gather information external to the firm that would assist management in strategic operations.

Further conceptualisation of SMA grew from Simmonds work. Bromwich (1990) defined SMA as *"the provision and analysis of financial information on the firm's product markets and competitors' costs and cost structures and the monitoring of the enterprise's strategies and those of its competitors in these markets over a number of periods"* (p. 28).

Lord (1996) identified three dimensions of SMA: collection of competitor information; exploitation of cost reduction opportunities; and matching of accounting emphasis with strategic position. Guilding, Cravens and Tayles (2000) saw SMA practices as exhibiting one or more of the following characteristics: an environmental or marketing orientation; a competitor focus; or a future-looking, long-term orientation.[1] More recently, Roslender and Hart (2003) provided a more refined definition of SMA as *"a generic approach to accounting for strategic positioning, defined by an attempt to integrate insights from management accounting and marketing management within a strategic management framework"* (p. 255).

It is notable that SMA practices have been suggested as having the potential to overcome the "fall" of management accounting (Johnson and Kaplan 1987) and restore the relevance of accounting information provided to the modern day manager (Johnson 1992). The SMA writings are significant to a consideration of the potential for CA as they highlight a developing awareness of the possibility of accountants assuming more of a strategic posture. This points towards the evolution of an environment that is more conducive to CA inception and development, as CA can be seen to be a particular example of SMA. It is also pertinent to recognise that, consistent with CA, SMA provides considerable impetus for greater communication and collaboration between the accounting and marketing functions (Roslender and Hart 2003).

---

[1]   It is noteworthy that these researchers failed to include any CA practices in their survey of SMA practices.

CUSTOMER ACCOUNTING – ACHIEVEMENTS TO DATE

Due to the limited amount of research and commentaries concerned with customer accounting, this section of the paper constitutes an attempt to provide a comprehensive review of all notable contributions to the customer accounting literature. In one of the earliest CA commentaries, Bellis-Jones (1989) discusses customer profitability analysis (CPA) in the context of the retail sector. As a result of a small number of major retailers being able to exert substantial pressure on suppliers to reduce prices, Bellis-Jones noted suppliers initiating activities tailored to certain customers in order to maintain competitiveness. Extending upon this idea, Ward (1992) sees CPA as a very important technique due to the increased focus it directs on customers as "*the most important assets which a company has*" (p. 168). He defines CPA as "*the total sales revenue generated from a customer or customer group less all the costs that are incurred in servicing that customer or customer group*" (p. 167). Ward argues that most customers require varying levels of customer service, which results in non-revenue related differentials in customer profitability levels. He sees CPA as an important analytical tool that can help firms distinguish between their profitable and unprofitable customers.

Smith and Dikolli (1995) further extend prior CPA discussions with an explicit reference to activity-based costing as a basis for tracing costs to customers. They identify four customer expense categories: purchasing patterns, delivery policy, accounting procedures and inventory holding. Each of these factors carries implications for a customer's profitability and a number of profitable and unprofitable customer characteristics can be identified within each category. Smith and Dikolli suggest that while a number of these characteristics can be directly traced and allocated to customers, other costs are more difficult to determine for each customer, and that these costs warrant the application of an activity-based costing approach.

Guilding, Kennedy and McManus (2001) extended the CA literature by investigating particular CA applications arising in the context of the hotel industry. Guilding et al. describe a technique that they refer to as "*supplementary purchasing CPA*" and explore the application of the technique by way of a hypothetical case study. This exposition demonstrates the potential importance of appraising revenue generating activities occurring after an initial hotel room sale. These "supplementary" sources of revenue include restaurant meals, bar sales, telephone calls, and room service. Guilding et al. then promote the idea of segmenting a hotel's customer base according to differentials apparent in customer purchasing patterns of such "supplementaries". They also explore the potential of customer asset accounting (CAA) in the context of hotel management.

In terms of applied applications of CPA, Cooper and Kaplan (1991a, 1991b, 1991c) describe three CPA case studies: Kanthal, Winchell Lighting Inc., and Manufacturers Hanover Corporation. Adoption of CPA in these three companies, either on a customer or customer segment basis, was motivated by a quest to identify profitable customer relationships that should be maintained and enhanced, as well as unprofitable customer relationships, to enable the initiation of actions designed to transform the accounts to a profitable standing or to terminate the trading relationship. The "Blue Ridge Manufacturing" case study, which was documented by Juras and Dierks (1994), was further analysed by Foster, Gupta and Sjoblom (1996) who undertook an ABC based CPA analysis and found that the largest customer segment which contributed 38% of the total company revenues, provided over 67% of the total operating income; and the small customer segment which represented 39% of company revenues, yielded a negative contribution towards operating income. Foster et al. (1996) noted several key issues arising from this case study. Firstly, that most management accounting systems only focus on products or departments and not on customers, and only seldom can a management accounting system produce customer profitability figures. Secondly, a customer's profitability depends not only on the product or service unit cost, but also on other costs such as marketing, customer service, and distribution. Additional applied CPA case studies have been conducted by McManus (2007) in a telecommunications company, Mulhern (1999) in three sales territories of a pharmaceutical manufacturer and Noone and Griffin (1999) in an Irish hotel.

Foster and Gupta (1994) undertook a broad overview of the interaction between the marketing and management accounting literatures concerned with the management of marketing costs. They also examined the opinions of marketing managers with respect to the value of the type of information made available by conventional accounting systems. Foster and Gupta identify a number of central themes, two of which are particularly relevant to customer accounting: the marketing focus on retaining profitable customers and the questionable accounting treatment of all marketing costs as period expenses. The authors also note that a minimally explored dimension of CPA is the lifetime profitability analysis of customers.

Guilding and McManus' (2002) study that investigated the incidence, perceived merit and antecedents of CA in a sample of Australian publicly listed companies stands in isolation in the literature as a survey of CA application. Three main findings were distilled from the study. Firstly, mean scores for three of the five CA practices appraised in the study were above the mid-point of the "used not at all – used to a large extent" measurement scale.[2] From this observation it was concluded that CA usage was greater than what might have been reasonably anticipated. In addition, mean scores of the perceived merit of all five CA practices appraised were above the mid-point of the measurement scale. The study's other main findings concerned an observed positive association between market orientation and CA, and a weak positive association between competition intensity and CA, although no support was found for a hypothesised inverted-U relationship between CA and competition intensity. Lind and Strömsten (2006) have added to the Guilding and McManus study by developing a framework to explain a company's choice of CA technique based on its customer resource interfaces.

It appears as highly significant that there are a growing number of accounting researchers appraising other customer related factors and non-financial performance measures such as customer loyalty, customer satisfaction, customer complaints, likelihood of return and market share (e.g. Banker, Potter and Srinivasan 2000; Banker and Mashruwala 2007; Cugini, Carù and Zerbini 2007; Davila and Foster 2005; Ghosh 2005; Ismail 2007; Ittner and Larcker 1998; Perera, Harrison and Poole 1997; Riley, Pearson and Trompeter 2003; Smith and Wright 2004). Perera et al. (1997) extended a study conducted by Abernethy and Lillis (1995) by examining whether companies that pursue a customer-focused manufacturing strategy also

---

[2]   The five CA practices appraised in the study were customer profitability analysis, customer segment profitability analysis, lifetime customer profitability analysis, valuation of customers or customer groups as assets, and customer accounting (i.e. holistic notion). One of the limitations of the Guilding and McManus (2002) study is that each of the CA practices was measured by a single item.

emphasise non-financial operations-based performance measures, and whether this emphasis results in improved company performance. The authors provided support for Abernethy and Lillis' findings concerning a positive association between a customer-focused manufacturing strategy and greater use of non-financial performance measures, but no support was found for the hypothesised link to improved company performance.

Ittner and Larcker (1998) focused exclusively on customer satisfaction as a lead indicator of a firm's financial performance and its value relevance using customer, business-unit and firm-level data. They found some support for their hypotheses that customer satisfaction is an indicator of customer purchase behaviour (measured by retention, revenue and revenue growth), growth in customer numbers and financial performance (measured by business-unit revenues, return on sales and profit margins). Evidence was also provided that customer satisfaction measures hold some value for stock markets but are not completely reflected in accounting book values. Ittner and Larcker also found that the relationship between customer behaviour (measured by retention, revenue and revenue growth) and financial performance are relatively stable over different ranges of customer satisfaction, but tend to diminish at high customer satisfaction levels.

Banker et al. (2000) investigated the performance impacts of using customer satisfaction (measured by the likelihood of return and customer complaints) in hotel managers' incentive contracts. This study's findings suggest that customer satisfaction measures are significantly associated with future financial performance measures and contain incremental information not reflected in past financial measures. In addition, it was found that both non-financial and financial performance measures (i.e. operating profit, revenue per available room, expense per available room and revenue contribution from toll-free lines) improve following the introduction of an incentive plan that includes non-financial performance measures.

More recently, Riley et al. (2003) examined the value relevance to investors of financial and non-financial performance variables. Riley et al. appraised the impact on stock returns of conventional accounting denominated financial measures (i.e., earnings and changes in abnormal earnings) as well as non-financial performance variables (i.e. customer complaints, revenue load factor, market share and ton miles) for seven of the largest United States airlines. It was found that financial and non-financial performance variables are significantly associated with stock returns. Of particular interest is the fact that non-financial performance variables were found to exhibit greater value relevance than traditional financial measures. While traditional financial measures were significantly associated with stock returns, no evidence was found of them providing any incremental explanatory power beyond that provided by the non-financial variables.[3]

Riley et al.'s (2003) findings provide support for the implementation of a more balanced set of internal performance measures in a manner such as that promoted in Kaplan and Norton's (1992) seminal work on the balanced scorecard. The balanced scorecard incorporates internal and external performance indicators sub-divided according to four main dimensions of focus, one of which concerns a customer perspective. Kaplan and Norton (1992) note that a number of companies have missions that focus on customers. Greater importance attached to customer

---

[3]   It was found that non-financial variables explained 23% of the variability in stock returns. Adding EPS and changes in abnormal earnings did not improve the amount of variability explained.

based performance measures would appear to underscore such a mission. Customer focused performance measures promoted by Kaplan and Norton (1992) include customer satisfaction, customer retention and market share in target segments. It appears as significant that the balanced scorecard represents a performance evaluation framework providing considerable impetus for the marketing and management accounting paradigms assuming a greater degree of common ground.

CUSTOMER ACCOUNTING – INVESTIGATING UNREALISED POTENTIAL

There are several constructs of potential customer accountability that, despite extensive discussion in the marketing literature, have attracted minimal attention in the research based accounting literature or in accounting textbooks. This section of the paper will consider three of the most widely researched marketing orientated customer accountability constructs of customer satisfaction, customer loyalty and customer profitability, and provide a commentary on their potential as objects of accountability that could be added to the strategic management accountant's portfolio of accounting techniques. The selection of these three themes has resulted from a quest to identify those strands of the marketing literature concerned with dimensions of customer focused organisational achievement that provide scope for performance measurement and establishing domains of accountability. The remainder of this section is structured according to an overview of the marketing literature pertaining to these three constructs, with particular attention directed to ways that they may be measured. While customer profitability from an accounting perspective has already been considered, an examination of the marketing literature concerned with customer profitability reveals a number of distinct conceptualisations and lines of enquiry.

Customer satisfaction

Prior to an exploration of the large marketing literature concerned with customer satisfaction, it is pertinent to note that the balanced scorecard literature widely extols the importance of customer satisfaction. A fundamental challenge arising in any attempt to quantify customer satisfaction stems from the fact that it represents a state of mind. Customers compare their expectations prior to a purchase with their performance perceptions after the purchase (Oliver 1996; Westbrook and Oliver 1991). The satisfaction literature focuses on customer satisfaction as an outcome of "*global satisfaction*" (the offer in total), rather than "*domain-specific satisfaction*" (each part of the offer) (Oliver 1996). Satisfaction is therefore a cognitive judgment that lies on a continuum ranging between low satisfaction where expectations exceed perceptions of performance, and high level satisfaction where performance is perceived as exceeding initial purchase expectations. As noted by Kotler (2000, p. 36) "*There is general agreement that: Satisfaction is a person's feelings of pleasure or disappointment resulting from comparing a product's perceived performance (or outcome) in relation to his or her expectations*".

A large body of research has focused on the antecedents and consequences of customer satisfaction (Anderson, Fornell and Lehmann 1994; Gómez, McLaughlin and Wittink 2004; Oliver 1997; Reinartz, Krafft and Hoyer 2004). The relationship between customer satisfaction, customer loyalty and profitability/performance has received interest from both academics and managers (Donio', Massari and Passiante

2006; Lowenstein 1996; Peterson and Wilson 1992). This interest stems from a widely-held belief that improved customer satisfaction will have a positive effect on business profitability/performance through increased customer loyalty (Anderson, Fornell and Lehmann 1994; Edvarsson, Johnson, Gustafsson and Strandvik 2000; Hallowell 1996; Heskett, Jones, Loveman, Sasser and Schlesinger 1994; Reichheld, Markey and Hopton 2000; Reichheld and Sasser 1990; Rust, Zahorik and Keiningham 1995; Schneider and Bowen 1995; Storbacka, Strandvik and Grönroos 1994). The causal mechanism underlying this linkage is fairly straightforward. It is assumed that satisfied customers are more likely to show loyalty to the business via repeat purchases (and increased customer retention). It is also thought that high levels of customer satisfaction will result in increased sales resulting from word of mouth referrals. This view is supported by the findings of several empirical studies (Anderson, Fornell and Mazvancheryl 2004; Holmes and Lett 1977; Singh and Pandya 1991; Swan and Oliver 1989).

It appears as a cornerstone to marketing theories that customer satisfaction has a positive impact on long-term business performance and a number of empirical studies have found a positive relationship between customer satisfaction and customer loyalty (Anderson and Sullivan 1993; Donio', Massari and Passiante 2006; Fornell 1992; Reichheld and Sasser 1990; Taylor and Baker 1994). Other studies have focused on customer retention as a manifestation of customer loyalty, providing evidence of a positive association between customer satisfaction and customer retention (Bearden and Teel 1982; Ennew and Binks 1996; LaBarbera and Mazursky 1983). The positive linkage between customer satisfaction, loyalty and retention, has been posited to favourably impact on a firm's profits as retained customers are cheaper to service than new customers (Anderson, Fornell and Mazvancheryl 2004; Hallowell 1996; Reichheld 1993).

A firm's long term profitability is also expected to benefit from increased customer satisfaction, as retained customers can be less price sensitive. To date, evidence concerning this relationship is mixed, however. While Zeithaml, Berry and Parasuraman (1996) found that price sensitivity was present in particular situations, Anderson (1996) showed that satisfied customers were less price sensitive and less likely to switch when a firm increases prices.

While there is limited evidence concerning a direct customer satisfaction / profitability link, the above studies provide a strong case for expecting that increased customer satisfaction will have a beneficial impact on financial performance. Research examining the link between satisfaction and performance from a cross-sectional perspective has yielded inconclusive findings (Anderson, Fornell and Mazvancheryl 2004; Boulding, Kalra, Staelin and Zeithaml 1993; Rust and Zahorik 1993; Rust, Zahorik and Keiningham 1995). For example, Yeung and Ennew (2000) found some evidence that satisfaction does have a positive financial impact but that the direct effects were generally small. Nelson, Rust, Zahorik, Rose, Batalden and Siemanski (1992) found a positive relationship between customer satisfaction levels and a range of profitability measures – earnings, net revenues and return on assets. Anderson, Fornell and Lehmann (1994) also provided evidence suggesting heightened customer satisfaction levels increase profitability. On the other hand, Tornow and Wiley (1991) report a negative association between customer satisfaction and profits, and Wiley (1991) suggested that all elements of customer satisfaction were negatively related to financial performance. Interestingly, Bernhardt, Donthu and Kennett (2000) examined the relationship between customer satisfaction and performance in a longitudinal setting and found that while an increase in customer satisfaction had no effect on firm performance in the short run, in the long-term, increased customer satisfaction had a significant positive effect on profits. While more recently, Anderson, Fornell and Mazvancheryl (2004) found a positive association between customer satisfaction and shareholder value that varied significantly across industries and firms.

A positive relationship between customer satisfaction and non-financial firm performance was documented by Schneider (1991). Further, although Tornow and Wiley (1991) found no association between customer satisfaction and financial performance, their results indicated a positive relationship between customer satisfaction, customer retention and perceptions of product quality.

Relationships between customer satisfaction, service quality and purchase intentions have also been examined. Cronin and Taylor (1992) found a positive relationship between perceived service quality and satisfaction, and satisfaction and intent to repurchase. Several other studies provide support for these findings (Bearden and Teel 1983; Dabholkar and Thorpe 1994; LaBarbera and Mazursky 1983; Oliver 1980; Oliver and Swan 1989; Rust and Zahorik 1993). In an earlier critical review of the consumer satisfaction literature, Yi (1990; p. 104) concluded *"Many studies found that customer satisfaction influences purchase intentions as well as post-purchase attitude"*.

Customer loyalty

Many marketing researchers have argued that retained loyal customers result in increased profits due to decreased costs and increased revenues (Berry and Parasuraman 1991; Choi, Kim, Kim and Kim 2006; Kumar and Shah 2004; Lee, Barker and Kandamputty 2003; Perrien, Paradis and Banting 1995; Pitta, Franzak and Fowler 2006; Sonnenberg 1994; Zeithaml, Parasuraman and Berry 1990). It is suggested that loyal customers result in lower costs due to lower acquisition expenses and efficiencies from servicing experienced customers; and revenues are increased as a result of repeat purchases and customer referrals. Reichheld and Sasser (1990) concluded that, depending on the industry, a company could improve profitability by between 25% - 85% by reducing customer defections by 5%. Also, Reichheld (1993) claims that in the life insurance industry, a 5% increase in customer retention reduces the cost per policy by 18%. These factors underscore Srivastava, Shervani and Fahey's (1998) view of customer loyalty as a valuable commercial asset of a business.

Customer loyalty can be defined in two ways (Jacoby and Kyner 1973). Firstly, loyalty can be defined as an attitude where customer attachment is developed to a product, service, brand or an organisation. From a purely cognitive perspective, such attachment defines a customer's degree of loyalty (Hallowell 1996). Secondly, loyalty can be defined in terms of behaviour. Yi (1990) provides examples of loyalty behaviour such as continuing to purchase from the same supplier, recommending a particular seller, or increasing the scale of a relationship with a supplier.

Customer loyalty has been a major focus in many industries over recent years as companies seek to increase customer loyalty by instigating loyalty reward programmes such as frequent flyer programmes, loyalty club cards and fly buy cards (Lewis 1999; Liebermann 1999). However, recent research has questioned the value of spending marketing resources in an attempt to build loyalty that may or may not result in improved profits (Reinartz and Kumar 2002). Dowling and Uncles (1997) mirror this sentiment by specifically questioning whether customer loyalty programmes actually work. In support of this view, Reinartz and Kumar (2002) studied four companies from different industries and found that the correlation between profitability and each firm's measure of customer loyalty was weak. This suggests customer loyalty programmes are much more strongly linked to customer spending or frequency of usage than customer profitability.

Empirical research concerned with behavioural loyalty has employed a number of different loyalty measures. These measures include probability of purchase (Farley 1964; Massey, Montgomery and Morrison 1970), probability of product repurchase (Lipstein 1959; Kuehn 1962), proportion of purchase (Cunningham 1966), purchase frequency (Brody and Cummingham 1968) and repeat purchase behaviour (Brown 1952). These measures focus on purchase behaviour or propensity to purchase. Kumar and Shah (2004), however, note that loyalty programmes that reward customer purchase behaviour without linking this behaviour to profitability are likely to fail and point to a number of inadequacies of current loyalty programmes. These inadequacies include the fact that the current measure of profitability used by loyalty programmes focuses on the past (Reinartz and Kumar 2003) as customers are rewarded for actions made today or actions made in the past accruing from accumulated points. This signifies that loyalty programmes fail to consider the future potential of a customer. This factor can be important as research suggests that customers who have provided profits to a business in the past may not continue to act in the same way in the future (Reinartz and Kumar 2002; 2003).

Attitudinal loyalty has been defined as a customer's long-term commitment to a business that cannot be deduced by measuring the customer's purchase behaviour. It has often been described in the context of brand loyalty (Kumar and Shah, 2004). Attitudinal loyalty is important as it can indicate a customer's predilection to demonstrate behaviours such as making recommendations about a company (Reichheld 2003) or the probability of future product or service usage (Liddy 2000). Dick and Basu (1994) believe that failure to account for attitudinal loyalty can lead to misleading gauging of customer loyalty. Like behavioural loyalty, measuring attitudinal loyalty presents some fundamental challenges, it is not surprising therefore that several researchers have advocated the use of both approaches to loyalty measurement (e.g. Day 1969; Pritchard, Howard and Havitz 1992).

Customer profitability

Consistent with the accounting literature, it appears the marketing literature tends to conceive of customer profitability as revenues less costs generated by a customer over a given time period (van Raaij 2005; van Raaij, Vernooij and van Triest 2003; van Triest 2005; Wayland and Cole 1994). An extension to this approach is offered by Jain and Singh (2002), however, who suggest recognition should also be given to other customer revenues and costs such as customer acquisition and retention costs.

A second departure from the accounting literature concerns the marketing literature's greater consideration given to two distinct customer profitability temporal perspectives. Firstly, customer profitability can be viewed in a manner analogous to the accounting notion of profit, i.e. a historically orientated measure pertaining to a specific past period of time. This type of analysis has been discussed at several different levels of profit reporting level, e.g. gross contribution margin level (Wang and Splegel 1994) or net profit level (Howell and Soucy 1990). Additionally, customer profitability has been considered in terms of marketing metrics that identify the profitability of marketing expenditures (Helgesen 2007); managing customer profitability using portfolio matrices (Ang and Taylor 2005) and financial approaches to customer segmentation (Helgesen 2005). It has also been considered in a relative sense through the calculation of *"customer return on assets"*, i.e. customer profitability divided by customer oriented assets, i.e. accounts receivable and inventory (Rust, Zahorik and Keiningham 1996). The second customer profitability time period concerns the future. This form of customer profitability is referred to as the *"lifetime value"* of the customer (Jain and Singh 2002). It is most often referred to in terms of some form of net present value calculation (Gupta, Lehmann and Stuart 2004). For example, Berger and Nasr (1998) describe a basic structural model of customer lifetime value (CLV) as customer revenues less customer costs discounted to present value over the periods of the projected trading relationship with a customer. CLV has also been termed *"customer equity"* (Bauer and Hammerschmidt 2005). Blattberg and Deighton (1996) suggested that customer equity could be measured by calculating the expected contribution of each customer, discounting the contributions to the net present value and adding all customer discounted contributions together.

The popularity of CLV stems from it being a forward-looking metric that incorporates revenues, expenses and customer behaviour that drives future profitability (Kumar and Shah 2004). It is widely claimed that CLV is a superior measure compared to customer profitability because of its forward looking nature (Reinartz and Kumar 2000). Jain and Singh (2002) in their review article of CLV research in marketing suggest that it is extremely important for marketing management to understand CLV, as CLV models represent an efficient way for firms to evaluate their relationships with customers.

According to Jain and Singh (2002) the literature on CLV research in mainstream marketing has embarked on a number of distinct directions, with three points of focus being prominent. Firstly, there is a body of research concerned with the development of models to calculate the CLV for each customer. Research in this area has commented on the inclusion of customer acquisition costs, retention costs, other marketing costs and also the customer revenue stream in the determination of CLV. Jain and Singh (2002) describe the second area of CLV research as *"customer base analysis"*. In this analysis, various methods have been proposed to analyse information about the customer base and predict the value of future customer transactions. Researchers have focused on individual customers and customer segments and have used empirical methods to determine which customers should be attracted and retained (Venkatesan and Kumar 2004). The third area of CLV research has concentrated on analysing the implications of CLV for management decision making through analytical models. Jain and Singh note that a particular interest in this sphere of research concerns the effect of loyalty programmes on CLV and a firm's profitability. Kumar, Shah and Venkatesan (2006) show that maximum positive impact to CLV occurs when the customer cross-purchases, shows multi-channel shopping behaviour, stays longer with the firm, buys specific product categories and purchases more frequently with the firm.

CLV models serve a variety of uses in organisations, as they can support strategic as well as tactical decision making (Jain and Singh 2002). Strategic decision making can be informed by CLV through the identification of a firm's customers, the nature of their characteristics, and which customers should be targeted over the long run (Venkatesan and Kumar 2004). Tactical decisions can be supported in areas such as informing short-term marketing resource allocations and also determining what marketing activities should be pursued (Ryals and Knox 2005). Knowledge of the potential profit of customers enables firms to develop customer-specific marketing programmes that can increase the efficiency and effectiveness of marketing strategies.

Dwyer (1997) extended the basic CLV model to incorporate a prediction of customer purchase behaviour founded on past purchase behaviour. While Dwyer's model can be seen as an advancement over the basic structural model as it incorporates the random nature of customer purchases, it does still have similar weaknesses such as the time period is fixed, cash flows are assumed to occur at the same time within the same period and predicted customer purchase behaviour depends only on the last purchase period.

Other model advancements have also been suggested. Blattberg and Deighton (1996) proposed a managerial model for finding the optimum balance between spending on customer acquisition and customer retention in order to maximise CLV. Berger and Nasr-Bechwati (2001) proposed a method that uses decision calculus to maximise total customer value by considering the optimal promotional expenditure allocation between customer acquisition, customer retention and other promotional outlays. Pfeifer and Carraway (2000) proposed Markov Chain Models as a method to model both customer retention and customer migration situations. Schmittlein, Morrison and Colombo (1987) proposed the Pareto/NBD model which incorporates a calculation of the probability that a customer is still active. Reinartz and Kumar (2000) propose a model that is an extension of the Pareto/NBD model as it incorporates the probability of a customer still being active as a dichotomous "*alive/dead*" measure.

A close examination of these models reveals that CLV is operationalised in each by considering customer retention as the most important attribute of customer management. Other customer-related attributes such as service usage, cross buying and positive referrals have been typically ignored, although Lee, Lee and Feick (2006) empirically investigate the effect of word of mouth effects in estimating CLV. Further advancements to CLV models can be expected to result once recognition is given to the range of customer behaviours evident in the client base of most medium to large organisations.

Analysis of customer profitability has been particularly important in firms operating direct marketing sales approaches (Shepard 1990). Even so, Mulhern (1999) notes that there can be difficulties in obtaining accurate information on an individual customer's purchasing behaviour. Measuring customer profitability requires information on customer purchases and variable marketing costs over a period of time. Contrary to this view, Blattberg and Deighton (1991) argue that customer profitability analysis is now increasingly possible because of the availability of customer databases containing a history of customer transactions.

Several studies provide particular insights in connection with customer profitability measurement issues. Schmittlein, Cooper and Morrison (1993) and Mulhern (1999) both provide major overviews of issues confronted in measuring customer profitability. Berger and Nasr (1998) discuss structural modelling aspects for building profitability models. Storbacka (1997) provides a description of customer profitability as a fundamental facet of relationship marketing and discusses measures for evaluating the distribution of profitability across customers. Schmittlein, Morrison and Colombo (1987) and Schmittlein and Peterson (1987) provide modelling procedures for determining whether a customer is still active and what to expect in terms of future purchase behaviour. While Berger et al. (2006) address the relationship between CLV and shareholder value.

It appears that customer profitability and customer lifetime value (CLV) have been the subject of increasing attention in recent years (Berger and Nasr 1998; Gupta et al. 2006; Kumar, Lemon and Parasuraman 2006; Mulhern 1999; Reinartz and Kumar

2000, 2003; Rust, Lemon and Zeithaml 2004). Mulhern (1999) sees this greater attention given to customer profitability in the marketing literature as strengthening managers' ability to target communications to worthy individual customers.

Wyner (1996) feels that the importance of customer profitability analysis is such that it can reposition the traditional marketing practice by treating the customer as an asset equivalent to other economic units. In this context, marketing decisions are similar to investment decisions as expenditure is evaluated in terms of expected returns. From this perspective, customer profitability becomes an important point of reference in the management of customer relationships (Morgan and Hunt 1994). Mulhern (1999) suggests that knowledge of customer profitability can improve decision making for many aspects of marketing including service and product development, pricing and all forms of marketing communications including personal selling and promotion.

DISCUSSION AND CONCLUSION

This paper has attempted to progress a synthesis of the marketing and management accounting literatures concerned with customer accounting. The work represents a novel contribution as it is believed to constitute the first study to draw the two literatures together within the context of a single paper. The extent of any claimed contribution has to be tempered, however, by a need to acknowledge that the synthesis achieved may be characterised as more partial than profound. This is because, in structuring the paper, the decision was made that highlighting the distinct marketing and accounting literatures on customers could be best served by commenting on them sequentially and not as a single integrated whole. While this might be interpreted as a shortcoming of the paper, the need to highlight the distinctive perspectives of the marketing and accounting literatures was believed to be important. Viewed in this light, the paper can be seen to lay important groundwork for any future studies that seek a more profound integration between the marketing and accounting literatures on customer accounting.

The study has revealed that the accounting literature addressing customer accounting can be described as little more than fledgling. This is particularly the case when it is considered in the context of the size and breadth of the marketing literature concerned with customer focused dimensions of organisational performance. This difference between the two literatures is clearly apparent when one reflects on the overview of the customer-oriented accounting and marketing literatures presented in Table 1. When reviewing this table, it should be born in mind that, although representing a greater quantum, the marketing customer focused studies cited represent much less of a comprehensive listing than the accounting literature customer focused studies cited.

The literature review conducted has yielded little in terms of case based research insights concerning how customers are appropriated between the accounting and marketing functions for internal debate. It is notable, however, that this divide between the accounting and marketing functions might lessen, together with the imbalance in the amount of attention directed to customer issues by accountants and marketers, if an organisational perspective commented on by Chenhall (forthcoming) grows in popularity. Chenhall draws on the works of Ostroff (1999); Schonberger (1996); and Galbraith (2005) to provide an accounting perspective

TABLE 1 Summary of customer-orientated accounting and marketing literatures

	Accounting Literature	Marketing Literature
Customer Accounting	Foster and Gupta (1994); Guilding et al. (2001); Guilding and McManus (2002); Lind and Strömsten (2006)	Helgesen (2007)
Customer Profitability	Bellis-Jones (1989); Cooper and Kaplan (1991a, 1991b, 1991c); Ward (1992); Foster and Gupta (1994); Smith and Dikoli (1995); Foster et al. (1996); Foster and Young (1997); Noone and Griffin (1999); Andon et al. (2001); Guilding et al. (2001); Chenhall (2003); Luft and Shields (2003); Cardinaels et al. (2004); Davila and Foster (2005); McManus (2007)	Howell and Soucy (1990); Schmittlein et al. (1993); Morgan and Hunt (1994); Wang and Splegel (1994); Wayland and Cole (1994); Rust et al. (1996); Wyner (1996); Berger and Nasr (1998); Storbacka (1997); Mulhern (1999); Reinartz and Kumar (2000); Jain and Singh (2002); van Raaij et al. (2003); Gupta et al. (2004); Ang and Taylor (2005); Helgesen (2005); van Raaij (2005); van Triest (2005); Helgesen (2007)
Customer-orientated Performance Measures	Kaplan and Norton (1992); Abernethy and Lillis (1995); Perera et al. (1997); Riley et al. (2003); Bryant et al. (2004); Banker and Mashruwala (2007); Cäker (2007); Ismail (2007)	
Customer Satisfaction	Ittner and Larcker (1998); Banker et al. (2000); Ghosh (2005); Cugini et al. (2007)	Holmes and Lett (1977); Bearden and Teel (1982); Bearden and Teel (1983); LaBarbera and Mazursky (1983); Swan and Oliver (1989); Reichheld and Sasser (1990); Yi (1990); Schneider (1991); Singh and Pandya (1991); Tornow and Wiley (1991); Wiley (1991); Westbrook and Oliver (1991); Cronin and Taylor (1992); Fornell (1992); Nelson et al. (1992); Peterson and Wilson (1992); Anderson and Sullivan (1993); Boulding et al. (1993); Rust and Zahorik (1993); Anderson et al. (1994); Dabholkar and Thorpe (1994); Heskett et al. (1994); Storbacka et al. (1994); Taylor and Baker (1994); Rust et al. (1995); Schneider and Bowen (1995); Anderson (1996); Edvarsson et al. (1996); Ennew and Binks (1996); Lowenstein (1996); Oliver (1996); Zeithaml et al. (1996); Bernhardt et al. (2000); Reichheld et al. (2000); Yeung and Ennew (2000); Gómez et al. (2004); Reinartz et al. (2004); Donio' et al. (2006)

Cont'd...

	Accounting Literature	Marketing Literature
Customer Loyalty	Smith and Wright (2004)	Day (1969); Reichheld and Sasser (1990); Yi (1990); Zeithaml et al. (1990); Berry and Parasuraman (1991); Fornell (1992); Peterson and Wilson (1992); Pritchard et al. (1992); Anderson and Sullivan (1993); Reichheld (1993); Dick and Basu (1994); Heskett et al. (1994); Sonnenberg (1994); Storbacka et al. (1994); Taylor and Baker (1994); Perrien et al. (1995); Rust et al. (1995); Schneider and Bowen (1995); Hallowell (1996); Lowenstein (1996); Dowling and Uncles (1997); Srivastava et al. (1998); Edvarsson et al. (2000); Liddy (2000); Reichheld et al. (2000); Reinartz and Kumar (2002); Lee et al. (2003); Reichheld (2003); Reinartz and Kumar (2003); Kumar and Shah (2004); Choi et al. (2006); Donio' et al. (2006); Pitta et al. (2006)
Customer Lifetime Value	Andon et al. (2001)	Schmittlein et al. (1987); Blattberg and Deighton (1996); Dwyer (1997); Berger and Nasr (1998); Pfeifer and Carraway (2000); Reinartz and Kumar (2000); Berger and Nasr-Bechwati (2001); Jain and Singh (2002); Gupta and Lehmann (2003); Gupta et al. (2004); Kumar and Shah (2004); Venkatesan and Kumar (2004); Bauer and Hammershcmidt (2005); Ryals and Knox (2005); Berger et al. (2006); Kumar et al. (2006); Gupta et al. 2006); Lee et al. (2006); Villanueva (2007)

on the evolving *"Horizontal Organisation"* philosophy to internal organisational structuring. The key distinguishing facet of this philosophy concerns a move away from conventional functionally based internal organisation structures towards more team based multifunctional groupings that have a customer oriented focus. Should this philosophy become a popularised approach, accountants will be drawn closer to marketing colleagues and we could witness the advent of a range of customer oriented accounting procedures that may well lie beyond the scope of the techniques reviewed in this paper.

The current accounting literature on CA appears dominated by a focus on cost allocation procedures, with frequent reference made to activity based costing. The marketing literature on CA is more broad-ranging with much greater attention directed to less measurable facets of customer related performance, lifetime customer valuation analysis and also ways that CA measures can be used to further decision making and control. Further, there is a much greater range of customer profitability measurement issues acknowledged and explored in the marketing literature. From a review of these two literatures, one is left with little doubt that marketing academics see a greater potential in the development and application of customer accounting procedures.

It is notable that a significant accounting development occurring around two decades ago concerned the coining of the term 'cost objects' (Cooper and Kaplan

1988). A cost object is the construct that is the subject of a costing exercise. This suggests a cost object constitutes a point of accountability. Conventional cost objects have been products or services. However Cooper and Kaplan's work promoted the notion of also costing activities such as machinery set ups, maintaining equipment, inspecting products, etc. Given the attention directed to the availability of choice in determining objects of accountability which has been underscored by Cooper and Kaplan's commentary, it appears we are overdue for similar new objects of accountability developing with respect to customers. From the discussion above, it seems that much that has been written in the marketing literature could serve to take the lead in this regard. The marketing literature's extensive discussion in connection with customer loyalty and customer satisfaction measurement issues appears as particularly pertinent. When the achievements of the marketing literature with respect to such constructs are recognised, the stunted status of CA in the accounting literature is particularly striking.

The lack of accounting research on CA is also surprising when we recognise that one of the four balanced scorecard dimensions of measurement promoted by Kaplan and Norton (1992) is the customer perspective. The balanced scorecard is an accounting innovation that has attracted considerable attention in the practice and research communities alike. In light of this, it appears as anomalous that greater accounting debate directed towards ways to account for customer performance has not been forthcoming. Of the three marketing oriented dimensions of customer performance reviewed in this paper, it is notable that customer loyalty and customer satisfaction both command explicit recognition in commentaries on the balanced scorecard. Niven, (2002: p.127) identifies them first and second in his listing of 34 possible customer measures.

Despite this, it appears that customer lifetime value provides greatest promise as the performance dimension that can be most easily assimilated into an accountant's portfolio of performance measures. This is because customer lifetime value is a monetarily denominated measure. If a bank is seeking to determine how much it can justify expending on a promotional campaign at a university campus, the answer would appear to lie in the expected customer lifetime value of accounts that will be opened. As long as the amount spent is not more than the customer lifetime value of the accounts opened, then a positive return on investment will result from the promotional exercise. This suggests customer lifetime value analysis can provide useful quantitative input to a marketing decision. Failure of the accounting function to grasp the nettle in providing such potentially useful information would appear to reinforce claims made around two decades ago concerning a cultural divide between marketing managers and management accountants (Ratnatunga, Pike and Hooley 1989).

It is notable that the apparently stunted accounting interest in CA continues despite an increased acceptance that non-financial customer related measures of performance can fall within the scope of management accounting. There is now increased recognition that non-financial performance measures are available to management accountants and increased acknowledgement of the important role such measures can play in motivating managers (Banker et al. 2000) and the incremental lead indicator information that they can encompass (Ittner and Larcker 1998; Riley et al. 2003). In light of all of the above, further research designed to determine what factors contribute to accounting's continued lack of interest in customer accounting would be welcome.

In addition to this, further research could build on the initiative of this study in the following ways:

- Those organisations that have adopted the balanced scorecard can be expected to have relatively advanced customer accounting systems due to the fact that one of the four pillars of the balanced scorecard focuses on the customer value creation dimension of performance. In light of this, case study research conducted in organisations that have adopted the balanced scorecard have the potential to advance our understanding of the potential of, and issues surrounding the application of, advanced customer accounting practices. As noted earlier, it appears that the balanced scorecard represents a performance evaluation framework providing considerable impetus for the marketing and management accounting paradigms assuming a greater degree of common ground.

- Case studies designed to determine the nature of particular facets of customer accounting would likely be productive endeavours in business contexts that lend themselves to customer accounting. For example, it is to be expected that valuable insights with respect to leading edge customer accounting practice would be found in banks and insurance companies. In both of these contexts, a long standing account can be expected to ensue from a new customer acquisition.

- To date accountants have not entered into discourse concerning the valuation of customer equity. Given accountants' background in performance measurement and financial modelling, there would appear to be an opportunity for accounting commentators to develop customer equity valuation models. A key factor determining marketing's take up of any model developed is likely to be its complexity, as more complex models can be expected to meet with resistance from marketers.

- More accounting research in regard to customer metrics that have received significant attention from marketing researchers (eg. customer satisfaction, customer loyalty, customer retention) and the impact of these customer metrics on firm performance is also to be welcomed. Such research could provide improved understanding of linkages between these customer-oriented constructs and also financial outcomes.

REFERENCES

Abernethy, M. A. and Lillis, A. M. (1995), "The Impact of Manufacturing Flexibility on Management Control System Design", *Accounting, Organizations and Society*, Vol. **20**, No. 4, pp. 241-258.

Anderson, E. W., Fornell, C. and Lehmann, D.R. (1994), "Customer Satisfaction, Market Share and Profitability: Findings from Sweden", *Journal of Marketing*, Vol. **58**, No. 3, pp. 53-66.

Anderson, E. W., Fornell, C. and Mazvancheryl, S. K. (2004), "Customer Satisfaction and Shareholder Value", *Journal of Marketing*, Vol. **68**, No. 4, pp. 172-185.

Anderson, E. W. and Sullivan, M. W. (1993), "The Antecedents and Consequences of Customer Satisfaction for Firms", *Marketing Science*, Vol. **12**, No. 2, pp. 125-143.

Ang, L. and Taylor, B. (2005), "Managing Customer Profitability Using Portfolio Matrices", *Journal of Database Marketing & Customers Strategy Management*, Vol. **12**, No. 4, pp. 298-304.

Banker, R. D., Potter, G. and Srinivasan, D. (2000), "An Empirical Investigation of an Incentive Plan that Includes Nonfinancial Performance Measures", *The Accounting Review*, Vol. 75, No. 1, pp. 65-92.

Banker, R. D. and Mashruwala, R. (2007), "The Moderating Role of Competition in the Relationship Between Nonfinancial Measures and Future Financial Performance", *Contemporary Accounting Research*, Vol. 24, No. 3, pp. 763-793.

Bauer, H. H. and Hammerschmidt, M. (2005), "Customer-based Corporate Valuation: Integrating the Concepts of Customer Equity and Shareholder Value", *Management Decision*, Vol. 43, No. 3, pp. 331-348.

Bellis-Jones, R. (1989), "Customer Profitability Analysis", *Management Accounting*, Vol. 67, No. 2, pp. 26-28.

Berger, P. D., Eechambadi, N., George, M., Lehmann, D. R., Rizley, R. and Venkatesan, R. (2006), "From Customer Lifetime Value to Shareholder Value: Theory, Empirical Evidence and Issues for Future Research", *Journal of Service Research*, Vol. 9, No. 2, pp. 156-167.

Berger, P. D. and Nasr, N. I. (1998), "Customer Lifetime Value: Marketing Models and Applications", *Journal of Interactive Marketing*, Vol. 12, No. 1, Winter, pp. 17-30.

Berger, P. D. and Nasr-Bechwati, N. (2001), "The Allocation of Promotion Budget to Maximize Customer Equity", *OMEGA: The International Journal of Management Science*, Vol. 29, No. 1, pp. 49-61.

Bernhardt, K. L., Donthu, N. and Kennett, P. A. (2000), "A Longitudinal Analysis of Satisfaction and Profitability", *Journal of Business Research*, Vol. 47, No. 2, pp. 161-171.

Berry, L. L. and Parasuraman, A. (1991), *Marketing Services: Competing Through Quality*, Lexington, MA: Free Press/Lexington Books.

Bhimani, A. and Keshtvarz, M. H. (1999), "British Management Accountants: Strategically Orientated", *Journal of Cost Management*, Vol. 13, No. 2, pp. 25-31.

Blattberg, R.C. and Deighton, J. (1996), "Manage Marketing by the Customer Equity Test", *Harvard Business Review*, Vol. 74, No. 4, pp. 136-144.

Boulding, W., Kalra, A., Staelin, R. and Zeithaml, V. (1993), "A Dynamic Process Model of Service Quality: From Expectations to Behavioral Intentions", *Journal of Marketing Research*, Vol. 30, No. 1, February, pp. 7-27.

Brody, R. P. and Cunningham, S. M. (1968), "Personality Variables and the Consumer Decision Process", *Journal of Marketing Research*, Vol. 5, No. 1, pp. 50-57.

Bromwich, M. (1990), "The Case for Strategic Management Accounting: The Role of Accounting Information for Strategy in Competitive Markets", *Accounting, Organizations and Society*, Vol. 15, No. 1, pp. 27-46.

Brown, G. H. (1952), "Brand Loyalty – Fact or Fiction?", *Advertising Age*, Vol. 23, No. 9, pp. 53-55.

Bryant, L., Jones, D.A. and Widener, S.K. (2004), "Managing Value Creation within the Firm: An Examination of Multiple Performance Measures", *Journal of Management Accounting Research*, Volume 16, No. 1, pp. 107-131.

Cardinaels, E., Roodhooft, F. and Warlop, L. (2004), "Customer Profitability Analysis Reports for Resource Allocation: The Role of Complex Marketing Environments". *ABACUS*, Vol. 40, No. 2, pp. 238-251.

Chenhall R. H. (2008), "Accounting for the horizontal organization: A review essay", *Accounting, Organizations and Society,* Vol. 33, No. 4/5, pp. 517-550.

Chenhall. R. H. (2003), "Management Control Systems Design Within Its Organizational Context: Findings from Contingency-Based Research and Directions for the Future", *Accounting, Organizations and Society*, Vol. 28, No. 1-2, pp. 127-168.

Chenhall, R. H. and Langfield-Smith, K. (1998a), "Adoption and Benefits of Management Accounting Practices: An Australian Study", *Management Accounting Research*, Vol. 9, No. 1, pp. 1-19.

Choi, D.H., Kim, C.M, Kim, S.I and Kim, S,H. (2006), "Customer Loyalty and Disloyalty in Internet Retail Stores: Its Antecedents and its Effect on Customer Price Sensitivity", *International Journal of Management*, Vol. 23, No. 4, pp. 925-936.

Coad, A. (1996), "Smart Work and Hard Work: Explicating a Learning Orientation in Strategic Management Accounting", *Management Accounting Research*, Vol. 7, No. 4, pp. 387-408.

Cooper, R. and Kaplan, R.S. (1988), "Measure Costs Right: Make the Right Decisions", *Harvard Business Review*, Vol. **66**, No. 5, pp. 96-103.

Cooper, R. and Kaplan, R. S. (1991a), "Kanthal (A)". In: Cooper, R. and Kaplan, R. S., *The Design of Cost Management Systems: Text, Cases and Readings,* Englewood Cliffs, New Jersey: Prentice-Hall Inc., pp. 48-56.

Cooper, R. and Kaplan, R. S. (1991b), "Manufacturers Hanover Corporation: Customer Profitability Report". In: Cooper, R. and Kaplan, R. S., *The Design of Cost Management Systems: Text, Cases and Readings*, Englewood Cliffs, New Jersey: Prentice-Hall Inc., pp. 10-22.

Cooper, R. and Kaplan, R. S. (1991c), "Winchell Lighting, Inc. (A)". In: Cooper, R. and Kaplan, R. S., *The Design of Cost Management Systems: Text, Cases and Readings*, Englewood Cliffs, New Jersey: Prentice-Hall Inc., pp. 27-39.

Cronin, J. J. and Taylor, S. A. (1992), "Measuring Service Quality: A Reexamination and Extension", *Journal of Marketing*, Vol. **56**, No. 2, pp. 55-68.

Cugini, A., Carù, A, and Zerbini, F. (2007), "The Cost of Customer Satisfaction: A Framework for Strategic Cost Management in Service Industries", *European Accounting Review*, Vol. **16**, No. 3, pp. 499-530.

Cunningham, S. M. (1966), "Brand Loyalty – What, Where, How Much?", *Harvard Business Review*, Vol. **44**, No. 1, January-February, pp. 116-128.

Dabholkar, P. A. and Thorpe, D. I. (1994), "Does Customer Satisfaction Predict Shoppers Intentions?", *Journal of Consumer Satisfaction, Dissatisfaction, and Complaining Behavior*, Vol. **7**, No. 1, pp. 161-171.

Davila, A. and Foster, G. (2005), "Management Accounting Systems Adoption Decisions: Evidence and Performance Implications from Early-Stage/Startup Companies", *The Accounting Review*, Vol. **80**, No. 4, pp. 1039-1068.

Day, G. S. (1969), "A Two-Dimensional Concept of Brand Loyalty", *Journal of Advertising Research*, Vol. **9**, No. 3, pp. 29-35.

Dick, A. S. and Basu, K. (1994), "Customer Loyalty: Toward an Integrated Conceptual Framework", *Journal of the Academy of Marketing Science*, Vol. **22**, No. 2, pp. 99-113.

Donio' J., Massari, P. and Passiante, G. (2006), "Customer Satisfaction and Loyalty in a Digital Environment: An Empirical Test," *Journal of Consumer Marketing*, Vol. **23**, No. 7, pp. 445-457.

Dowling, G. R. and Uncles, M. (1997), "Do Customer Loyalty Programs Really Work?", *Sloan Management Review*, Vol. **38**, No. 4, pp. 71-82.

Edvardsson, B., Johnson, M. D., Gustafsson, A. and Strandvik, T. (2000), "The Effects of Satisfaction and Loyalty on Profits and Growth: Product versus Services", *Total Quality Management*, Vol. **11**, No. 7, pp. 917-928.

Ennew, C. T. and Binks, M. R. (1996), "The Impact of Service Quality and Service Characteristics on Customer Retention: Small Businesses and Their Banks in the UK", *British Journal of Management*, Vol. **7**, No. 3, pp. 219-230.

Erevelles, S. and Leavitt, C. (1992), "A Comparison of Current Models of Consumer Satisfaction/Dissatisfaction", *Journal of Consumer Satisfaction, Dissatisfaction, and Complaining Behavior*, Vol. **5**, No. 1, pp. 104-114.

Farley, J. U. (1964), "Why Does Brand Loyalty Vary Over Products?", *Journal of Marketing Research*, Vol. **1**, No. 4, pp. 9-14.

Fornell, C. (1992), "A National Customer Satisfaction Barometer: The Swedish Experience", *Journal of Marketing*, Vol. **56**, No. 1, January, pp. 6-21.

Foster, G. and Gupta, M. (1994), "Marketing, Cost Management and Management Accounting", *Journal of Management Accounting Research*, Vol. **6**, No. 1, pp. 43-77.

Foster, G., Gupta, M. and Sjoblom L. (1996), "Customer Profitability Analysis: Challenges and New Directions", *Cost Management,* Vol. **10**, No. 1, Spring, pp. 5-17.

Foster, G. and Young, S.M. (1997), "Frontiers of Management Accounting Research", *Journal of Management Accounting Research*, Vol. 9, No. 1, pp. 63-77.

Fournier, S. and Mick, D.G. (1999), "Rediscovering Satisfaction", *Journal of Marketing*, Vol. 63, No. 4, pp. 5-23.

Galbraith, J. (2005), *Designing the customer-centric organization, a guide to strategy, structure, and process*, San Francisco: Josey-Bass.

Galloway, D. and Waldron, D. (1988), "Throughput Accounting: The Need For a New Language For Manufacturing", *Management Accounting*, Vol. 66, No. 10, pp. 34-35.

Ghosh, D. (2005), "Alternative Measures of Managers' Performance, Controllability, and the Outcome Effect", *Behavioral Research in Accounting*, Vol. 17, No. 1, pp. 55-70.

Gómez, M. I., McLaughlin, E. W. and Wittink, D. R. (2004), "Customer Satisfaction and Retail Sales Performance: An Empirical Investigation", *Journal of Retailing*, Vol. 80, No. 4, pp. 265-278.

Guilding, C., Cravens, K. S. and Tayles, M. (2000), "An International Comparison of Strategic Management Accounting Practices", *Management Accounting Research*, Vol. 11, No. 1, pp. 113-135.

Guilding, C., Kennedy, D. J. and McManus, L. (2001), "Extending the Boundaries of Customer Accounting: Applications in the Hotel Industry", *Journal of Hospitality and Tourism Research*, Vol. 25, No. 2, pp. 173-194.

Guilding, C and McManus, L. (2002), "The Incidence, Perceived Merit and Antecedents of Customer Accounting: An Exploratory Note", *Accounting, Organizations and Society*, Vol. 27, No. 1-2, pp. 45-59.

Gupta, S., Hanssens, D., Hardie, B., Kahn, W., Kumar, V., Lin, N., Ravishanker, N. and Sriram, S. (2006), "Modelling Customer Lifetime Value", *Journal of Service Research*, Vol. 9, No. 2, pp. 139-155.

Gupta, S., Lehmann, D.R. and Stuart, J.A. (2004), "Valuing Customers", *Journal of Marketing Research*, Vol. 41, No. 1, pp. 7-18.

Hallowell, R. (1996), "The Relationships of Customer Satisfaction, Customer Loyalty, and Profitability: An Empirical Study," *International Journal of Service Industry Management*, Vol. 7, No. 4, pp. 27-42.

Helgesen, Ø. (2005), "Customer Segments Based on Customer Account Profitability", *Journal of Targeting, Measurement and Analysis for Marketing*, Vol. 14, No. 3, pp. 225-237.

Helgesen, Ø. (2007), "Customer Accounting and Customer Profitability Analysis for the Order Handling Industry – A Managerial Accounting Approach", *Industrial Marketing Management*, Vol. 36, No. 6, pp. 757-769.

Heskett, J. L., Jones, T. O., Loveman, G. W., Sasser, Jr., W. E. and Schlesinger, L. A. (1994), "Putting the Service Profit Chain to Work", *Harvard Business Review*, Vol. 72, No. 4, March-April, pp. 105-111.

Holmes, J. H. and Lett, J. D. (1977), "Product Sampling and Word-of-Mouth Intentions", *Journal of Consumer Research*, Vol. 4, No. 2, pp. 35-40.

Howell, R.A. and Soucy, S.R. (1990), "Customer Profitability: As Critical as Product Profitability", *Management Accounting*, Vol. 72, No. 4, October, pp. 43-47.

Ismail, T.H. (2007), "Performance Evaluation Measures in the Private Sector: Egyptian Practice", *Managerial Auditing Journal*, Vol. 22, No. 5, pp. 503-513.

Ittner, C.D. and Larcker, D.F. (1998), "Are Nonfinancial Measures Leading Indicators of Financial Performance? An Analysis of Customer Satisfaction", *Journal of Accounting Research*, Vol. 36, No. 3, pp. 1-35.

Jacoby, J. and Kyner, D.B. (1973), "Brand Loyalty vs. Repeat Purchasing Behaviour", *Journal of Marketing Research*, Vol. 10, No. 1, pp. 1-9.

Jain, D. and Singh, S. S. (2002), "Customer Lifetime Value Research in Marketing: A Review and Future Directions", *Journal of Interactive Marketing*, Vol. 16, No. 2, pp. 34-46.

Johnson, H. T. (1992), *Relevance Regained: From Top-Down Control to Bottom-Up Empowerment*, New Jersey: The Free Press.

Johnson, H. T. and Kaplan, R. S. (1987), *Relevance Lost: The Rise and Fall of Management Accounting*, Boston: Harvard Business School Press.

Juras, P. E. and Dierks, P. A. (1994), "Student Case Competition Case: Blue Ridge Manufacturing", *Management Accounting*, Vol. 76, No. 6, December, pp. 57-59.

Kaplan, R. S. and Norton, D. P. (1992), "The Balanced Scorecard – Measures that Drive Performance", *Harvard Business Review*, Vol. 70, No. 1, January-February, pp. 71-79.

Kotler, P. (2000), *Marketing Management, International Edition*, Englewood Cliffs, NJ: Prentice Hall.

Kuehn, A. (1962), "Consumer Brand Choice as a Learning Process", *Journal of Advertising Research*, Vol. 2, No. 1, March-April, pp. 10-17.

Kumar, V., Lemon, K .N. and Parasuraman, A. (2006), "Managing Customers for Value: An Overview and Research Agenda", *Journal of Service Research*, Vol. 9, No. 2, pp. 97-94.

Kumar, V. and Shah, D. (2004), "Building Sustaining *Profitable* Customer Loyalty for the 21st Century", *Journal of Retailing*, Vol. 80, No. 4, pp. 317-329.

Kumar, V., Shah, D. and Venkatesan, R. (2006), "Managing Retailer Profitability – One Customer at a Time", *Journal of Retailing*, Vol. 82, No. 4, pp. 277-294.

LaBarbera, P. A. and Mazursky, D. (1983), "A Longitudinal Assessment of Consumer Satisfaction/Dissatisfaction: the Dynamic Aspect of the Cognitive Process", *Journal of Marketing Research*, Vol. 20, No. 4, pp. 393-404.

Lee, S.C., Barker, S. and Kandampully, J. (2003), "Technology, Service Quality, and Customer Loyalty in Hotels: Australian Managerial Perspectives", *Managing Service Quality*, Vol. 13, No. 5, pp. 423-432.

Lee, J., Lee, J. and Feick, L. (2006), "Incorporating Word-of-Mouth effects in Estimating Customer Lifetime Value", *Database Marketing and Customer Strategy Management*, Vol. 14, No. 1, pp. 29-39.

Lewis, H. G. (1997), "Does Your "Loyalty" Program Inspire Any Loyalty?", *Direct Marketing*, Vol. 60, No. 2, pp. 46-48.

Liebermann, Y. (1999), "Membership Clubs as a Tool for Enhancing Buyers' Patronage", *Journal of Business Research*, Vol. 45, No. 3, pp. 291-297.

Liddy, A. (2000), "Relationship Marketing, Loyalty Programmes and the Measurement of Loyalty", *Journal of Targeting, Measurement Analysis for Marketing*, Vol. 8, No. 4, pp. 351-362.

Lind J. and Strömsten, T. (2006), "When Do Firms Use Different Types of Customer Accounting?", *Journal of Business Research*, Vol. 59, No. 12, pp. 1257-1266.

Lord, B. (1996), "Strategic Management Accounting: The Emperor's New Clothes", *Management Accounting Research*, Vol. 7, No. 3, pp. 347-366.

Lowenstein, M. W. (1996), "Keep Them Coming Back", *Marketing Tools*, Vol. 3, No. 3, May, pp. 54-57.

Luft, J. and Shields, M. (2003), "Mapping Management Accounting: Graphics and Guidelines for Theory-Consistent Empirical Research", *Accounting, Organizations and Society*, Vol. 28, No. 2/3, pp. 169-249.

Massey, W. F., Montgomery, D. B. and Morrison, D. G. (1970), *Stochastic Models of Buyer Behavior*, Cambridge: MIT Press.

McManus, L. (2007), "The Construction of a Segmental Customer Profitability Analysis", *Journal of Applied Management Accounting Research*, Vol. 5, No. 2, pp. 59-74.

Morgan, R. M. and Hunt, S. D. (1994), "The Commitment-Trust Theory of Relationship Marketing", *Journal of Marketing*, Vol. 58, No. 3, pp. 20-38.

Mulhern, F. J. (1999), "Customer Profitability Analysis: Measurement, Concentration, and Research Directions", *Journal of Interactive Marketing*, Vol. 13, No. 1, pp. 25-40.

Nelson, E. C., Rust, R. T., Zahorik, A., Rose, R. L., Batalden, P. and Siemanski, B. A. (1992), "Do Patient Perceptions of Quality Relate to Hospital Financial Performance?", *Journal of Health Care Marketing*, Vol. 12, No. 4, pp. 6-13.

Niven, P. R. (2002), *Balanced Scorecard Step by Step*, New York: John Wiley and Sons.

Noone, B. and Griffin, P. (1999), "Managing the Long-Term Profit Yield from Market Segments in a Hotel Environment: A Case Study on the Implementation of Customer Profitability Analysis", *Hospitality Management*, Vol. 18, No. 2, pp. 111-128.

Nyamori, R. O., Perera, M. H. B. and Lawrence, S. R. (2001), "The concept of strategic change and implications for management accounting research", *Journal of Accounting Literature*, Vol. 20, No. 1, pp. 62-83.

Oliver, R. L. (1980), "A Cognitive Model of the Antecedents and Consequences of Satisfaction Decisions", *Journal of Marketing Research*, Vol. 17, No. 4, pp. 460-469.

Oliver, R. L. (1996), *Satisfaction: A Behavioral Perspective on the Consumer*, New York, NY: McGraw-Hill.

Oliver, R. L. and Swan, J. E. (1989), "Consumer Perceptions of Interpersonal Equity and Satisfaction in Transaction: A Field Survey Approach", *Journal of Marketing*, Vol. 53, No. 2, pp. 21-35.

Ostroff, F. (1999), *The horizontal organization*, Oxford University Press: New York.

Perera, S., Harrison, G. and Poole, M. (1997), "Customer-Focused Manufacturing Strategy and the Use of Operations-Based Non-Financial Performance Measures: A Research Note", *Accounting, Organizations and Society*, Vol. 22, No. 6, pp. 557-572.

Perrien, J., Paradis, S. and Banting, P. M. (1995), "Dissolution of a Relationship: The Salesforce Perception", *Industrial Marketing Management*, Vol. 24, No. 4, pp. 317-327.

Peterson, R. A. and Wilson, W. R. (1992), "Measuring Customer Satisfaction: Fact and Artifact", *Journal of the Academy of Marketing Science*, Vol. 20, No.1, pp. 61-71.

Pitta, D., Franzak, F. and Fowler, D. (2006), "A Strategic Approach to Building Online Customer Loyalty: Integrating Customer Profitability Tiers", *Journal of Consumer Marketing*, Vol. 23, No. 7, pp. 421-429.

Pfeifer, P. E. and Carraway, R. L. (2000), "Modelling Customer Relationships as Markov Chains", *Journal of Interactive Marketing*, Vol. 14, No. 2, pp. 43-55.

Pritchard, M. P., Howard, D. A. and Havitz, M. E. (1992), "Loyalty Measurement: A Critical Examination and Theoretical Extension", *Management Science*, Vol. 38, No. 7, pp. 155-164.

Ratnatunga, J., Pike R., and Hooley G., (1989), "New Evidence on the Accounting - Marketing Interface", *British Accounting Review*, Vol. 21, No. 4, pp. 351-370.

Reichheld, F. F. (1993a), *The Loyalty Effect*. Boston, MA: Harvard Business School Press.

Reichheld, F. F. (1993b), "Loyalty-based Management", *Harvard Business Review*, Vol. 71, No. 2, March-April, pp. 64-73.

Reichheld, F. F. (1996), *The Loyalty Effect: The Hidden Force Behind Growth, Profits and Lasting Value*, Boston, MA: Harvard Business School Press.

Reicheld, F. F. (2003), "The One Number You Need to Grow", *Harvard Business Review*, Vol. 81, No. 12, pp. 46-54.

Reichheld, F. F., Markey Jr., R. G. and Hopton, C. (2000), "The Loyalty Effect – The Relationship Between Loyalty and Profits", *European Business Journal*, Vol. 12, No. 3, pp. 134-141.

Reichheld, F. F. and Sasser, W. E. (1990), "Zero Defections: Quality Comes to Services", *Harvard Business Review*, Vol. 68, No. 5, pp. 105-111.

Reinartz, W. J., Krafft, M. and Hoyer, W. D. (2004), "The Customer Relationship Management Process: Its Measurement and Impact on Performance", *Journal of Marketing Research*, Vol. 41, No. 3, pp. 293-305.

Reinartz, W. J. and Kumar, V. (2000), "On the Profitability of Long-Life Customers in a Noncontractual Setting: An Empirical Investigation and Implications for Marketing", *Journal of Marketing*, Vol. 64, No. 4, pp. 17-35.

Reinartz, W. J. and Kumar, V. (2002), "The Mismanagement of Customer Loyalty", *Harvard Business Review*, Vol. 80, No. 7, p. 86.

Reinartz, W. J. and Kumar, V. (2003), "The Impact of Customer Relationship Characteristics on Profitable Lifetime Duration", *Journal of Marketing*, Vol. 67, No. 1, pp. 77-99.

Riley, R. A., Pearson, T. A. and Trompeter, G. (2003), "The Value Relevance of Non-financial Performance Variables and Accounting Information: The Case of the Airline Industry", *Journal of Accounting and Public Policy*, Vol. **22**, No. 3, pp. 231-254.

Roslender, R. and Hart, S. J. (2003), "In Search of Strategic Management Accounting: Theoretical and Field Study Perspectives", *Management Accounting Research*, Vol. **14**, No. 3, pp. 255-279.

Rust, R. T., Lemon, D. and Zeithaml, V. A. (2004), "Return on Marketing: Using Customer Equity to Focus Marketing Strategy", *Journal of Marketing*, Vol. **68**, No. 1, pp. 109-127.

Rust, R. T. and Zahorik, A. J. (1993), "Customer Satisfaction, Customer Retention, and Market Share", *Journal of Retailing*, Vol. **69**, No. 2, pp. 193-215.

Rust, R. T., Zahorik, A. J. and Keiningham, T. (1995), "Return on Quality (ROQ): Making Service Quality Financially Accountable", *Journal of Marketing*, Vol. **59**, No. 2, pp. 58-70.

Ryals, L. J. and Knox, S. (2005), "Measuring Risk-Adjusted Customer Lifetime Value and its Impact on Relationship Marketing Strategies and Shareholder Value", *European Journal of Marketing*, Vol. **39**, No. 5/6, pp. 456-472.

Schneider, B. (1991), "Service Quality and Profits: You Can Have Your Cake and Eat it Too", *Human Resource Planning*, Vol. **14**, No. 2, pp. 151-157.

Schneider, B. and Bowen, D.E. (1995), *Winning the Service Game*, Boston, M.A.: HBS Press.

Schonberger, R. J. (1996), *World class manufacturing: The next decade*, New York: The Free Press.

Schmittlein, D. G., Cooper, L. G. and Morrison, D. G. (1993), "Truth in Concentration in the Land of (80/20) Laws", *Marketing Science*, Vol. **12**, No. 2, pp. 167-183.

Schmittlein, D. G., Morrison, D. G. and Colombo, R. (1987), "Counting Your Customers: Who Are They and What Will They Do Next?", *Management Science*, Vol. **33**, No. 1, January, pp. 1-24.

Schmittlein, D. G. and Peterson, R. A. (1994), "Customer Base Analysis: An Industrial Purchase Process Application", *Marketing Science*, Vol. **13**, No. 1, Winter, pp. 41-67.

Shepard, D. (1990), *The New Direct Marketing*, Homewood, IL: Business One Irwin.

Shields, M. D. (1997), "Research in Management Accounting by North Americans in the 1990s", *Journal of Management Accounting Research*, Vol. **9**, No. 1, pp. 3-61.

Simmonds, K. (1981), "Strategic Management Accounting", *Management Accounting*, Vol. **59**, No. 4, pp. 26-29.

Singh, J. E. and Pandya, S. (1991), "Exploring the Effects of Complaint Behaviours", *European Journal of Marketing*, Vol. **25**, No. 9, pp. 7-21.

Smith, M. and Dikolli, S. (1995), "Customer Profitability Analysis: An Activity-Based Costing Approach", *Managerial Auditing Journal*, Vol. **10**, No. 7, pp. 3-7.

Smith, R. E. and Wright, W. F. (2004), "Determinants of Customer Loyalty and Financial Performance", *Journal of Management Accounting Research*, Vol. **16**, No. 1, pp. 183-205.

Sonnenberg, F. K. (1994), "The Age of Intangibles", *Management Review*, Vol. **83**, No. 1, pp. 49-53.

Spreng, R. A. and Page Jr., T. J. (2001), "The Impact of Confidence in Expectations on Consumer Satisfaction", *Psychology and Marketing*, Vol. **18**, No. 11, pp. 1,187-1,204.

Srivastava, R. K., Sherwani, T. A. and Fahey, L. (1998), "Market-Based Assets and Shareholder Value: A Framework for Analysis", *Journal of Marketing*, Vol. **62**, No. 1, January, pp. 2-18.

Storbacka, K. (1997), "Segmentation Based on Customer Profitability – Retrospective Analysis of Retail Bank Customer Bases", *Journal of Marketing Management*, Vol. **13**, No. 5, pp. 479-492.

Storbacka, K., Strandvik, T. and Grönroos, C. (1994), "Managing Customer Relationships for Profit: The Dynamics of Relationship Quality", *International Journal of Service Industry Management*, Vol. **5**, No. 5, pp. 21-38.

Swan, J. E. and Combs, L .J. (1976), "Product Performance and Consumer Satisfaction: A New Concept", *Journal of Marketing*, Vol. **40**, No. 2, pp. 25-33.

Swan, J. E. and Oliver, R. L. (1989), "Postpurchase Communications by Consumers", *Journal of Retailing*, Vol. 65, No. 4, pp. 516-533.

Taylor, S. A. and Baker, T. L. (1994), "An Assessment of the Relationship Between Service Quality and Customer Satisfaction in the Formation of Consumers' Purchase Intentions", *Journal of Retailing*, Vol. 70, No. 2, pp. 163-178.

Tomkins, C. and Carr, C. (1996), "Introduction to the Special Issue on Strategic Management Accounting", *Management Accounting Research*, Vol. 7, No. 2, pp. 165-167.

Tornow, W. W. and Wiley, J. W. (1991), "Service Quality and Management Practices: A Look at Employee Attitudes, Customer Satisfaction and Bottom-Line Consequences", *Human Resource Planning*, Vol. 14, No. 2, pp. 105-115.

Tse, D. K. and Wilton, P. C. (1988), "Models of Consumer Satisfaction Formulation: An Extension", *Journal of Marketing Research*, Vol. 25, No. 3, August, pp. 204-212.

van Raaij, E.M. (2005), "The Strategic Value of Customer Profitability Analysis", *Marketing Intelligence & Planning*, Vol. 23, No. 4/5, pp. 372-381.

van Raaij, E. M., Vernooij, M. J. A. and van Triest, S. (2003), "The Implementation of Customer Profitability Analysis: A Case Study", *Industrial Marketing Management*, Vol. 32, No. 7, pp. 573-583.

van Triest, S. (2005), "Customer Size and Customer Profitability in Non-Contractual Relationships", *The Journal of Business and Industrial Marketing*, Vol. 20, No. 2/3, pp. 148-155.

Venkatesan, R. and Kumar, V. (2004), "A Customer Lifetime Value Framework for Customer Selection and Resource Allocation Strategy", *Journal of Marketing*, Vol. 68, No. 4, pp. 106-125.

Villanueva, J. (2007), *Customer Equity: Measurement, Management and Research Opportunities*, Boston: Now Publishers.

Wang, P. and Splegel, T. (1994), "Database Marketing and Its Measurement of Success", *Journal of Direct Marketing*, Vol. 8, No. 2, pp. 73-84.

Ward, K. (1992), Accounting for Marketing Strategies. In: Drury, C. (ed.). *Management Accounting Handbook*, Oxford: Butterworth-Heinemann.

Wayland, R. E. and Cole, P. M. (1994), "Turn Customer Service into Customer Profitability", *Management Review*, Vol. 83, No. 7, pp. 22-24.

Westbrook, R. A. and Oliver, R. L. (1991), "The Dimensionality of Consumption Emotion Patterns and Consumer Satisfaction", *Journal of Consumer Research*, Vol. 18, No. 1, June, pp. 84-91.

Wiley, J. W. (1991), "Customer Satisfaction: A Supportive Work Environment and Its Financial Costs", *Human Resource Planning*, Vol. 14, No. 2, pp. 117-127.

Wyner, G. A. (1996), "Customer Profitability: Linking Behavior to Economics", *Marketing Research*, Vol. 8, No. 2, pp. 36-38.

Yeung, M. C. H. and Ennew, C. T. (2000), "From Customer Satisfaction to Profitability", *Journal of Strategic Marketing*, Vol. 8, No. 2, pp. 313-326.

Yi, Y. (1990), A Critical Review of Consumer Satisfaction. In: Zeithaml, V. (ed.). *Review of Marketing*, Chicago, IL: American Marketing Association, pp. 47-95.

Zeithaml, V. A., Berry, L. L. and Parasuraman, A. (1996), "The Behavioural Consequences of Service Quality", *Journal of Marketing*, Vol. 60, No. 2, pp. 31-46.

Zeithaml, V. A., Parasuraman, A. and Berry, L. L. (1990), *Delivering Quality Service*, New York, NY: The Free Press.

Examining the theoretical influences of customer valuation metrics

Kenneth Weir, *Heriot Watt University, UK*

Abstract Within the previous two decades there has been an intensification of marketing activity from which there has emerged a series of concepts relating to customer profitability and value. These developments have led to the establishment of a series of techniques regarding customer valuation and can be separated into three distinct categories: customer profitability calculations; customer lifetime value; and customer equity. This paper seeks to clarify and discuss the theoretical influences upon these categories, whilst also presenting some implications for the future development of customer valuation metrics.

INTRODUCTION

Customers have always been included in, and been central to, marketing for many years, but within the last 40 years there has been an intensification of marketing activity (Brown 1995) and the past two decades have witnessed the emergence of a series of developments in which customer loyalty, profitability and valuations have risen to prominence. Consistent with the observation that some customers are more equal than others (Peppers and Rogers 1997), more recent literature has sought to provide allocation of marketing resources resulting from the outcomes of value calculations (for example see Boyce 2000). This surge in the "value" literature, arguably, stemmed from an increase in global competition and a loss of (American) competitiveness, in addition to a realisation that a strategic planning focus on competitors and market dominance did not lead to business success (Webster 1988; Boyce 2000). Concomitant with these marketing concerns, the 1990s witnessed a boom in interest regarding market-oriented management accounting research (Foster and Gupta 1994; Helgesen 2007), where attention was drawn to customer accounting and, in particular, customer profitability analysis (Bellis-Jones 1989; Cooper and Kaplan 1991; Foster and Gupta 1994; Guilding and McManus 2002; Helgesen 2007). These developments placed the customer at the forefront of consideration and allowed previously unexplored avenues of research to be opened up.

Concepts regarding customer valuation and profitability have predominantly been written about in the marketing literature, and to a lesser extent, papers have appeared within the accounting, hospitality, and banking literatures. Broadly conceived in the accounting literature, these valuation and customer profitability metrics are referred to holistically as customer accounting (see Guilding and McManus 2002; Lind and Strömsten 2006). On synthesising these wide sources on customer valuation, it is evident that there are three stages of development, each related to a set of techniques. The first stage concerns simple customer profit calculations, such as Customer Profitability Analysis and Customer Segment Profitability Analysis; the second considers the lifetime value of customers, as examined through Customer Lifetime Value and Lifetime Customer Profitability Analysis; and the third builds upon lifetime value to construct notions of Customer Equity.

Thus, as a meta-practice and as an holistic theory, customer accounting and customer valuation comprises of three related areas of investigation. However, it has been opined that there is still much to learn about these techniques and areas of study (Guilding and McManus 2002). This paper takes the form of a literature review and attempts to synthesise work in field, with an emphasis to tease out the underlying theoretical influences of each set of metrics. That is to write that the main thrust of the paper is to determine the rationale and the theories that have informed the development of customer valuation metrics, specifically focusing upon which schools of thought and specific theories have influenced the development of each metric. The purpose of such a literature review is to examine the progress of customer valuation techniques and practices, as described in the literature, and to speculate where it can go in the future.

The paper is structured as follows. In the next section, the foundations of customer profitability will be explored. Following from this, the third section will elaborate upon customer value concepts. The fourth section will look at customer equity and examine the most recent advancements in customer valuation. The fifth section will provide an ideal place to recapitulate the arguments thus far, whilst the final concluding section will draw together what has been discussed and illuminate some potential implications for marketing management.

FIRST STAGE OF DEVELOPMENT: CUSTOMER PROFITABILITY ANALYSIS

Attention is now drawn to the first stage of the development of customer valuation metrics. Customer profitability calculations exist in the guise of several techniques; for example within accounting articles, such calculations are referred to as Customer Profitability Analysis [CPA], and Customer Segment Profitability Analysis [CSPA] (Guilding and McManus 2002; Lind and Strömsten 2006), whilst in the marketing literature a generic approach termed Customer Accounting Profitability [CAP] has been identified (Foster and Gupta 1994).

As posited by some writers (Bellis-Jones 1989; Foster and Gupta 1994) the logic behind understanding customer profitability is that company's revenues can differ across customers purchasing the same product. Foster et al. (1996) acknowledge that some "dollars", and hence some customers (cf Pfeifer et al. 2005) contribute more than others to the net revenue of the firm. Hence there is a platform for managers to understand the net effect of these differences between customers; and it is here that customer accounting is of use (Cooper and Kaplan 1991; Kaplan and Narayanan 2001).

The first widely recognised instance of CA in accounting appeared in 1989 with the publication of Bellis-Jones' article (Guilding and McManus 2002). Prior to this, customer accounting and profitability analysis existed in the form debated by Schiff and Mellman (1962). However, in the late 1980s, the topic received more attention, coinciding with the advent of alternative costing techniques. Bellis Jones' (1989) comments complemented two articles published in *Harvard Business Review* urging companies to recognise the importance that should be afforded to customer profits (Shapiro et al. 1987) and the related analysis of customer costs (Dudick 1987), contrary to the predominant focus which was placed on sales (Shapiro et al. 1987), whereby customer profitability was determined by assigning selling, general and administration costs [SG&A] (Dudick 1987). The original platform of using SG&A would typically allocate costs to customers on a pro-rata basis, for example, a customer that produced 10% of total sales would be allocated a total of 10% of SG&A costs, and with the resulting arithmetic difference being the customer's related profit. This type of analysis was deemed to be inappropriate (Bellis-Jones 1989; Dudick 1987; Shapiro et al. 1987), particularly given the "80-20 Rule", where it is advanced that 20% of customers generate 80% of profits. Bellis-Jones (1989) also highlighted the failures of traditional measures and urged companies to develop metrics of customer profitability analysis in order to quantify the trading relationship. The approach advanced by Bellis-Jones (1989) involved tracing overheads to customers on an activity basis, thus implicitly the profitability analysis relied upon advances in costing- particularly those in activity based costing [ABC].

In a similar vein, Cooper and Kaplan's (1991) case study found that Kanthal was using an ABC type framework in order to analyse customer revenues and costs. The article demonstrates the benefits of using such an ABC approach over the perceived pitfalls of the traditional SG&A cost allocation in relation to customer profitability analysis. The Kanthal case is typical of many academic case studies in that ABC is ultimately recommended when the customer is placed at the heart of the analysis (Guilding and McManus 2002). In fact, numerous commentaries focus on how ABC is, or can be used, in CPA and how it is beneficial to the organisation, most notably, in that the use of ABC in a customer context, can lead to improved decision making (Bellis-Jones 1989; Cooper and Kaplan 1991; Guilding et al. 2001; Noone and Griffin 1997). Furthermore, the nature of ABC allows overhead costs to be traced along the organisation and then applied to customers on an activity basis. Despite the existence of several approaches to calculate customer profits, each technique essentially breaks down to following simple calculation:

Customer Revenues *less* Customer Costs = Customer Profit (loss)

The differences that exist between varying papers stem from the type of costs that are traced to customers and the costing systems that is used to do so. The types of costs that can be allocated to customers include discounts and commissions, packaging and documentation, marketing and sales support, inventory holding costs, delivery, handling customer inquiries, and customer service, technical and administrative support, quality control, credit terms, financing, accounts receivable days, collection costs, order entry processing, (Bellis-Jones 1989; Howell and Soucy 1990; Smith and Dikoli 1995; Foster et al. 1996; Pearce 1997; Boyce 2000; Van Triest 2005). Whereas the literature is not so clear on how these types of costs should be allocated.

Typically, an ABC cost hierarchy consists of order-related, channel, and customer-specific costs (Kaplan and Narayanan 2001). Foster et al. (1996) build upon the typical ABC hierarchy and posit the approach to CPA where Customer-specific costs are subtracted from revenues to yield customer-specific contribution. From this Customer- line costs are deducted to find the Customer- line contribution, and the next step is to take off company enterprise cost to come to the operating profit.

Several authors, however, have constructed their own hierarchies, for example, Van Triest (2005) asserts that costs can be separated into four distinct categories; these being product costs, exchange costs, targeted customer costs and pro-rata allocated costs. Elaborating this brief list, exchange costs include logistics costs (which are charged directly per order by the third party that performs all logistics activities) and customer administration costs (allocated per order); whereas targeted customer costs extend to the costs of technical service mechanics and customer consultants (these are allocated per hour spent with customer); whilst the final scheme pro rata allocated costs covers general marketing activities (and are allocated as a percentage of sales within that sector). Ultimately, though, users will decide how many levels of cost analysis will be placed in any hierarchy (Pfeifer et al. 2005).

Therefore, what is immediately evident from even a brief glance at the literature is that progress within management accounting theory and practice has expanded theories in customer costing. Thus the advances in customer costing have engendered a development in customer profit measurement. Without customer costing, customer profits cannot be determined. Any customer costing system will generate cost numbers that reproduces the varying resource usage of each customer or transaction in a measurable form and thus there is an importance placed upon any system of customer costing. Helgesen (2007) offers the alternatives of marginal or absorption costing to ABC for use in customer cost analyses, but concludes by stating that ABC is most appropriate in the context of customer costing, which is a sentiment offered elsewhere (Cooper and Kaplan 1991; Noone and Griffin 1997). Accordingly it appears that advances in customer costing are mainly limited to the influence afforded to ABC.

As the literature has indicated (for example see Kaplan and Narayanan 2001) ABC probes further into realms of costs than marginal or absorption costing, and thus it is claimed by ABC advocates as being more realistic (Macintosh, 2002). In an ABC-type example overhead costs would be assigned to those customers to whom services were provided. In doing so, customer revenues and direct costs produced by customers are evaluated, allowing the net profitability effect to demonstrate the financial contribution of each customer to the overall profitability of the business entity.

With the increase in global competition, the rhetoric of ABC and subsequent claims that ABC yields clearer insights and increased accuracy in tracing customer costs (for example see Noone and Griffin 1997) is appealing. However, there have been more advances in costing since ABC was first introduced to an academic audience in the late 1980s. The strategic advances in management accounting, for example, have contained a number of developments that might serve as an additional or an alternative basis for use in constructing customer valuation metrics (Roslender and Hart 2004), for example Target Costing (TC). TC is a Japanese development which takes as its starting point the selling price which is determined by market considerations (Feil et al. 2004), and then a target cost is achieved following the deduction of a desired profit margin. The whole TC process is contradictory to traditional costing logic, which takes internal costs as the starting point and determines the selling price based on a desired margin. In addition the whole consideration of what constitutes an acceptable level of cost is determined by what the customer is prepared to pay for the product. Research has shown (for example, Dekker and Smidt 2003) that benefits to a firm utilising TC include a reduction in costs, as well as better quality control. Since TC has an explicit focus on the customer, it might be possible to seek cooperation with customers and, for example, product design could be employed with the main needs of customers being transformed into technical requirements for a product (cf Ansari and Bell 1997). This would have the advantage of knowing exactly what materials are required; hence what direct material costs are then attributable to customers can also be known. A problem might arise, though, in the treatment of overheads, as costs determined through TC might ultimately be subject to the same manipulation that ABC costs are subject to.

Despite this potential, however, TC and other costing methods, such as marginal or absorption costing, are under-represented in the CPA literature. In fact the CPA literature, from an accounting perspective, has largely accepted ABC as a theoretical base from which to build upon, with relatively few authors prepared to offer alternatives (Noone and Griffin 1997; Guilding et al. 2001; Roslender and Hart 2004; Helgesen 2007), which is worrying given the plethora of criticism and negative attention that ABC has received (for example see Armstrong 2002; Jones and Dugdale 2002; Roslender 1996).

A particularly damning critique (Armstrong 2002) revealed that in an ABC system, costs are, ultimately, whatever the company or manager wants them to be. In the context of customer accounting, the costs levied at customers can be whatever the company wants them to be, which has far-reaching ethical implications, in that managers are free to assign whatever costs they wish to a particular customer or customer group. Furthermore, criticisms have revealed that ABC is central to power struggles, since ABC can be used in a rhetorical battle to gain material advantage in selling ideas of control (Armstrong 2002; Jones and Dugdale 2002). The original idea (Armstrong 2002) is that ABC is used to abstract knowledge of activities, in particular middle management, in order to make them a variable cost. Their work then becomes evaluated according to whether it adds value to the firm, and if it does not, they can be unemployed. A similar situation arises in customer accounting, where customers are examined, in calculative terms, in order to find whether a particular customer or customer group is value-adding. If they are not, then resources can be allocated away from them (Gordon 1998; Boyce 2000) and they too can face termination from the company. However, it should be noted that in some cases, profitability reports might also be used to identify loss-making customers so that they can be urged to change their purchase habits in order to convert them into profitable customers.

Contemporaneously accountants are becoming more exposed to alternative customer metrics (Kaplan and Narayanan 2001), such as those contained within the balanced scorecard. Yet within the accounting literature, CPA has been identified as being the most widely recognised CA practice (Guilding and McManus 2002). Similarly, accountants are also able to choose from a larger pool of costing techniques, such as target costing, throughput accounting, life cycle costing, quality costing, and others that have been identified under the umbrella of SMA. This adds some concern to the potentially negative social effects that the use of these metrics might encourage, particularly given the monopoly of influence that ABC has brought to the research. Therefore it is important to question the influence of ABC in customer accounting, especially given the numerous alternatives that exist elsewhere.

In the next section emphasis is placed upon more sophisticated techniques that focus on the notion of customers as assets. These metrics disaffiliate from the traditional accounting frameworks and are largely absent from the accounting literature.

SECOND STAGE OF DEVELOPMENT: CUSTOMER LIFETIME VALUE

In this section, awareness is turned to customer valuation metrics. Interestingly, it is in this area where there is a recognised gulf between accounting and marketing disciplines (Guilding and McManus 2002; Roslender and Hart 2004). Whilst both disciplines are similar in their approach to profitability, vis-à-vis CPA and CAP, the marketing literature appears to have advanced beyond the focus of current levels of profit and has extended the analysis to future periods, emulating a type of NPV calculation. The marketing literature also advances a case for customer value, under the auspices of customer lifetime value [CLV] and customer equity [CE]. Whilst these metrics are advocated in the marketing literature, the accounting literature appears to have adopted a restricted focus on notions of customer value, with the only documented approaches that examine customer value are identified to as Lifetime Customer Profitability Analysis [LCPA] and the Valuation of Customers or Customer Groups as Assets [VCA] (Guilding and McManus 2002; Lind and Strömsten 2006).

Previous customer relationship research in accounting, particularly within the management accounting literature, primarily focused on non-financial information as a means to measure performance (Mouritsen 1997; Vaivio 1999; Malmi et al. 2004). Given this ostensible unimportance afforded to customer valuation within accounting studies, it is still surprising to note that LCPA is an under-represented metric, with only one case study documenting its application (Cooper and Kaplan 1991; Guilding and McManus 2002). The one documented case is offered by Cooper and Kaplan (1991) in a study which involves an attempt by a bank to uncover which customers are profitable. The conceptual model tendered in the article involves a 3-part calculation that ostensibly merges a loan-pricing model with a typical customer profitability calculation, and then adjusts the resulting figures with a risk-adjusted Return on Equity calculation. In this manner, what was presented to the bank was a risk-adjusted number that placed a value on the financial commitments of the customer over the lifetime of the loan agreement; subsequently, LCPA broadens the time frame of the analysis to include previous years and the future (Berliner and Brimson 1988; Foster and Gupta 1994), where future costs and revenues connected to a specific customer are calculated on accrual principles (Guilding and McManus 2002; Pfeifer et al. 2005; Lind and Strömsten 2006). Similarly, VCA is relatively unexplored within the accounting literature. The first published study by Foster et al. (1996) still being the most widely cited (Guilding and McManus 2002)

As above, there appears to be a chasm between the metrics developed by accountants and those generated by marketers, as lifetime value concepts have been widely published in the marketing literature.

Throughout the last 40 or so years marketing has become increasingly focused around customers (Brown 1995; Rust et al. 2004) consistent with related developments and studies such as market orientation and customer value (Rust et al. 2004). Stemming from the latter study, customer lifetime value studies have been gaining increased attention in the marketing literature (Blattberg and Deighton 1996; Berger and Nasr 1998; Reinartz and Kumar 2000; Gupta and Lehmann 2003; Rust et al. 2004; Bauer and Hammerschmidt 2005; Berger et al. 2002; 2006; Gupta et al. 2006). Consideration of these studies reveal that several metrics have been proposed for valuing customers over future periods, however despite the myriad techniques advanced for measuring CLV, not one has been generally accepted as a superior approach (Jain and Singh 2002; Bauer and Hammerschmidt 2005), nor has any synthesis taken place (Bauer and Hammerschmidt 2005). Consequently, there exist numerous techniques that place contradictory importance on different aspects of the customer relationship (see Gupta et al. 2006). For example, they note that some authors neglect retention rates, whilst others do not.

In addition to the above observations, there appears to be some confusion regarding the correlation between customer retention and profitability. Reichheld and Sasser (1990) found that a 5% increase in retention rates could increase firm profitability from 25% to 85%. However, Reinartz and Kumar (2000) suggested that the length of the customer relationship is not the decisive factor, as customer revenue drives the lifetime value. This contrary position was strengthened when Reinartz and Kumar (2002) conducted further study and their findings of weak to moderate correlation between customer tenure and profitability also opposed Reichheld and Sasser's earlier work. What emerges is the idea that there are conflicting theories regarding the importance of certain variables within the metrics.

Nevertheless, it is claimed that any model of CLV examines specific linkages between marketing strategies or programmes, customer retention, customer acquisition, customer expansion, and firm value (Bauer and Hammerschmidt 2005; Berger et al. 2002; 2006; Gupta et al. 2006). This process is shown in Figure 1.

FIGURE 1 Framework for modelling CLV, adapted from Gupta et al. (2006)

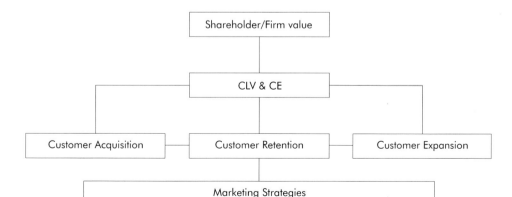

A generic approach

Gupta et al. (2006) evaluates the CLV literature to date and concludes that six different types of CLV model exist: RFM models; probability models; econometric models; persistence models; computer science models; and diffusion/growth models. However, each model contained similar variables in that each involved calculating a customer's future gross profits and discounting them over the tenure that the customer is expected to remain loyal. Furthermore, each approach considered customer retention and acquisition rates. In addition to these variables the marketing resources allocated to the customer (see for example, Berger et al. 2006) will also affect a CLV model. Thus the elements of CLV can be identified as retention rate; acquisition rate; revenues; and costs. These components will constitute the generic approach that will be discussed in this section. Firstly, in order to demonstrate the idea behind the arithmetic, a basic CLV calculation without retention rates and acquisitions costs, taken from Berger et al. (2006), is numerated below:

$$CLVi = \sum_{t=1}^{n} \frac{(\text{future gross profits } _{it} - \text{future costs } _{it})}{(1 + r)^t} \qquad (1)$$

Where
i = customer index,
t = time index,
n = forecast horizon, and
r = discount rate

In this simple model, future gross profits are based on future revenue following the deduction of cost of goods sold and other marginal and/or variable costs. Future costs refer to those that are traced to the individual customer, for example, service costs.

Following "time value of money" from financial theory, future customer revenue streams are discounted in order to express the customer's potential profitability in contemporary money terms. This exercise is a common element to (almost) any CLV metrics and is a point that most researchers agree upon (Pfeifer et al. 2005). The time period can be any set by the company, and is often the expected length of relationship that the firm has with the customer.

The approach of using a customer or customer groups' lifetime value regards customers as assets (Rust et al. 2004), which create future cash flows and are then discounted, which, in finance terms, is a standard methodology for the financial evaluation of assets (Arnold 2002). Customers are ostensibly viewed as investments that are subject to net present value calculations. Consequently, the influence of financial theory upon the CLV model is evident.

What is also critical to CLV is the idea that both customers and products have different purchase cycles, and that at any time, a customer can engage in cross buying. During such times, the firm is not receiving 100% of the customer (Dowling and Uncles 1997; Berger et al. 2002), hence models can emulate switching behaviour in order to establish more reliable estimates of customer and competitor behaviour within a certain time frame (Berger et al. 2002). The impact of this upon CLV models is in the inception of retention-based, and migration-based models.

Retention based models differ from migration models in their treatment of the buyer-seller relationship. Migration models assume that customers have several suppliers and that they decide when to transact with a particular firm or supplier. Rust et al. (2004) note, it is impossible to retain all customers, since some are "*lost for good*" (Jackson 1985; Rust et al. 2004), and implicitly, it is difficult to keep and satisfy all customers. As a proxy, migration models use the date of last purchase to predict the probability of a future transaction (Dwyer 1997), simulating, albeit weakly, the effect of customer exit or migration. But these migration models are sometimes neglected in CLV models (Gupta et al. 2006), and are not a common element.

Retention models, on the other hand, measure the amount of customers that remain loyal to a company in a given period. Reasons given for customers remaining loyal range from customer satisfaction (Kaplan and Narayanan 2001) to high switching costs (Dwyer 1997) such as exit fees or customer knowledge of a product or service.

As a result, research in customer behaviour has enabled researchers to build variables into CLV metrics that deal with retention and migration rates.

There are several ways to estimate retention and migration at a particular period, with researchers choosing to advocate econometric models and probability models (see Gupta et al. 2006). Also advanced is the use of Markov chain models (Villaneuva and Hanssens 2007). Thus, statistical modelling has been used to determine fluctuations in the customer base.

Bauer and Hammerschmidt (2005) conducted a review of CLV models in the marketing literature and revealed that analysis can be extended to include additional variables such as termination of customer relationship costs. Moreover, the refinement of customer value theories has led to the elaboration of CLV models (for example see Gupta et al. 2006). What can readily be seen from this is that it becomes increasingly complicated to determine a CLV figure, and that the metric itself becomes 'messier' as it becomes more steeped in financial calculus.

However in spite of the increase in variables, even the extended and more complicated models have the same theoretical grounding as the more simplistic models, in that both sets of CLV techniques resemble an NPV calculation. That is that both use the discounted cash flow model in order to calculate the return generated from a particular customer of customer segment over a period of years. Consistent with customer profitability metrics considered above, the literature does not reconcile issues regarding costs, consequently, there are a great number of costs that can be considered when calculating CLV.

In recent years, some researchers have looked at evaluating the possibility of moving beyond CLV calculations. Specifically, certain researchers have sought not to solely *measure* customer value, but to *maximise* it.

THIRD STAGE OF DEVELOPMENT: CUSTOMER EQUITY

A recent and an increasing body of contributions seek to observe the impact of customer investment upon firm value. Returning to the previous section and figure 1, it is evident that CLV calculations mainly examine the impact of variables upon customer value. However, recent articles have issued calls to consider the overall impact upon firm value, and they place this at the centre of reflection. This movement within the literature, labelled customer equity, was first written about by Blattberg and Deighton (1996), and this is where attention is focused to in this section.

Customer Equity [CE] is commonly described as the sum of individual discounted lifetime values of both present and future customers for the duration of the time they continue to transact with the company (Blattberg and Deighton 1996; Bayon et al. 2002, Rust et al. 2004). However, various approaches have been developed and, akin to the related earlier developments in CLV, no overall model has been conceived that synthesises previous attempts.

The approach was first proposed as a measure to determine the optimal balance between the acquisition of customers and customer retention (Blattberg and Deighton 1996), with the optimal level occurring when CE was at its highest. And in recent years CE has been advocated as a process to increasing returns to shareholders (Doyle 2000; Bayon et al. 2002), embracing a value-based approach (Bayon et al. 2002, Rust et al. 2004), as well as acting as a proxy for firm value (Gupta et al. 2006). Advances in consumer behaviour studies, such as cross-buying and duration of customer retention (Bayon et al. 2002), and the developments in CLV influenced researchers and facilitated the extension of studies in customer value by providing a conceptual basis on which to construct notions of CE, where the essential principle is a steady creation of value with reference to individual customer lifetime values (Bayon et al. 2002; Richards and Jones 2008). Behavioural studies have provided a platform for understanding customers, hence aiding marketers and managers in seeking and identifying potential new customers, based on, for example, their cross-buying potential or their retention frequency. Furthermore insights proffered from research in CLV have provided the means for marketers to identify the customers that contribute to CE. Richards and Jones (2006) also highlight the contemporary importance of CE to marketers by claiming that CE focuses on two important marketing concerns: customer relationships, and financial accountability.

With respect to the latter concern, it is claimed that top managers viewed marketing expenditures as short-term costs, instead of long-term investments (Rust et al. 2004), but CE adds a dimension of financial accountability in that the effects of strategic marketing expenditures can be measured against any resulting increases in CE levels in order to ascertain if particular marketing strategies have resulted in a favourable increase in CE.

A generic approach

In developing a model for CE, different authors have sought to highlight dissimilar areas of the customer relationship and have accordingly emphasised alternative rationales for their metrics. However, a common approach (Bauer and Hammerschmidt 2005) would split the model into three areas. Firstly, lifetime values for individual customers are calculated, per equation (1) above. Secondly, data is gathered about customer acquisitions during a particular period, and CLV calculations are performed on these newly acquired customers. Finally, a CE calculation can be conducted, which is simply to add the resulting figures derived from the previous tasks and then to discount to the present period.

When these tasks are completed, they can be compounded into a single equation (Bauer and Hammerschmidt 2005):

$$CE = \sum_{s=0}^{T} \frac{1}{(1+d)^s} \sum_{k=(v_{s-1}+1)}^{v_s} \sum_{t=s}^{T} r_i^t \frac{(R_{ti} - C_{ti})}{(1+d)^t}$$

Equation (2) (source: Bauer and Hammerschmidt 2005, eqn. 5)

FIGURE 2 Simplified customer equity model

$$CE = \sum_{s=0}^{T} \underbrace{\frac{1}{(1+d)^s}}_{C} \underbrace{\sum_{k=(v_{s-1}+1)}^{v_s}}_{B} \underbrace{\sum_{t=s}^{T} r_i^t \frac{(R_{ti} - C_{ti})}{(1+d)^t}}_{A}$$

Whilst it appears to be complex, the formula is easy to understand. In Figure 2, A refers to the first task mentioned in Equation (2), where CLV calculations are performed for existing customers; B to the second task in which the rate of newly acquired customers is derived; C to the sum of the equities previously calculated, which are discounted to the current period – this represents the summation of the value of the current customer base, as well as the value of acquired customers.

Considering figure 2, the influence of customer behaviour studies is most apparent in B, where customer acquisition is the key element. CLV metrics built upon the idea of *"polygamous loyalty"* (Dowling and Uncles 1997), where customers have numerous suppliers at once. Studies, such as the one by Ganesh et al. (2000), suggested that such customers may be dissatisfied with one or more of their suppliers and that they can be targeted for acquisition.

An early general quantitative approach to determine acquisition rates was advanced by Blattberg and Deighton (1996). Their estimation is based on the current level of acquisition spending, the resulting acquisition rate, as well as a constant that expresses the effectiveness of acquisition activities and an upper threshold of customer acquisitions in the absence of any limiting factor or constraints. However, it has been noted in the literature that acquisition rates assume a never-decreasing pool of customers (Pfeifer et al. 2005), which may not be the case in practice. Next is to estimate margins of future acquired customers. Bauer and Hammerschmidt (2005) suggest that it can be easily achieved using past archived customer data and determining profit patterns. By projecting these patterns into future periods, it is possible to estimate future values.

In addition to the influence of finance on CE models, an idea behind CE management is that the CE metric can provide a basis for calculating the ROI of any strategic investment. Some writers have even extended the analysis to consider how CE impacts upon firm equity (Andon et al. 2001; Rust et al. 2004; Bauer and Hammerschmidt 2005; Gupta et al. 2006), and can be calculated as:

$$ROI = (\Delta CE - E)/E.$$

Equation (3) (Source: Rust et al. 2004, eqn. 8)

In this example, the financial impact of a marketing initiative can be measured by the return on investment, where the present value of investment is subtracted from the change in customer equity as a result of the marketing action. This adds a level of accountability to CE (Richards and Jones 2008), and hence embraces ideas central to accounting (see Catasús 2007).

In addition to the generic approach described above, further sub-components or sub-drivers of CE value have been considered by researchers (Zeithaml 1988; Rust et al. 2000; Lemon et al. 2001; Richards and Jones 2008): value equity, relationship equity and brand equity. These additional sub-drivers also consider research from customer behaviour studies as they each place an importance upon customers' perceptions. To elaborate, consider value equity.

Value equity is characterised as the customer's assessment of the brand based on their utility position (Richards and Jones 2008), specifically customers evaluate the opportunity cost of obtaining the brand in order to establish this aspect of equity (Zeithaml 1988; Richards and Jones 2008). In addition, the customer's evaluation of price, quality and convenience is seen to impact upon the value equity (Rust et al. 2000; Lemon et al. 2001; Richards and Jones 2008). Value equity is seen as an important aspect in CE theory, as customers must perceive that they are increasing their utility with each purchase, otherwise there is no incentive for customers to make repeat transactions (Rust et al. 2004; Richards and Jones 2008). This aspect of repeat transactions impacts upon retention rates, which can also affect the resulting CE figure.

Under relationship equity, retention programs, loyalty schemes and affinity programs, are used to capture and measure the link between the customer and the brand (Rust et al. 2004; Richards and Jones 2008) particularly because these plans place an impetus upon the customer and are aimed at building relationships (see for example, Verhoef 2003).

These subjective aspects can affect the overall perception of a firm's goods or services and thus alter retention and attraction rates. But, these sub drivers, particularly brand equity, can mean many things, and are often used by researchers with different meanings (Feldwick 1996; Villaneuva and Hanssens 2007). In fact, there are those who feel that both customer and brand equity share similarities (for example, Kumar et al. 2006), in that they both measure the intangible value of marketing assets and both view customer loyalty as a fundamental construct (Villaneuva and Hanssens 2007). Consequently, the literature on loyalty has impacted upon CE in a way that was not realised under CPA, and to an extent CLV (see Rust et al. 2004).

However, the literature supplies no concrete agreement concerning the role of these sub drivers in customer equity. Blattberg and Deighton (1996), for example, portray customers as the true source of value and wealth creation, suggesting that brands are but one mechanism of increasing customer equity and that brands are never as important as the customers that buy them. Equally the converse is supplied, whereby it is argued that brands are more important than customers, as they attract the customer. Nevertheless, in both arguments, brands and customers are seemingly linked in a positive association, with proponents of both arguments highlighting brand power as an apparatus for attracting new customers and securing existing customers. Therefore, as would be expected, theories of brand power are linked with brand equity, and also can be seen to underlie both value and relationship equity drivers of value. Resultantly, it is fair to assert that such theories are also important to the development of CE.

Role of resources

Inexorably linked with both CLV and CE is Customer Relationship Management (CRM), which is claimed to underpin theories on customer value (Mitussis et al. 2006). CRM is defined as the management of a mutually beneficial relationship from the perspective of the seller (LaPlaca, 2004). That is; that CRM is the process of identifying, acquiring and retaining the most "valuable" customer in order to produce increasing profits. The crux is that during cooperative and collaborative relationships, value is created both for the customer and the firm, which benefits all those in the relationship (Tzokas and Saren 1997; Parvatiyar and Sheth 2000; Mitussis et al. 2006).

However, Winer (2001) laments contemporary debates on CRM, offering that as a notion CRM is ill defined, highlighting in particular that CRM means "*different things to different people*" (p.91). From a practical perspective, at least, CRM is seen to align business processes with customer strategies in order to increase customer loyalty and maximise profits over time (Rigby et al. 2002). Simply put then, CRM is concerned with identifying profitable/valuable customers and then allocating the majority of resources and attention to these groups.

Furthermore, empirical research has indicated that many organisations operate a pluralistic approach to marketing – with CRM being conducted in conjunction with transaction marketing (Brodie et al. 1997; Möller and Halinen 2000; Palmer et al. 2005), where transaction marketing is used to gain new customers (Lindgreen et al. 2004). This might add a strategic dimension to CRM (see Richards and Jones 2008), and consequently import an overall strategic objective to CRM and CE, implying that the strategy literature has had an impact upon the development of CE models.

However, the strategic perspective might derive from the overall result of such a pluralistic approach to marketing. By focusing upon the exploitation of economic exchanges of the customer relationship, customers are commodified and traded on the basis of their perceived future and present cash flows, with enhanced or deeper relationship management being offered to those privileged customers that are conveyed as being more valuable. Tied with this are the references by some writers to a portfolio of customers built upon value (Dhar and Glazer 2003; Van Raaij et al. 2003), which suggests that CE writers' view of a portfolio view of customers might have been influenced by investment and portfolio theories. For example, comparing a customer group to a stock or share holding, risk of low returns can be traded away by creating an investment portfolio of customers that, according to the calculations, are expected to yield much higher returns. There are, naturally, social concerns related to this, and these will be addressed in the concluding section of the paper.

From the above analysis, it appears that the influence of econometric modelling is most evident in the area of customer equity. In addition to the generic model (eqn 2) described above, alternatives are available to researchers where one can examine customer migration models, where the models predict behaviour based on historical instances of purchase, and by examining the number of periods since last purchase; these models can predict the likelihood of customer migration (see Berger and Nasr 1998). Other alternatives available include stochastic models (Villanueva and Hanssens 2007), models based on survey data (Rust et al. 2000; 2004) and managerial judgement (Villanueva and Hanssens 2007). Consequently, there is a wealth of theoretical influence in the area of customer equity. Similarly, the same wealth of influence exists for the other two areas of customer valuation that have been explored in this study. Thus, it would be useful to summarise the debate so far.

RECAPITULATION: CONSIDERING THE THEORETICAL INFLUENCES

Since the techniques are extensions on each other, it is fair to assert that the customer valuation techniques discussed share similar underlying principles. However, by grouping them into separate areas of development, it is possible to see that whilst the three stages do indeed share a common core of ascertaining profits and revenue flows arising from a customer or particular group of customers, advancements in other fields have impacted upon the development of customer valuation metrics.

Metrics and calculations that were amongst the first customer valuation techniques included CPA, and arose out of dissatisfaction over existing means of assigning customer costs. Advancements in costing at the time led researchers to trace costs to customers, and such exercises were underpinned by the focus to expose the most/ least profitable customers within a firm.

To do this, techniques built upon simple accounting logic vis-à-vis profit calculations, where customer profits were the difference between customer revenues and customer costs. Thus, as a foundation, CPA and related models lean more toward accounting, theoretically, as CPA is more noticeably influenced by accounting concepts and conventions; in particular, the customer profit calculation represents a specific application of traditional profit measurement. Furthermore ABC heavily influenced the advances in customer costing that took place around the late 1980s. This influence is still present in CPA techniques today. It is doubtful whether customer costing would have made such progress without the advancement and academic refinement of ABC and related costing developments, because this provided the platform to overcome perceived deficiencies of the SG&A cost allocation practices.

Thus, it is fair to assert that the first stage of valuation techniques were heavily influence by accounting theories.

CLV models extend the simplicity of CPA models by building upon the focus on income in the previous models by adding elements of forecasting. Whilst CPA models were established to uncover past customer profits, CLV models and metrics became forward-looking through the introduction of a DCF type analysis. The idea reinforcing this DCF analysis within CLV is to expose the most/least valuable customers in both current and future periods, where "value" is equated to aggregated present value returns. The focus upon aggregated returns, adds a dimension of financial theory to the calculations, one that was absent in previous models.

There is no indication that the costing structure used in previous metrics has been abandoned or changed under CLV, consequently it can be assumed that CLV is still influenced by ABC. Furthermore it can be argued that CLV is a form of strategic management accounting technique (as previously hinted by Guilding and McManus, 2002) because of the future-oriented perspective and the use of externally generated information. However, the main theoretical link in CLV is the "marriage" of finance and marketing.

Also important in CLV are the retention and migration models. Advances in customer behaviour studies have influenced these models – for example theories of cross buying and customer switching patterns- thus customer behaviour research has become an important influence upon the customer valuation literature; an influence that was previously missing under the first stage metrics.

The third stage of development saw the introduction of models that not only measured lifetime values of customers, but also sought to maximise them. Customer Equity metrics built upon CLV to consider larger groups of customers, and extended its links with finance by going beyond customer valuation to include elements of firm valuation. Hence, finance theory is an important influence in the development of CE, and is arguably becoming more influential to customer valuation research as a whole.

As with some CLV calculations, econometric and statistical modelling is prevalent in the development of CE. An influence that, tied also to the impact of customer behaviour studies, has led to the establishment of customer acquisition rates within the models.

As with CLV then, the most influential theories upon CE have come from finance. Furthermore, CE has introduced an ROI type measure to the valuation literature, which further stresses the links with financial theory. In addition, the ROI figure has sought to address the need for a platform of accountability, and thus re-introduces an accounting logic to the technique.

Whilst the first stage relied heavily upon accounting, the second stage of development borrowed from finance theory in order to construct a lifetime value model, which was elaborated by customer behaviour studies. The same studies and financial stresses are prevalent in the third stage of development, but the third stage also seeks more outside influence in the form of statistical and econometric modelling, while accounting is also seen as an influence in the form of the ROI measure.

CONCLUSION AND IMPLICATIONS

What has been broadly conceived in various business and management literatures as customer valuation, and customer accounting, groups together numerous calculative practices and metrics. The various techniques that have been written about under these labels can be easily separated into three main areas of development: customer profitability analysis, customer lifetime value, and customer equity. The main focus of this paper has been to review, albeit in rather a brief and simplistic manner, the main streams of techniques that exist under the customer valuation label. Each stage of development received a specific examination wherein generic techniques were introduced, elaborated upon and finally discussed with reference to their main theoretical bases. It was found that customer profitability metrics were a specific application of the accounting profit equation, and were consequently steeped in accounting theories. The second stage, however, represented a move away from accounting in favour of a more financially inclined set of metrics. The final stage of development simultaneously introduced solutions of accountability and value maximisation to marketing managers and thus broadened the focus to an interdisciplinary arena whereby accounting, finance and marketing intermingle theoretically.

What is evident from the recent advances in the area is that customer valuation is becoming a separate area of study which can be conceived of as an interdisciplinary practice (see Roslender and Hart 2004). No specific area or discipline enjoys a monopoly of influence upon the development of customer valuation metrics. Nor is it likely to have in future years. However, given the recent trends in customer equity literature (see Villanueva and Hanssens 2007) it is likely that econometric modelling may have more of an influence than in previous periods of research.

Some benefits relating to the advancement of the metrics pertain to knowing more about customers. With the vast databases that are available, firms have the potential to extract all sorts of knowledge(s) and understandings relating to their current and potential customers, which firms can then use to customise goods or services according to the information contained in their databases. Placing this idea within the "satisfaction-loyalty-profitability" chain, the logic is that customers will benefit from this customised service and will be satisfied and more likely to enter into future transactions with the firm again, eventually building up a loyalty to the organisation.

Through this loyalty, the customers will become more valuable and profitable to the company, resulting in higher profit levels from the customers, aggregating to an overall increase in profitability for the firm. In this scenario, both customer and firm benefit from the metrics and the databases that can be developed.

However, this is not necessarily good news. Given the previous two stages of development, it is evident that financial theories are becoming more prominent and involved in the metrics. This increasing sway from finance implies that the metrics will become more complex and abstract in nature, as can be evidenced by examining some of the models of customer equity in the literature. Such a position carries a readily apparent consequence in that the metrics might become so complex that they become difficult to implement in practice.

Furthermore, whilst the metrics and the theories of customer valuation expand, so too does the number of variables that have to be included. But, so far formulae have focused on only quantitative aspects of the business relationship, neglecting qualitative factors such as satisfaction and quality, which on a technical basis, should be included into the metrics where the aim is to get closer to and getting to know the customer better (Duboff 1992; Treacy and Wiersema 1993).

Another practical issue arises when consider the role of firm capacity. For example, the idea that only valuable customers are worth having means that, the loss-making customers are discarded (Bellis-Jones 1989; Gordon 1998; Boyce 2000, Kaplan and Narayanan 2001), with resources often transferred to more valuable customers or customer groups (Boyce 2000; Rust et al. 2004; Gupta and Lehmann 2005). However, if only x% of customers are profitable (cf Cooper and Kaplan 1991), hence valuable, then (100-x)% are not worth building relationships with because they are loss-makers. But if a company only deals with x customers, then the company is likely to be under-capacity, which would increase overheads and reduce the apparent profitability or value of these customers. This might negate any value in an exercise of calculating the value of customers, and reduce metrics to an exercise of futility.

There are also social issues and concerns that relate to customer valuation. There is a fear expressed by some (Andon et al. 2001; Boyce 2000) that relying solely on the metrics could engender a situation whereby managers handle customers based on the numbers produced by the metrics, leading to management at a distance, which has the potential of alienating specific customers or customer groups. To recap, underpinning the metrics are notions of a clearer understanding of the customer, which enables better management of the customer; however, the reality is more akin to a financial appraisal of customers in order to determine which are valuable and thus deserving of attention. What follows from this is the creation of value hierarchies, where customers are grouped according to their profitability: a "Loyal" grouping for profitable and potentially valuable customers, and a "Disloyal" grouping for unprofitable customers. This loyalty dialectic is then used as the basis of constructing a customer portfolio (Dhar and Glazer 2003; Van Raaij et al. 2003) where the company creates a customer base akin to an investment portfolio in which customers are included on their potential contribution to shareholder value. A recent case in Britain exemplified these worries whereby HSBC were publicly criticised for setting up a branch exclusively for richer customers (Heming 2007; Smith 2007). This, as above in section 4, points to the notion that customers are commodified in the customer valuation metrics.

In a similar vein, perhaps the drive in customer equity, like that in CLV, is taking focus away from the customer, despite them being placed at the heart of the analysis, the over-arching focus is on increasing shareholder value. Accordingly the benefit is not for the customer, but for shareholders, further commodifying customers. During this commodification process, it has been feared by Boyce (2000) that some customers will ultimately be alienated from the firm.

In spite of some of these implications, as the paper has documented, customer valuation models and research has a rich influence and a solid conceptual base. Given the given the evidence of recent customer valuation research becoming an interdisciplinary topic, it is perhaps worthy to encourage interdisciplinary research projects, as various insights could be gained by a collaborative effort. For example, Roslender and Hart (2004) previously suggested that much could be gained from a project ensuring cooperation between marketing and accounting.

Regarding empirical work, the models discussed have yet to fully consider uncertainty in lifetime valuations. From finance theory (see Arnold 2002), cash flows are not deterministic meaning that the models may not accurately predict cash flows. In addition to cash flow problems, customer valuation metrics do not cover risk or volatility of future customer cash flows/values - thus risk and uncertainty are inadequately covered in current models, and could be an area of future empirical research. In addition, research could be undertaken that looks at qualitative factors, as noteworthy in their absence from customer valuation metrics.

Future research should also be encouraged, particularly paying attention to potential social issues as a result of valuation techniques. By engaging with notions of emancipation, Roslender and Fincham (2004) challenged the managerialist intentions of intellectual capital reporting, and proposed intellectual capital self-accounting as an emancipatory solution, whereby employees would write blogs of their experiences within a firm. Such an idea stemmed from the idea that accounting could be conceived as a system of "story-telling" and built upon narrative approaches to reporting intellectual capital information to interested parties. A similar approach could be applied to customer valuation. This would allow customers to recount their stories and experiences, and promote a voice that has been missing in previous attempts at customer valuation – ironically the customer. The key idea is that customers are given a space to speak for themselves, which distances them from the calculus that captures them as a financial number. Future research might include an agenda to see if such a solution is practical, or even possible.

Similarly, the allocation of marketing resources has been to profitable and valuable customers, who represent a less risky investment. A novel or experimental analysis might also consider if there is indeed such a value-risk trade-off in practice – is it prudent to build a customer bases of only profitable customers?

REFERENCES

Andon, P., Baxter, J. and Bradley, G. (2001), "Calculating the economic value of customers to an organisation", *Australian Accounting Review*, Vol. 11, No. 1, pp. 62-72.

Ansari, S. L. and Bell, J. (1997), *Target Costing: The Next Frontier in Strategic Cost Management*, USA: MacGraw-Hill.

Armstrong, P. (2002), "The costs of activity-based management", *Accounting, Organizations and Society*, Vol. 27, No. 1-2, pp. 99-120.

Arnold, G. (2002), *Corporate Financial Management*, 2nd edition, Financial Times/ Prentice Hall: London.

Bauer, H. H. and Hammerschmidt, M. (2005), "Integrating the concepts of customer equity and shareholder value", *Management Decision*, Vol. 43, No. 3, pp. 331-348.

Bayon, T., Gutsche, J. and Bauer, H. (2002), "Customer equity marketing: Touching the intangible", *European Management Journal*, Vol. **20**, No. 3, pp. 213–222.

Bellis-Jones, R. (1989), "Customer Profitability Analysis", *Management Accounting*, Vol. **67**, No. 2, pp. 26-28.

Berger, P. D. and Nasr, N. I. (1998), "Customer Lifetime Value: Marketing models and applications", *Journal of Interactive Marketing*, Vol. **12**, No. 1, pp. 17-30.

Berger, P. D., Bolton, R. N., Bowman, D., Briggs. E., Kumar, V., Parasuraman, A. and Terry, C. (2002), "Marketing Actions and the Value of Customer Assets: A Framework for Customer Asset Management", *Journal of Service Research*, Vol. **5**, No. 1, pp. 39-54.

Berger, P. D., Naras E., Morris G., Lehmann, D. R., Rizley, R. and Venkatesan, R. (2006), "From Customer Lifetime Value to Shareholder Value: Theory, Empirical Evidence, and Issues for Future Research," *Journal of Service Research*, Vol. **9**, No. 2, pp. 156-167.

Berliner, C. and Brimson, J. A. (1988), *Cost management for today's advanced manufacturing - the CAMI conceptual design*, Boston: Harvard Business School Press

Blattberg, R. C. and Deighton, J. (1996), "Manage marketing by the customer equity test", *Harvard Business Review*, Vol. **74**, No. 4, pp. 136-144.

Boyce, G. (2000), "Valuing customers and loyalty: The rhetoric of customer focus versus the reality of alienation and exclusion of (de valued) customers", *Critical Perspectives on Accounting*, Vol. **11**, No. 6, pp. 649-689.

Brodie, R. J., Coviello, N. E., Brookes, R. W. and Little, V. (1997), "Towards a paradigm shift in marketing: an examination of current marketing practices", *Journal of Marketing Management*, Vol. **13**, No. 5, pp. 383-406.

Brown, S. (1995), "Life begins at 40? Further thoughts on marketing's 'mid-life' crisis", *Marketing Intelligence and Planning*, Vol. **13**, No.1, pp. 4-17.

Catasús, B. (2007), "In Search of Accounting Absence", Critical Perspectives on Accounting, In Press, doi:10.1016/j.cpa.2007.02.002 [Accessed 29 March 2007]

Cooper, R. and Kaplan, R.S. (1991), *The Design of Cost Management Systems: Text, Cases, and Readings*, Englewood Cliffs, New Jersey: Prentice-Hall

Dekker, H. and Smidt, P. (2003), "A survey of the adoption and use of target costing in Dutch firms", *International Journal of Production Economics*, Vol. **84**, pp. 295-305

Dhar, R. and Glazer, R. (2003), "Hedging Customers," *Harvard Business Review*, Vol. **81**, No. 5, pp. 3-8.

Dowling, G. R. and Uncles, M. (1997), "Do customer loyalty programs really work?" *Sloan Management Review*, Vol. **38**, No. 4, pp. 71–82.

Doyle, P. (2000), "Value-based marketing", *Journal of Strategic Marketing*, Vol. **8**, No. 4, pp. 299-311.

Duboff, R. S. (1992), "Marketing to maximise profitability", *Journal of Business Strategy*, Vol. **13**, No. 6, pp. 10-13.

Dudick, T. S. (1987), "Why SG&A doesn't always work", *Harvard Business Review*, Vol. **65**, No. 1, pp. 30-33.

Dwyer, F. R. (1997), "Customer lifetime valuation to support marketing decision making", *Journal of Direct Marketing*, Vol. **11**, No. 4, pp. 8-15.

Feil, P., Yook, K. H. and Kim, I. W. (2004), "Japanese Target Costing: A historical perspective", *International Journal of Strategic Cost Management*, Vol. **2**, No. 4, pp. 10-19.

Feldwick, P. (1996), "What is brand equity anyway, and how do you measure it?", *Journal of Market Research Society*, Vol. **38**, pp. 85–104.

Foster, G. and Gupta, M. (1994), "Marketing, cost management and management Accounting", *Journal of Management Accounting Research*, Vol. **6**, No. 1, pp. 43-77.

Foster, G., Gupta, M. and Sjoblom, L. (1996), "Customer profitability analysis: challenges and new directions", *Journal of Cost Management*, Vol. **10**, No.1, pp. 5-17.

Ganesh, J., Arnold, M. J. and Reynolds, K. E. (2000) "Understanding the Customer Base of Service Providers: An Examination of the Differences Between Switchers and Stayers", *Journal of Marketing*, Vol. **64**, No. 3, July, pp. 65-87.

Gordon, I. H. (1998), *Relationship Marketing: New Strategies, Techniques and Technologies to Win the Customers You Want and Keep Them Forever*, Toronto: Wiley

Guilding, C., Kennedy, J. and McManus, L. (2001), "Extending the boundaries of customer accounting- applications in the hotel industry", *Journal of Hospitality and Tourism Research*, Vol. 25, No. 2, pp. 173-194.

Guilding, C. and McManus, L. (2002) "The incidence, perceived merit and antecedents of customer accounting: An exploratory note", *Accounting, Organizations and Society*, Vol. 27, No. 1, pp. 45–59.

Gupta, S. and Lehmann, D. R. (2003), "Customers as assets", *Journal of Interactive Marketing*, Vol. 17, No.1: 9-24

Gupta, S., and Lehmann, D. R. (2005), *Managing Customers as Investments*, Philadelphia: Wharton School Publishing

Gupta, S., Hanssens, D., Hardie, B., Kahn, W., V. Kumar, Lin, N., Ravishanker, N., and Sriram, S. (2006), "Modelling Customer Lifetime Value", *Journal of Service Research*, Vol. 9, No. 2, pp. 139-155

Helgesen, Ø. (2007), "Customer Accounting and Customer Profitability Analysis for the Order Handling Industry - A Managerial Accounting Approach", *Industrial Marketing Management*, Vol. 36, No. 6, pp. 757-769

Heming, T. (2007), "Happy Serving Big Customers", *The Sun*, London, 12th April.

Howell, R. A. and Soucy, S. R. (1990), "Customer Profitability: As Critical as Product Profitability", *Management Accounting*, Vol. 72, No. 4, pp. 43–47.

Jackson, B. B. (1985), *Winning and Keeping Industrial Customers*, Lexington, MA: D.C. Heath and Company

Jain, D. and Singh, S. S. (2002), "Customer lifetime value research in marketing: a review and future directions", *Journal of Interactive Marketing*, Vol. 16, No. 2, pp. 34-46.

Jones, T. C. and Dugdale, D. (2002), "The ABC bandwagon and the juggernaut of Modernity", *Accounting, Organizations and Society*, Vol. 27, No. 1-2, pp. 121-163.

Kaplan, R. S. and Norton, D. P. (1992), "The Balanced Scorecard - Measures that drive performance", *Harvard Business Review*, Vol. 70, No. 1, pp. 71–79.

Kaplan, R. S. and Narayanan, V. G. (2001), "Measuring and managing customer profitability", *Journal of Cost Management*, September/October 2001, pp. 5-15.

Kumar, V., Leman, N. K. and Parasuraman, A. (2006), "Managing customers for value: An overview and research agenda", *Journal of Service Research*, Vol. 9, No. 2, pp. 87–94.

LaPlaca, P. J. (2004), "Letter from the editor: Special issue on customer relationship management", *Industrial Marketing Management*, Vol. 33, No. 6, pp. 463–464.

Lemon, K. N., Rust, R. T. and Zeithaml, V. A. (2001), "What drives customer equity?", *Marketing Management*, Vol. 10, No. 1, pp. 20–25.

Levitt, T. (1962), Innovation *in Marketing: New Perspectives for Profit and Growth*, London: Pan

Lind, J., and Strömsten, T. (2006), "When do firms use different types of customer accounting", *Journal of Business Research*, Vol. 59, No. 12, pp.1257–1266.

Lindgreen, A., Palmer, R., and Vanhamme, J. (2004), "Contemporary marketing practice: theoretical propositions and practical implications", *Marketing Intelligence and Planning*, Vol. 22, No. 6, pp. 673-692.

Macintosh, N. B., (2002), *Accounting, Accountants and Accountability: poststructuralist positions*. London: Routledge

Malmi, T., Raulas, M., Gudergan, S., and Sehm, J. (2004), "An empirical study on customer profitability accounting, customer orientation and business unit performance" Discussion paper. Available at: http://wwwdocs.fce.unsw.edu.au/accounting/news/seminars2004_s2/paper06.pdf Accessed: 25th February 2007.

Mitussis, D., O'Malley, L., and Patterson, M. (2006), "Mapping the Re-engagement of CRM with Relationship Marketing", *European Journal of Marketing*, Vol. 40, No. 5/6, pp.572-589.

Möller, K. and Halinen, A. (2000), "Relationship marketing theory: its roots and direction", *Journal of Marketing Management*, Vol. **16**, Nos. 1-3, pp. 29-54.

Mouritsen, J. (1997), "Marginalizing the customer: Customer orientation, quality and accounting performance", *Scandinavian Journal of Management*, Vol. **13**, No. 1, pp. 5-18.

Noone, B., and Griffin, P. (1997), "Enhancing yield management with customer profitability analysis", *International Journal of Contemporary Hospitality Management*, Vol. **9**, No. 2, pp. 75–79.

Palmer, R., Lindgreen, A., and Vanhamme, J. (2005), "Relationship marketing: schools of thought and future research directions", *Marketing Intelligence and Planning*, Vol. **23**, No. 3, pp. 313-330.

Pearce, S. L. (1997), "Activity-based Costing: A practical approach", *Industrial Distribution*, Vol. **86**, No. 5, pp. 82-90.

Peppers, D. and Rogers, M. (1997), *Enterprise One to One: Tools for Competing in the Interactive Age*, New York, NY: Currency Doubleday

Pfeifer, P. E., Haskins, M. E., and Conroy, R. M. (2005), "Customer lifetime value, customer profitability, and the treatment of acquisition spending", *Journal of Managerial Issues*, Vol. **17**, No. 1, pp. 11-25.

Reichheld, F. F., and Sasser, W. E. (1990), "Zero defections: Quality comes to services", *Harvard Business Review*, Vol. **68**, No. 5, pp. 105-111.

Reinartz, W. J. and Kumar, V. (2000), "On the profitability of long-life customers in a noncontractual setting: an empirical investigation and implications for marketing", *Journal of Marketing*, Vol. **64**, No. 4, pp. 17-35.

Reinartz, W., Krafft, M., and, Hoyer, W.D. (2004), "The customer relationship management process: Its measurement and impact on performance", *Journal of Marketing Research*, Vol. **41**, No. 3, pp. 293-305.

Richards, K. A. and Jones, E, (2008), "Customer relationship management- Finding value drivers" *Industrial Marketing Management*, Vol. **37**, No. 2, pp. 120-130.

Rigby, D. K., Reichheld, F. F., and Schefter, P. (2002), "Avoid the four perils of CRM", *Harvard Business Review*, Vol. **80**, No. 2, pp. 101–109.

Roslender, R. (1996), "Relevance lost and found: critical perspectives on the promise of management accounting", *Critical Perspectives on Accounting*, Vol. **7**, No. 5, pp. 533-561.

Roslender, R. and Fincham, R. (2004), "Intellectual capital: who counts, controls?", *Accounting and the Public Interest*, Vol. **4**, No. 1, pp. 1-23.

Roslender, R. and Hart, S. (2004), "Broadening the focus of customer accounting", University of Stirling Discussion paper.

Rust, R. T. and Oliver, R. L. (2000), "Should we delight the customer?" *Journal of the Academy of Marketing Science*, Vol. **28**, No. 1, pp. 86-94.

Rust, R. T, Lemon, K. N. and Zeithaml V. A. (2004), "Return on marketing: Using customer equity to focus marketing strategy", *Journal of Marketing*, Vol. **68**, No. 1, pp. 109-127.

Schiff, M., and Mellman, M. (1962), *Financial Management of the Marketing Function*, New York: Financial Executives Research Foundation

Shapiro, B. P., Rangan, V. K., Moriarty, R. T. and Ross, E. B. (1987), "Manage customers for profits (not just sales)", *Harvard Business Review*, Vol. **63**, No. 5, pp. 101-108.

Sheth, J. N. and Parvatiyar, A. (2000), *Handbook of Relationship Marketing*, Thousand Oaks, CA.: Sage Publications.

Smith, R. (2007), "Bank Bans the Poor", *Mirror*, London, 12th April.

Smith, M. and Dikoli, S. (1995), "Customer Profitability Analysis: An Activity-Based Costing Approach", *Managerial Auditing Journal*, Vol. **10**, No. 7, pp. 3-7.

Treacy, M. and Wiersema, F. (1993), "Customer intimacy and other value disciplines", *Harvard Business Review*, Vol. **71**, No. 1, pp. 84-93.

Tzokas, N. and Saren, M. (1997), "Building relationship platforms in consumer markets: a value chain approach", *Journal of Strategic Marketing*, Vol. **5**, No. 2, pp. 105-20.

Vaivio, J. (1999), "Examining 'The Quantified Customer'", *Accounting, Organizations and Society*, Vol. **24**, No. 8, pp. 689 -715.

Van Raaij, F., Vernooij M. J. A. and van Triest S. (2003), "The Implementation of customer profitability analysis: A case study", *Industrial Marketing Management*, Vol. **32**, No. 7, pp. 573-583.

Van Triest, S. (2005), "Customer size and profitability", *Journal of Business and Industrial Marketing*, Vol. **20**, No. 3, pp. 148–155.

Verhoef, P. C. (2003), "Understanding the effect of customer relationship management efforts on customer retention and customer share development", *Journal of Marketing*, Vol. **67**, No. 1, pp.30-45.

Villanueva, J. and Hanssens, D. M. (2007), "Customer Equity: measurement, management and research opportunities", *Foundations and Trends in Marketing*, Vol. **1**, No 1, pp. 1–95.

Webster, F. E. (1992), "The changing role of marketing in the corporation", *Journal of Marketing*, Vol. **56**, No. 4, pp. 1-17.

Winer, R. S. (2001), "A Framework for Customer Relationship Management", *California Management Review*, Vol. **34**, No. 4, pp. 89-105.

Zeithaml, V. A. (1988), "Consumer perceptions of price, quality and value: A means-end model and synthesis of evidence", *Journal of Marketing*, Vol. **52**, No. 1, pp. 2-22

APPENDIX – SUMMARY OF LITERATURE

TABLE 1 CPA Literature

Study	Aim	Research Category	Model/Method	Outcome/ Findings
Bellis-Jones (1989)	Discusses importance to managers of customer profitability	Theoretical	Engages with CPA by considering typical business situations	Introduces CPA model to a practical audience
Cooper and Kaplan (1991)	Synthesises case studies that authors have conducted	Theoretical and Empirical	Kanthal "A" case study is of relevance as it examines CPA application	Case study demonstrates allocation of costs to customers; discusses CPA in practical situation
Foster et al. (1996)	Discusses modifying cost systems to provide measures for CPA	Theoretical and Empirical	Uses ABC to illustrate customer costs and provides examples of how this cost info can be used with CPA models	Provides numerous managerial challenges faced when using CPA (eg estimation of future costs); future research opportunities and benefits of CPA usage are also debated

Cont'd...

Study	Aim	Research Category	Model/Method	Outcome/ Findings
Guilding and McManus (2002)	Examines how customer valuation practices are used	Empirical	Survey data is used to test hypotheses relating customer valuation to two contingency factors: intensity of competition and market orientation	Only hypotheses relating to market orientation were supported by survey data, albeit only partially supported – namely usage rates are higher in companies with a higher market orientation, and perceived managerial benefits of customer valuation use is higher in similar companies
Helgesen (2007)	Focuses on the profitability of holding and maintaining CP accounts	Theoretical and Empirical	Uses data from four exporting companies	Introduces a market-oriented accounting framework for managing customer accounts at a profit; managerial implications are also discussed
Kaplan and Narayanan (2001)	Reviews literature on CPA and considers impact on customer management relationship	Theoretical and Empirical	Considers CPA from a user perspective presenting typical usage problems and examples of customer cost assignment	Illustrates how and why CPA can be applied in practical situations; considers how CPA can be used in health care
Lind and Strömsten (2006)	Develops a framework to explain a company's choice of customer accounting technique based on its customer resource interfaces	Theoretical and Empirical	Explores two cases which ultimately support the framework	Main contribution is the framework
Noone and Griffin (1998)	Discusses a case study of CPA implementation	Theoretical and Empirical	Case study is used to test the feasibility of CPA implementation in a hotel	Introduce a step system for the development of a CPA system

Cont'd...

Study	Aim	Research Category	Model/Method	Outcome/ Findings
Roslender and Hart (2004)	Provides a review and critique of customer valuation techniques	Theoretical	Takes the form of a literature review and suggests ways in which customer valuation, specifically CPA, can be broadened	Suggests ways in which the focus of CPA can be broadened (eg by considering narrative aspects of customer relationships)

TABLE 2 CLV Literature

Study	Aim	Research Category	Model/Method	Outcome/ Findings
Andon et al. (2001)	Explore the economic value of customers to an organisation	Empirical	Exploratory case studies of three service organisations, examining CLV and CPA practices	Valuation changed existing management of customer relationships; concerns expressed over lack of management involvement with customers after valuation; customer reporting viewed by firm as stand-alone activity
Bauer and Hammerschmidt (2005)	Synthesis of CLV and shareholder value (SHV) approaches in order to develop a marketing based approach to firm valuation	Theoretical	Examines previous literature and models of CLV to guide the development of a new model	Authors seek to link the CE and the SHV approach to develop a new model and introduce scenarios and cases where their model may be beneficial; They find a CE-based valuation can guide marketing investments and can help to avoid misallocation of resources

Cont'd...

Study	Aim	Research Category	Model/Method	Outcome/ Findings
Berger and Nasr (1998)	Discuss CLV models	Theoretical	Reviews retention and migration models in CLV literature	Provides examples of CLV retention and migration models; suggests applications of CLV and possible directions for future research aimed at refining CLV models, viz. to include repeat purchasing variables
Berger et al. (2002)	Develops a framework for assessing how marketing actions affect a firm's CLV	Theoretical	Reviews CLV models and customer asset management literature;	Develops a framework for managing customers; identifies future research directions
Boyce (2000)	Outline and expose some broad social and ethical implications of customer valuation practices	Theoretical	Reviews CPA and CLV models; engages with ideas from critical accounting literature to consider impacts of valuation upon customers and customer groups	Main finding is that less-valuable customer groups face marginalisation and ultimately alienation from firms as a result of valuation exercises; other ethical implications, such as managing customer relationships, are discussed
Dwyer (1997)	Demonstrates how CLV could be used to support direct marketing decisions	Theoretical and Empirical	Two models were constructed for transaction relationships: retention model and a migration model	Several implications of CLV for managers were discussed; an implementation case was also used for illustrative purposes

Cont'd...

Study	Aim	Research Category	Model/Method	Outcome/ Findings
Gupta and Lehmann (2003)	Argues that customers are important intangible assets that should be valued and managed	Theoretical and Empirical	Using publicly available data, a model is developed to calculate average CLV	Discusses the limitations of previous CLV models; a CLV model is developed and instances where it could be used are suggested
Jain and Singh (2002)	Collate and review CLV research in marketing literature	Theoretical	Reviews and summarises previous CLV models	Limitations of CLV models are discussed; future research directions are sought and encouraged
Pfeifer et al. (2005)	Clarifies differences between CPA and CLV and offers definitions for both	Theoretical	Through a literature review, CLV models are compared with CPA models	Differences between CPA and CLV models are discussed, namely the treatment of acquisition variables; definitions of CLV and CPA are also refined; suggestions are provided regarding inclusion of additional variables
Reinartz and Kumar (2000)	Test the relationship between customer profitability and lifetime duration	Theoretical and Empirical	Reviews literature on CLV and tests four emerging hypotheses from data gathered from a catalogue retailer over 3 years	Findings challenge formulated hypotheses, for example data suggests that long life customers may not necessarily be profitable; marketing implications of the study are discussed; future directions of research are also considered

Cont'd...

Study	Aim	Research Category	Model/Method	Outcome/ Findings
Van Triest (2005)	Explores the relationship between customer size and profitability	Theoretical and Empirical	Five variables are identified and tested using a database from a business-to-business setting	Customer size is not a driver of the profitability margin, but other variables (mainly exchange efficiency) can affect margins; Practical implications for managing customer relations are also offered

TABLE 3 CE Literature

Study	Aim	Research Category	Model/Method	Outcome/ Findings
Bayon et al. (2002)	Reviews CE concept and models. In addition to redefine marketing from a shareholder's perspective	Theoretical	Reviews CE concept and CLV models in order to construct a CE model	Construction of a CE models; Provide a summary of CE management
Berger et al. (2006)	Propose a framework for understanding how CE affects shareholder value	Theoretical	Reviews previous literature and models to elaborate their framework	Main contribution is their framework; future directions for research are also discussed
Blattberg and Deighton (1996)	Introduce concept of CE to managers to aid in decisions relating to customer retention and acquisition	Theoretical	Using decision calculus authors develop a model of CE and framework to determine retention/ acquisition rates based on their model	Introduces concept of CE to wider audience; construct a model of CE
Gupta et al. (2006)	Reviews CLV models that can be implemented in practice and may be of use in conjunction with CE	Theoretical	Reviews CLV models and various approaches taken to modelling	Highlights advances in CLV and CE research; suggests 11 possible areas/ avenues for future research

Cont'd...

Study	Aim	Research Category	Model/Method	Outcome/ Findings
Lemon et al. (2001)	Develops a strategic marketing framework which considers customer value and growth	Theoretical	Describes the key drivers of firm growth (value, brand and relationship equities) to show how CE can be increased	Drivers of growth are discussed and links with CE are suggested; considers situations where each driver and related marketing actions might be of relevance when trying to increase firm value
Richards and Jones (2008)	Examines espoused CRM benefits and their ability to increase CE	Theoretical	Reviews CE and drivers of CE value and formulate 10 propositions to explore the effects of drivers on firm performance and CE	Explores 10 propositions, which then form the basis a framework used to measure CRM
Rust et al. (2004)	Introduces a strategic framework to show how marketing actions can be traded off by considering impact on CE	Theoretical and Empirical	Identifies drivers of CE which are then tested through Markov models in order to estimate switching patterns; CE models are then refined and applied in an airline context	Development of a model that includes info about the influence of competition on customer purchase patterns; authors tailor CE models to demonstrate how they can be used to show a return on investment on any marketing activity
Villanueva and Hanssens (2007)	Provides a comprehensive review of existing CE literature	Theoretical	Literature review is used to discuss CE models	The study provides a detailed consideration of CE metrics and variables used in each model; directions for future research are also discussed, particularly on how to refine CE models

Accounting is from Mars, marketing is from Venus: establishing common ground for the concept of customer profitability

Robin Gleaves, *Customer Value Associates, UK*
Jamie Burton, *Manchester Business School, UK*
Jan Kitshoff, *Customer Value Associates, UK*
Ken Bates, *Victoria University of Wellington, New Zealand*
Mark Whittington, *University of Aberdeen, UK*

Abstract Marketing and Management Accounting (MA) have traditionally been seen as poles apart in terms of both focus and approach. Innovative developments in MA measures and increasing pressure on marketers to "prove" their worth, combined with technological advancements in database management are, however, contributing to a need for more effective synergy. An examination of the treatment and coverage of customer profitability (CP) in both the MA and marketing literatures and in a sample of forty textbooks: (i) confirms apparent synergy in CP research, (ii) identifies how each discipline approaches the subject and (iii) examines similarities and differences in the approach to the measurement and management of CP. Both disciplines show a sporadic and variable interest in CP and there is still a long way to go in order to develop consistent definitions, language and application methods for the concept. The marketing literature shows confusion and contradiction in its understanding of this issue but does take an innovative approach to the subject. It advocates the measurement of future customer lifetime profit potential through two closely linked additional concepts – customer lifetime value (CLV) and customer equity (CE) both of which the management accounting literature largely ignores, perhaps highlighting the accountant's inbuilt conservatism and reluctance to wrestle with these more creative and judgement based measures. A conceptual model is presented as a means to clarify the differences between CP, CLV and CE, and to establish a common "platform of understanding" both within and between the two disciplines in order that further research progress can be made.

Keywords Customer profitability, Customer lifetime value, Customer equity, Management accounting, Marketing, Customer accounting

INTRODUCTION

Customer profitability (CP) assesses the financial value of a customer to the business and hence is a fundamental concept that links accounting and marketing. Many managers appreciate that revenues derive from customers and many costs are directly caused by customers. Whilst this concept is of immediate and apparent relevance to both marketing and management accounting (MA), academics and practitioners recognise that there are widespread differences in interpretation of the concept (Bauer and Hammerschmidt, 2005). In recent years there has been considerable and growing demand for research which develops improved approaches to marketing that encompass more analytical rigour and demonstrate a clearer linkage between marketing performance and business performance (Doyle 2000; Ambler 2003; Ward 2004; Anonymous 2006). Similarly, the emphasis in MA is increasingly on providing effective information for strategic decision-making as well as for reporting performance, for example Kaplan and Cooper (1998) propose the accurate measurement of activity costs combined with the reduction of costs through continuous improvements to enable accountants to *"shift from being the passive reporter of the past to a proactive influencer of the future"* (p.vii). However, Accounting and Marketing are distinct disciplines that are taught separately on undergraduate and postgraduate courses, occupy distinct areas in publishers' lists and have separate professional bodies and their own research journals. Accounting is stereotypically a "hard" subject - focused, analytical and numeric, whilst marketing is "softer", more creative and speculative. These distinctions perhaps reflect the long-running debate about the "two cultures" of science and humanities, which has found general currency since Snow (1998) first coined the term in his famous 1959 Rede lecture. Snow argued that *"a gulf of mutual incomprehension"* (p.4) prevented the two cultures from working together effectively and that the *"clashing point of two subjects [...] ought to produce creative chances"* (p.16). Customer accounting is such a clashing point between marketing and MA.

A clear and common understanding of the CP concept between the two disciplines is a necessary foundation for the successful development of the topic. CP is one of the keys to effective marketing and MA, enabling marketing and MA to address senior management concerns. Therefore, if CP is fundamental to the strategic success of both marketing and MA, not to mention business generally, it is important to establish the extent to which it is *commonly* understood in the literature and the published teaching resources of both disciplines.

The aims of this research are twofold. This paper will firstly examine how this concept is covered in the marketing and MA literature, highlighting the similarities and differences in approach and offer a conceptual shared definition of CP for the two disciplines. Secondly the paper will investigate the extent to which coverage of CP has been established in teaching resources, MA and marketing textbooks and case studies, which will, in time, influence future management practices. The empirical work conducted attempts to establish the level of shared understanding of CP management and the associated methods of customer lifetime value (CLV) forecasting and customer equity (CE) calculation by reviewing marketing and MA textbooks published since Moorman and Rust's (1999) claim that most marketing textbooks fail to systematically explain how marketers should manage financial accountability. It is hoped, that by establishing and agreeing the current state of understanding of the two disciplines in textbooks and journal papers, researchers from both sides can be encouraged to accept a shared definition of CP and become more accurate and consistent in their use of the term. This will create better teaching and understanding of the concept within both disciplines and will also create the opportunity for the development of a more robust conceptual framework on which to base the construction of CP measurement models. It should also provide increased possibilities for constructive collaboration between the two disciplines in both research and teaching. Such collaboration will need to address the many differences in terminology in the literature of the two disciplines. In particular, this paper shows how the marketing literature is often unclear and contradictory in its use of profit or cash flow within CP, CLV and CE and, whilst it does not focus on the detailed calculations beneath these terms, it highlights that this is an important issue for future research.

The rest of the paper is organised as follows. Firstly, the relevant literature from both marketing and MA is reviewed. Secondly, a survey of textbook content and a questionnaire to educators is considered. Thirdly, synergy between the two disciplines is assessed and a conceptual model to clarify the linkages between CP, CLV and CE is suggested. The paper ends by considering limitations, future research and conclusions.

A TALE OF TWO LITERATURES

This section reviews the literature from each discipline in order to identify similarities and differences in approach to CP.

Customer profitability in marketing literature

It is increasingly recognised that it makes sense to target marketing efforts and resources at the most profitable individual customers (Mulhern 1999) by identifying and allocating costs and revenues to each customer, an idea outlined over forty years ago by Sevin (1965). The progression of CP analysis in marketing over those forty years has been slow and, because of limitations in data collection, storage, retrieval, and analysis systems, CP analysis initially focused on groups of customers. Beik and Buzby (1973, p.48) noted that *"by tracing sales revenues to market segments and relating these revenues to marketing costs, the marketing manager can improve and control his decision making with respect to the firm's profit objective."* However, with recent advances in IT systems and flexible database development, the potential for effective CP analysis has grown.

Mulhern (1999, p.26) identified seven different ways that he perceived CP was referred to in the literature namely; lifetime value, customer lifetime value, customer valuation, customer lifetime valuation, customer relationship value, customer equity and customer profitability. The view that CP and CLV might be discrete terms is not obvious from the marketing literature and Mulhern points out that these terms are frequently used interchangeably. Jain and Singh (2002) highlight that, *"In the literature, CLV also appears under other names such as customer equity and customer profitability."* (p.37). Confusion is evident and it serves to compound the error by not recognising them as distinct concepts. This review of marketing literature on CP suggests that marketers eschew definitions of "customer profitability" and focus instead on calculating the profitability dependent "customer lifetime value" and "customer equity" with little or no discrimination between these two latter concepts and that of CP.

An inherent problem is that whilst a considerable number of CLV models have been developed to measure value from individual customers across their entire life cycle for a particular company, there is no consensus on the existence of a single best method of calculation (Jain and Singh 2002). One of the key reasons for this is that there are many variables that marketers might identify that can be omitted from a particular CLV calculation; cross-sales revenue, positive word-of-mouth, and retention/churn rates (Bauer and Hammerschmidt 2005) are three such categories. However, a more fundamental, and perhaps easier to solve problem, is that clarity and consistency of definition of CP and CLV is hard to find.

Marketers have been slow to promote the measurement of individual customer value to the firm. To date, a relatively small, but increasing number of marketing papers have proposed specific models for the measurement of individual customer value to the organisation (Blattberg and Deighton 1996; Berger and Nasr 1998; Pfeifer and Carraway 2000; Niraj, Gupta and Narasimham 2001). The methods proposed and variables measured are inconsistent. The use of historical customer data in marketing calculations of CP analysis is described as common (Blattberg and Deighton 1991, Storbacka 1997, Mulhern 1999 and Jacobs et al. 2001), however, Hoekstra and Huizingh (1999, p.258) declare that; *"lifetime value is a discounted measure for future income,"* and that at the very least its estimation should contain future predictions as well as historical customer data. Here we return to the inconsistency of language. Blattberg and Deighton (1996) propose the measurement of CE as the key criteria to enable firms to find the optimal balance between customer acquisition and retention. They suggest that to measure CE firms need to measure the sum of discounted individual current customer's expected lifetime of contributions to *"offsetting the company's fixed costs"* (p.137-8). The term CE is used to reflect the view that marketing, as Bell et al. (2002, p.77) put it, is seeing *"the beginnings of a focus on viewing the customer as an asset"* and this idea has also been promulgated by Gupta and Lehmann (2003, 2005) and Storbacka (2006).

The majority of marketers who tackle customer valuation focus on CLV *"The general principles of LTV* (lifetime value) *analysis- estimating the discounted benefits (gross profit) less burdens (e.g., account servicing, communication, claims) of customer"* (Dwyer 1997, p.8). CE then would appear to be a summation of CLV across all customers (Blattberg and Deighton 1996). However, it is in implementation of CLV where variation can be identified. Berger and Nasr, (1998) suggest that CLV is the excess of revenues over costs of attracting, selling and servicing (i.e. profit) derived over time, from a customer, however, they create a model to measure CLV that does not include customer acquisition costs or fixed costs. Further, they suggest that; *"The difference between customer equity and CLV is that customer equity takes acquisition cost into consideration."* (Berger and Nasr 1998, p.27). In contrast Bayón et al. (2002), Hogan, Lemon and Rust (2002) and Rust et al. (2004) suggest that CE is the monetary sum of the CLV of all current and future customers, which implicitly suggests that CLV and CE both include an allowance for customer acquisition. Hoekstra and Huizingh (1999, p.258), note that whilst there is generally agreement that lifetime value is future income, discounted to a present value, differences can occur in the specification of income with *"net profit"*, *"contributions to profit"* and *"contributions to overhead and profit"* being used. Additionally, Hoekstra and Huizingh (1999) note that *"lifetime value"* has been used to denote just the future value of new customers and that Blattberg and Deighton (1996) define CE as *"the monetary value of the customer"* (Hoekstra and Huizingh (1999, p.259). However, this assertion that CE is a financial valuation only, is subsequently brought into question by their proposed new definition of LTV; *"the total value of direct contributions (transactions) and indirect contributions (e.g., recommendations, new product ideas) to overhead and profit of an individual customer during the entire customer life cycle, that is from the start of the relationship until its projected ending."* (Hoekstra and Huizingh 1999, p.266). This refined definition is in-line with the views of Jacobs et al. (2001); Stahl et al. (2003) and Mulhern (1999) who suggest that other measures could be added to the concept of individual financial profitability, such as the propensity of the customer to positively influence other customers' perceptions of the organisation.

Jain and Singh (2002) attempt to bring some clarity by providing a categorisation of what they see as the three main areas of CLV research; (i) research developing models to measure CLV, incorporating revenue streams from customers set against customer acquisition and retention costs and "other" marketing costs; (ii) *"customer base analysis"* which involves analysis of customer information and calculation of probabilities of future transactions and (iii) the managerial implications of CLV in terms of effects on profitability and customer loyalty schemes. Pfeifer et al. (2005) highlight the confusion and frequent interchanging of CLV and CP and refer to Mulhern's (1999) identification of seven terms in the marketing literature for CP as a cause for concern, but do not delineate CE as a distinct term. Pfeifer et al. (2005) also highlight the problem of customer value or net present value of revenue streams from a customer over their lifetime being misinterpreted as customer profit.

In the face of potential misinterpretation within marketing, simple but flexibly interpreted definitions are desirable. Pfeifer et al. (2005) suggest that CP is simply: *"the difference between the revenues earned from and the costs associated with the customer relationship during a specified period."* (p.14), and that CLV is *"the present value of the future cash flows attributed to the customer relationship."* (p.17). However, we also find that CLV is *"the present value of all current and future profits generated from a customer over the life of his or her business with the firm."* (Gupta and Lehmann 2005, p.15). Here CLV is calculated as the forecasted net present value of the profits from a single customer over the rest of their lifetime with the company. Finally, it should be noted that the management of CE is seen by marketers as the key business driver of shareholder value (Bayón et al. 2002; Stahl et al. 2003) because *"the combined lifetime values of all current and future customers yield the value of the customer base (CE) which represents the entire operating cash flow of a firm"* (Bauer and Hammerschmidt 2005, p.332). Given the areas of disparity in the marketing literature in calculating CP, CLV and CE, there should be some concern both over the level and complexity of CP content in marketing textbooks widely used by students and managers.

The marketing literature also contains a few examples of the application of CP analysis to operational marketing such as Reinartz and Kumar (2000, 2002) who link CP in broad terms to customer loyalty, as do van Raiij et al. (2003) and more recently Wang and Hong (2006). Additionally, Reinartz et al. (2005) provide more general guidance in relation to using CP to balance appropriate levels of specific marketing activities such as customer acquisition and retention.

Customer profitability in management accounting literature

The task of providing information to management is that of the management accountant, rather than the financial accountant who is focused on external reporting to shareholders. Despite the rising importance of the Operating and Financial Review in company's annual accounts and customer satisfaction being one of the most common measure included in such a statement (Ittner and Larckner 1998), CP is primarily the concern of management accountancy and that is the literature we will concentrate on here.

Johnson and Kaplan (1987) tell a story of MA having lost its way after becoming subordinate to financial accounting some 50 years before. They explain that it stopped developing and changing in response to both management needs and an increasingly dynamic competitive environment. This book increased interest in the idea that MA was not just about providing managers with internal information, but also appropriate external information to inform decision making. Part of Johnson and Kaplan's story was that as approaches to business had changed, partly shown by the progress of marketing (Kotler 2003), MA had not. Kotler (2003) presents a timeline of marketing development from production and product focus to one of customer focus, whereas MA has always had a primary focus on product costing and profitability, not customer costing and profitability. If MA had since become dynamic and responsive, then one might assume CP would have achieved at least equal prominence in the literature alongside the traditional primary cost focus, the product.

However, there has been very limited CP focus within the MA literature until the last decade. Shields (1997) found no articles on CP in MA papers in major accounting journals in his seven-year survey. One might question whether academic journals are the place to look for latest practice, as surveys of the use of MA techniques find the use of CP by practitioners to be common (for example Innes and Mitchell (1995), Innes et al. (2000), Roslender and Hart (2003)). However, such surveys do not make clear how sophisticated the calculations of CP might be and the last survey, a more detailed look at a small number of companies, found more desire than achievement.

This picture of at best, slow change belies some notable work on CP. As long ago as 1955 Longman and Schiff wrote that analysis of selling and marketing costs can "...make possible computation of the costs and profits resulting from sales to individual customers. The customers may then be grouped to show cost and profit by district, route, class of trade, retail versus wholesale accounts, or by other customer classifications," (Longman and Schiff 1955, p. 181). Moreover, Sevin (1965) suggested that some customers actually lost money for the firm and that this loss needs to be calculated, and yet such ideas remained effectively dormant in the literature for many years.

Simmonds (1981; 1982) sparked interest in the need for the management accountant to get their hands dirty with analysing the environment and this led to a stream of literature generally referred to as strategic management accounting (SMA). Wilson (1990) took up the challenge and advocated the use of strategic cost analysis to measure relative competitive position and this involved not only measuring the firm's own cost of differentiation but also assessing the costs of competitors. One key theme that emerged was CP with Bellis-Jones (1989); Howell and Soucy (1990) and Ward (1992) highlighting the importance of CP, though Ward preferred the term customer account profitability to CP. Ward (1992) emphasised ranking the profitability of customers above the need to work out actual profitability as he considered that there were too many common costs. In the US the term SMA is not used, but Shank and Govindarajan (1989 and 1993) coined the phrases strategic cost analysis and strategic cost management focusing their attention on the need to have cost information presented in a way that could be used strategically.

A major development in MA was the rise of activity based costing (ABC), a method made practical by a dramatic reduction in computation costs. Smith (1993), recognising the need to focus on important strategic considerations, considered that ABC and total quality management (TQM) stressed product profitability when a more appropriate focus would be CP. Smith and Dikolli (1995) emphasised the potential usefulness of ABC in measuring CP and a significant proportion of the customer-related MA literature focuses on how ABC can be enhanced to provide CP as well as product profitability. This is in part because management accountants have traditionally focussed on product costs using complex costing systems to arrive at "factory gate" product costs and have paid little attention to the selling, general and administration (SG&A) costs. ABC can potentially be used to address CP by analysing SG&A costs according to factors thought to drive them, for example the number of orders or the distribution channel.

This approach is explained in Kaplan and Cooper (1998), where they emphasise customer costing over product costing and use the Kanthal case in which a large proportion of the customers were found to be unprofitable. Kaplan and Cooper (1998) should also be seen as a part of the balanced scorecard (BSC) literature, which develops a broader view of information and control than just the traditional financial focus. The BSC has had a customer perspective from the beginning (Kaplan and Norton 1992), and the concern for CP was explicitly included in 1996 (Kaplan and Norton 1996).

The growing importance of the services sector and the need to develop MA systems and measures that fit with this environment has also been important in the development of the literature. Of particular note here is case study based material and industry focused research, the financial services sector being particularly to the fore (Weiner 1995, Hudson 1994, Raihall and Hrechak 1994 and O'Sullivan 1997 would be early references for this sector). This highlights a key feature of good MA, that it is contingent on circumstances, hence it is logical that more progress might be made on fine tuning techniques when one industry alone is considered. According to Kaplan and Narayanan (2001), in service companies it is often the customer that determines the demand on the firm's operating activities and they describe how ABC-based CP can prompt actions to transform unprofitable customers to profitable ones, with three categories of action: process improvement, pricing decisions and relationship management.

Foster et al. (1996) find it a paradox that "... *most management accounting systems focus not on the customer, but on products, departments or geographic regions*" and claim that "*only rarely can a management accounting system produce customer profitability figures,*" (p.5). They develop a series of challenges facing the management accountant in developing CP information, these include good customer cost analysis and, without actual mention of CLV, the need for modelling longer time frames. The terms CE and CLV make few appearances in the MA literature and it would seem that working out a customer's profitability for a single period is a sufficiently daunting task. Guilding and McManus (2002) refer to the fledgling literature in customer accounting and seek to find evidence of different levels of customer accounting within top Australian firms. They found that over half the companies undertook some form of CP, by individual firm and by segment, but a much lower proportion used CLV or assessed customers as assets, a CE approach. With large samples it is difficult to ascertain the quality and depth of work the companies were doing, but a further question revealed managers to perceive the approaches to have more merit than their current use suggested. They also found some evidence that the use of customer accounting techniques was contingent on the level of competition in the industry and, not surprisingly, on the market orientation of the company. One factor in the seeming reluctance to adopt longer-term metrics might be the accountant's inbuilt conservatism that makes him or her draw back from more creative and judgement-based measures.

TEXTBOOK SURVEY

Having reviewed the varied coverage of CP as an overlapping issue in the accounting and marketing literature it is important to understand the extent to which such issues are represented in the teaching of the two subjects. In order to investigate the usage of different terms in accounting and marketing and the extent to which key terms are covered in the curriculum of undergraduate and postgraduate-level courses, accounting and marketing textbooks were examined. Textbook content is analysed for two reasons. Firstly it acts as a proxy for what is actually taught to business students, providing more depth of detail than lecture titles or indeed outlines. In light of the problems of circumventing access issues or actually attending multiple business course modules at multiple locations or analysing large volumes of course notes, this method provides an easily accessible and practical route to accessing in depth data on the curricula on which many marketing or MA modules are based. Secondly, textbooks provide a bridge between research and teaching, in that textbooks are based on the core understanding and knowledge within a research discipline. The research was planned to investigate the degree of consistency between researched and taught knowledge on CP in both disciplines. Today's students are the business managers of tomorrow, therefore it is important that there is rapid transfer of leading research on CP into the classroom. A small sample survey of academics involved in teaching MBAs was conducted to check whether classroom content matched textbook content.

Two research questions were therefore investigated:

RQ1) How frequently is CP covered in marketing textbooks?

RQ2) How frequently is CP covered in management accounting textbooks?

Marketing texts

The literature review of CP in the context of marketing has led us to identify three key concepts of relevance: CP, CLV and CE. In order to investigate RQ1, thirty-eight core-marketing textbooks, including UK, US and International editions, were identified and a sample of twenty-two analysed, varying in size from approximately 350 to over 1000 pages. The overall sample selected was based on availability from bookshops and university libraries. We define "core-marketing" as being focused on the whole of the general subject of marketing and not focused on a particular area or niche. Given the comparative infancy of CP in the marketing literature we only identified textbooks with editions published post-2000, thus deliberately analysing those published since Moorman and Rust's (1999) criticism of the lack of financial instruction in such textbooks. Whilst most textbooks have associated support materials, the research focuses only on the actual textbook content. Surprisingly, perhaps rather ironically, most of the books were reticent about explicitly identifying their target market, but they are all clearly aimed at undergraduate or postgraduate students and sometimes also practitioners. From the original population of 38 textbooks any that were aimed at students below undergraduate level were deliberately excluded leaving twenty-two books to be analysed all containing the word 'Marketing' in the title. Nine also contained the word 'Principles' or 'Management' and 'Practice/Practices' occurred in four titles each. 'Introduction' appeared in a further three titles while 'Essentials' and 'Strategies/Strategy' both appeared twice, although when identifying the population of thirty-eight books, 'Strategy' (rather than 'Marketing') focused textbooks were avoided. A full list of the sample analysed is available from the lead author.

The index, glossary, table of contents and key topic chapters (such as those dealing with profitability, segmentation, customer relationships/management) of these marketing textbooks were reviewed to check for the presence of the three key concepts identified above.

Management accounting texts

In order to investigate RQ2, core-MA textbooks, including UK, US and International editions, were identified and a sample of eighteen analysed, varying from approximately 350 to over 1100 pages. In a similar manner to the selection of the marketing texts, 'core-MA' is defined as being focused on the whole of the general subject of MA and not focused on a particular area or niche. For comparability only textbooks with editions published post-2000 were identified. The sample was based on ease of availability from bookshops and university libraries and the research focuses only on the textbooks (not any associated support materials). All the textbooks were clearly aimed at undergraduate or postgraduate students and sometimes also practitioners. Seventeen of the books analysed contained the words "management accounting" or "managerial accounting" in the title with one, Zimmerman (2003) entitled *Accounting for decision making and control*. The index, glossary, table of contents and key topic chapters and sections (such as those dealing with cost management, activity based costing, strategic cost accounting or management and strategic management accounting) of these MA textbooks were reviewed to check for content on CP, CLV and CE, including content on these areas under different titles. Again, a full list of the sample analysed is available from the lead author.

Results - marketing texts

As Table 1 shows only 7 (32%) of the marketing textbooks reviewed included 'customer profitability' in the index/glossary, table of contents or key topic chapters, 8 (36%) referred to 'customer equity' whilst 12 (55%) included the term "customer lifetime value". This higher figure for CLV is perhaps unsurprising given the relative popularity of this term in the marketing literature compared to the other two terms. However, the relative frequency of occurrence of all the terms is disappointingly low given the importance given to CP in the literature. One author, however, is consistently using CP terms and the percentage results would be considerably worse if the seven books co-authored or authored by Philip Kotler were removed from the sample, (falling to 6% for CE and CP and 31% for CLV).

TABLE 1 CP related text strings in marketing and management accounting textbooks

		Marketing textbooks				Management Accounting textbooks	
		Including Kotler texts		Excluding Kotler texts			
Number of books in survey:		22	100%	15	100%	18	100%
Number of texts indexing	Customer equity	8	36%	1	6%	0	0%
	Customer lifetime value	12	55%	5	31%	0	0%
	Customer profitability	7	32%	1	6%	7	39%

Results - management accounting texts

CP, Customer Profitability Analysis or equivalent was indexed or mentioned in the glossary or contents pages of only 7 (39%) of the MA textbooks and in a number of these texts, the content referred to by the index was very brief. In none of the sample texts was specific mention of CLV or equivalent found and given that CE is the summation of CLV for all customers it is perhaps unsurprising that it was also not mentioned. The two texts with most CP related content were Atkinson et al. (2004) and Langfield-Smith et al. (2003) both with 6 relevant pages referenced. Atkinson et al. (2004) prefer the term customer profitability measurement (CPM) and suggest that companies with market-oriented strategies should use ABC techniques to fully understand the cost of selling to or serving different customer segments. Langfield-Smith et al. (2003) use the term customer profitability analysis (CPA) and also advocate the use of ABC methodology, stressing that CPA can provide a different perspective on business profitability. They relate CPA to CRM but highlight the need to consider product life-cycles (not customer life cycles) and dismiss the identification of individual customer profitability as impractical unless there are only a few customers.

Comparing accounting and marketing textbooks

The fact that CP is covered in both the marketing and MA literature provides prima facie evidence that CP is an area where strong synergy between accounting and marketing would be expected. A key variation between marketing and accounting textbooks was found to be the coverage, or absence of coverage, of CLV and CE. Whilst none of the sampled MA texts indexed CLV or included it in their contents pages, Drury (2004) suggests the use of life-cycle profitability analysis to decide whether to retain or drop customers but gives no detailed explanation of how this is done and does not use the term CLV. A few other texts do discuss lifecycle costing, but what they describe is firmly based on products rather than customers.

Figure 1 summarises the findings for the three terms across both sets of textbooks. Within the marketing textbooks CLV was used considerably more frequently than "customer profitability". This perhaps highlights marketers' focus on long-term,

FIGURE 1 Comparison of key search term occurrences in management accountancy and marketing textbooks.

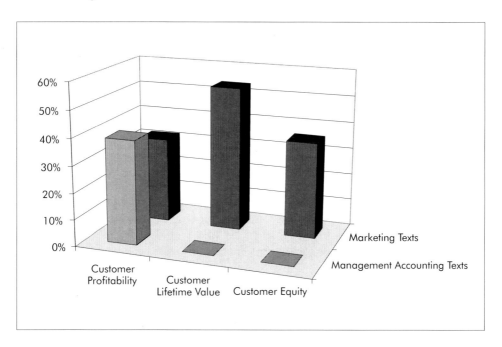

future value for the business compared to accountants who are traditionally accused of having a rather shorter-term financial focus or are, as we suggested earlier, unwilling to grapple with the more creative and judgement-based measures.

Survey evidence

An Internet based survey of MBA teaching at 20 leading UK business schools showed that whilst most had an obligatory full core marketing course most did not have a full, compulsory core course titled management accounting; instead they included MA content in an initial compulsory accounting module alongside financial accounting. Questionnaires were sent to a convenience sample of marketing and MA academics involved in teaching MBA modules at these schools to find further evidence on the depth of coverage of CP techniques. The marketing returns included a range of responses with CP being the most likely to be taught, or at least mentioned. CLV might also be introduced as a general concept, but CE was not mentioned. There was a general view that textbooks should include more CP content. One marketing academic commented:

> More needs to be covered on the inter-link between marketing and finance in general. Both are lateral functions, integrating managerial functions across boundaries. They are ironically seen as antagonistic extremes; marketing as fluffy, finance as hard-nosed but with no relationship with managerial demands. Both of these views are caricatures.

Another marketing academic commented that:

> It would be useful to see these concepts (CP, CLV and CE) addressed in accounting

modules, although the two perspectives often sit uneasily because of differences of opinion in terms of cost allocation.

The MA questionnaires also revealed a variety of coverage with some courses not mentioning CP at all, and most only briefly mentioning the concept. CLV was not mentioned in most courses and CE was not included in any. Again there was a desire for more customer-focused content in mainstream textbooks. One MA academic raised a concern that;

> *Management Accounting is becoming a crowded teaching area with more and more things being included in isolation. This is reflective of a course/area that is suffering too much from 'add-ons' and greatly in need of a review of what is its core and has that core moved/transformed in the past two decades.*

These two small surveys provide evidence that the low level of coverage of CP in the textbooks is reflected in what is actually taught. There was no evidence that either group of academics viewed CP as a topic that should belong only to the other discipline and some encouragement that the inter-linking of marketing and MA should be more specifically covered.

SYNERGY BETWEEN MARKETING AND MANAGEMENT ACCOUNTING

Crittenden and Wilson (2006) found that the use of cross-functional teaching was limited on US undergraduate courses. Our results support their findings, suggesting that coverage of the financial value of customers in general marketing and accounting texts is limited and that there is perhaps a need for writers from both disciplines to work together and produce joint research and textbooks focusing on customers' financial value to the firm as a core concept of business management. One explanation may be that CP is taught as a specialist elective topic, (although we found no evidence of this) but this does suggest that the majority of marketing or management accounting students are able to graduate without gaining grounding in CP; a topic that the authors believe should play a key role in the strategic development of both disciplines. This paper has primarily focused on CP within the accounting and marketing literature and textbooks. It is clear that when marketers talk about CP and CLV they are utilising two basic accounting concepts – the periodic income statement which reconciles revenues and costs into a single account in order to calculate profit or loss for an accounting period, typically one year, and the net present value calculation which discounts future years into a single present value. However, whilst the concepts are complementary, the actual usage of the term *CP* varies considerably and, especially in the marketing literature, there are additional terms, which can become blurred with CP including the terms CLV and CE which should have very specific meanings. There is also some vague or confused use of costing terms in the marketing literature where collaboration with MA specialists should lead to greater clarity.

Representing the financial value of customers to a firm

As previously discussed, Pfeifer et al. (2005) define CP as *"the difference between the revenues earned from and the costs associated with the customer relationship during a specified period*" (p.14) and CLV as "*the present value of the future cash flows attributed to the customer relationship*" (p.17) and hence make clear the linkages between the key concepts of CP and CLV. Pfeifer et al. (2005) also recognise that many authors define or use CLV as a discounted measure of future customer profit flows. If we use this definition for CLV (e.g. Gupta and Lehmann 2005), it should be noticed that CP is in fact a special case of CLV – with the lifetime period set at one accounting year[1] (with no discounting therefore applied and with some care taken with the distinction between cash flow and profit).

Pfeifer et al. (2005) do not identify CE as a separate term but Rust et al. (2004, p110) defined CE as "*the total of the discounted lifetime values summed over all of the firm's current and potential customers*" This was acknowledged as being consistent with Blattberg and Deighton (1996) but also allows for the possibility of new customers (Bayón et al. 2002; Hogan, Lemon, and Libai 2002; Bauer and Hammerschmidt 2005). Thus it is possible to provide clear definitions of CP, CLV and CE which are robust, self-consistent and which recognise their inter-relation.

If, as is proposed in this paper, CP can be considered, with some adjustments, equivalent to the CLV over a period of one accounting year, it is possible to see the inter-relation of these two terms. Since CE is defined as the sum of all current and future customers' lifetime values, we can clearly link CE with CLV by adding the NPV of future customers to the sum of the individual CLVs of all existing customers. Hence we have now clarified how these three concepts may be linked together. The key distinctions between these three parameters, which all measure customer value, relate either to the timescales being analysed (and hence the need for discounting or not) or to whether the analysis is for one or all of the customers. Answering one very simple question will assist with the construction of a profound and fully coherent model: what is the sum of all customers' individual customer profitability? The answer to this question, whilst perhaps self-evident, is that the sum of the profitability of each individual customer is the total profit generated in the period by all customers. If we consider this to be the total annual operating profit of the business (where operating profit ignores income from investments and other financial instruments) then we can complete a model (Figure 2) showing how all of these key concepts inter-relate. This may not only be used for teaching purposes, in order to clarify the differences between these concepts and to show their inter-linkage, but could also be used in the development of future CP research to ensure clarity of the interrelationships between the concepts.

Thus four concepts – CP, CLV, total annual operating profit and CE can be related diagrammatically in a two by two matrix which delineates one customer from all customers and one accounting period from all future accounting periods. The following definitions could be adopted, but may need some care over the less tangible aspects of value in the customer relationship and consideration of whether talking of future profits or cash flows:

- Customer profitability is: "*the difference between the revenues earned from and the costs associated with the customer relationship during a specified period.*" (Pfeifer et al. 2005 p.14). In the case of Figure 2, this term is set at one accounting period (usually a year) and all costs have been allocated or traced to customers.

---

[1] This assumption of a one-year accounting period is for demonstration purposes only; it is accepted that for some industries the purchase cycle that should be measured is not one year (Reichheld 1996) and in MA one could measure CP by month, quarter, half year and/or year.

FIGURE 2 The inter-relation of customer profitability, customer lifetime value, customer equity and period operating profit

	Current accounting period, e.g. one year	All future accounting periods (NPV basis)
All customers	PERIOD OPERATING PROFIT	CUSTOMER EQUITY
A single customer	CUSTOMER PROFITABILITY	CUSTOMER LIFETIME VALUE

- CLV is *"the present value of all current and future profits generated from a customer over the life of his or her business with the firm."* (Gupta and Lehmann 2005 p.15). Thus CLV is calculated as the forecasted net present value of the profits from a single customer over the rest of their lifetime with the company. (This is distinct from another definition of CLV which is *"the present value of the future cash flows attributed to the customer relationship."* (Pfeifer et al. 2005 p.17).

- CE is *"the combined lifetime values of all current and future customers"* (Bayón et al. 2002, p.213). Thus CE is the sum of all customers' lifetime values. (Clearly since CE is frequently defined in terms of CLV and there are two main distinct definitions of CLV, there is the potential for two different definitions of CE).

- Annual operating profit is the sum of the customer profitability from all customers the firm has served within a single accounting year, (again with all costs having been traced to customers).

It should be noted for consistency and to promote further synergy in future research that the sum of earnings for all customers for all future accounting periods (with appropriate discounting) could also be equated to the enterprise value of the business, a thesis first put forward by Williams (1938) with methods still used to the present day.

LIMITATIONS AND FUTURE RESEARCH

There is a need for marketers and accountants to search for further synergies between the two disciplines. The results discussed here suggest that coverage of the financial value of customers in marketing and MA texts is limited and that there is perhaps a need for writers from both disciplines to come together and produce joint work which focuses on customers' financial value to the firm as a core concept of business management.

This research focuses on 'traditional' core or basic marketing and MA textbooks. However, marketing is changing and the interface between marketing and strategy is becoming more blurred. Further research should consider marketing strategy textbooks. For example, Wilson and Gilligan, (2005), have written a strategic marketing textbook which shows the benefits of a textbook written by authors who, between them, have extensive expertise of both marketing and accounting.

This research has used textbook content as a proxy measure to gauge what CP content is being taught to management students. Further research could focus on reviewing the syllabi of business school marketing and accounting courses more directly. Finally, the confusion and variation in the literature suggests a need for a detailed, full and comprehensive review of the accounting and marketing literature at the intersection of CP and CP related issues. One issue that needs to be addressed by such a review is that of calculation. The calculations behind the terms CP, CLV and CE need further clarification not only in terms of calculation of customer acquisition costs, for example, but also on the use of profit or cash-based numbers. The marketing literature suggests, from an accountant's perspective, a lack of understanding and clear use of such terms, whilst much of the management accounting literature fails to ask what it is that marketing actually wishes to measure.

The model developed from this research, and shown in Figure 2, presents a simplified view of the inter-relation between the key concepts (CP, CLV, CE and period operating profit) but masks a plethora of complex questions. In particular what is the appropriate treatment of customer acquisition costs? Whilst these are assumed to be traceable to existing customers, CLV would need to exclude sunk customer acquisition costs occurring in prior years. Another question would be whether all costs can be allocated or traced to individual customers - the treatment of research and development costs will be a particular problem here. This also raises the question of how CP should deal with 'business-sustaining' costs. Further questions include; should CLV be measured on a profit or cash flow basis; how does CLV deal with predicting customer lifetime; how does CE deal with the addition of future customers and how should the intangible value of customers (e.g. word of mouth) be taken into account?

Once these questions have been researched, there are other questions that need to be considered including which sectors and industries are most suited to the use of CP and what strategic and tactical actions can be taken as a result of calculating CP? Some of these have been partially answered in the literature, often by case analysis, but frequently without a complete and consistent recognition of CP, CLV and CE.

CONCLUSIONS

In this paper we have highlighted a growing interest in providing more effective links between marketing activity and bottom line performance, the need for more relevant management accounting information and that areas of business activity can be identified that are of interest from both an accounting and marketing perspective. Whilst we find that scope for synergy should exist between marketing and MA approaches to Customer Accounting (CA), our review of both marketing and MA texts shows a disappointingly low level of content which is not surprisingly reflected in the low level of CA coverage in MBA teaching. Of particular significance is the disturbing absence of coverage of CLV and CE in mainstream MA texts. MBA teachers appear to recognise that CP is a concept of importance in both marketing and MA, but find little space for detailed coverage, whilst CLV and CE are hardly covered at all.

At present there are differences in the research literature of and between both disciplines about the definition and approach to CP, CLV and CE. This lack of a consistent approach is restricting knowledge development and it is hoped that this paper will facilitate synergy between the two disciplines by promoting debate on the use of common definitions and terminology and a greater understanding of the detailed approaches and provisos that each discipline brings to this subject.

There is also some concern from survey evidence that companies are more interested in CP as a concept and for making strategic decisions than the researchers and teachers of either discipline. This could mean that graduates and postgraduates are ill-equipped to address the needs of the organisations that recruited them and will lead to a further continuation of the problems caused by this lack of a consistent approach. It also means managers already in place are less able to interact with a common language and understanding. The seemingly silo-like mentality of the two professions needs to end for both to move forward with value relevance. Unless both the marketing and MA communities correct this as a matter of urgency the professions run the risk of failing to deliver what their customers, students in the case of academics and senior management in the case of practitioners, have a right to expect. There is therefore considerable scope for future research in order to define common concepts and calculative techniques. This should recognise the potential for synergy - marketing brings an understanding of the supplier-customer interface, whilst MA offers tools to evaluate strategic options and the potential for integrating marketing information and costs with those of the rest of the organisation.

MA typically treats CP as an extension to ABC, adding additional cost elements driven by the customer relationship. Marketing has introduced two extended concepts related to CP, namely CLV and CE, and prefers to look strategically to the future whilst perhaps not fully recognising the scope, limitations and complexity of CP itself. In addition, Marketing has given rise to two different versions of CLV – one based on discounted future profits from the customer, the other based on discounted future cash flows. Since CE is usually defined on the basis of CLV this means that there are also at least two different possible definitions for CE. Marketing therefore requires the input of MA to shore-up and clarify these issues. The conceptual model in Figure 2 is put forward as a means to clarify the differences between CP, CLV and CE and to establish a common 'platform of understanding' both within and between the two disciplines in order to provide a tool for teaching and as a stepping-stone for future research.

ACKNOWLEDGEMENTS

The authors would like to acknowledge the help and constructive input of two anonymous referees and the editors' comments in refining and developing previous drafts of this paper.

REFERENCES

Ambler, Tim. (2003), *Marketing and the Bottom Line*, 2nd edition, Harlow: FT Prentice Hall, Pearson Education Limited.

Anonymous (2006), *"Hard-Edged Marketing,"* (online), Berkshire: Chartered Institute of Marketing. Available at: http://www.shapetheagenda.com/ins/agendas.cfm?choice=HEM (Accessed 31/01/2007).

Atkinson, A., et al. (2004), *Management Accounting*, 4th edition, New Jersey: Pearson Education.

Bauer, H. and Hammerschmidt, M. (2005), "Customer-Based Corporate Valuation: Integrating the Concepts of Customer Equity and Shareholder Value", *Management Decision*, Vol. 43, No.3, pp. 331-348.

Bayón, T., Gutsche, J. and Bauer, H. (2002), "Customer Equity Marketing: Touching the Intangible", *European Management Journal*, Vol. 20, No.3, pp. 213-222.

Beik, Leland, L., and Buzby, Stephen, L. (1973), "Profitability Analysis by Market Segments", *Journal of Marketing*, Vol. 37, pp. 48-59.

Bell D., Deighton J., Reinartz W. J., Rust R. T. and Swartz G. (2002), "Seven Barriers to Customer Equity Management", *Journal of Service Research*, Volume 5, No. 1, pp. 77-85.

Bellis-Jones, R. (1989), "Customer Profitability Analysis", *Management Accounting (UK)*, Vol. 67, No.2, pp. 26-28.

Berger, P. D. and Nasr, N. I. (1998), "Customer Lifetime Value: Marketing Models and Applications", *Journal of Interactive Marketing*, Vol. 12, No. 1, Winter, pp. 17-30.

Blattberg, R. A. and Deighton, J. (1991), "Interactive Marketing: Exploiting the Age of Addressability", *Sloan Management Review*, Vol. 33, No. 1, Fall, p. 5-14.

Blattberg, R.A. and Deighton, J. (1996), "Manage Marketing by the Customer Equity Test", *Harvard Business Review*, Vol. 74, No.4, July-August, p. 136-144.

Crittenden, V. and Wilson, E. (2006), "An Exploratory Study of Cross-Functional Education in the Undergraduate Marketing Curriculum", *Journal of Marketing Education*, Vol. 28, No.1, April, pp. 81-86.

Doyle, P. (2000), *Value-Based Marketing*, Chichester, UK: John Wiley and Sons Ltd.

Drury, C. (2004), *Management and Cost Accounting*, 6th edition, London: Thomson Learning.

Dwyer, F. R. (1997), "Customer Lifetime Valuation to Support Marketing Decision Making", *Journal of Direct Marketing*, Vol. 11, No. 4, Fall, pp. 6-13.

Foster, G., Gupta, M. and Sjoblom, L. (1996), "Customer Profitability Analysis: Challenges and New Directions", *Journal of Cost Management*, Vol. 10, No. 1, pp. 5–17.

Guilding, C. and McManus, L. (2002), "The Incidence, Perceived Merit and Antecedents of Customer Accounting: An Exploratory Note." *Accounting, Organisations and Society*, Vol. 27, No. 2, pp. 45 -59.

Gupta S and Lehmann D. R. (2005), *Managing Customers as Investments: The Strategic Value of Customers in the Long Run*, Upper Saddle River, NJ: Wharton School Publishing, Pearson Education, Inc.

Gupta S. and Lehmann D. R. (2003), "Customers as Assets", *Journal of Interactive Marketing*, Vol. 17, No. 1, pp. 9-24.

Hoekstra, J. C. and Huizingh, E. K. R. E. (1999), "The lifetime value concept in customer-based marketing", *Journal of Market Focused Management*, Vol. 3, No. 3, pp. 257-74.

Hogan, J. E., Lemon, K. N. and Libai, B. (2002), "Quantifying the ripple: word of mouth and advertising effectiveness", *Journal of Advertising Research*, Vol. 44, No. 3, pp. 271-280.

Hogan, J. E., Lemon, K. N. and Rust, R. T. (2002), "Customer Equity Management: Charting New Directions for the Future of Marketing", *Journal of Service Research*, Vol. 5, No. 1, August, pp. 4-12.

Howell, R. A. and Soucy, S. R. (1990), "Customer Profitability: As Critical As Product Profitability", *Management Accounting*, Vol. 72, No. 4, October, pp. 43–47.

Hudson, P. (1994), "Big Banks Focus on Customers, Too." *Bank Marketing*, Vol.26, No.11, p.60.

Innes, J., Mitchell, F. and Sinclair, D. (2000), "Activity based costing in the UK's largest companies: a comparison of 1994 and 1999 survey results", *Management Accounting research*, Vol. 11, No. 3, pp. 348-362.

Innes, J. and Mitchell, F. (1995), "A survey of activity based costing in the UK's largest companies", *Management Accounting Research*, Vol. 6, No. 2, pp. 137-153.

Ittner, C. D. and Larcker, D. F. (1998), "Are Nonfinancial Measures Leading Indicators of Financial Performance? An Analysis of Customer Satisfaction", *Journal of Accounting Research*, Vol. 36, Supplement, pp. 1-46.

Jacobs, F., Johnston, W. and Kotchetova, N. (2001), "Customer Profitability: Prospective vs. Retrospective Approaches in a Business-to-Business Setting", *Industrial Marketing Management*, Vol. 30, No. 4, pp. 353-363.

Jain, D. and Singh, S. (2002), "Customer Lifetime Value Research in Marketing: A Review and Future Directions", *Journal of Interactive Marketing*, Vol. 16, No.2, pp. 34-46.

Johnson, H. T. and Kaplan, R. S. (1987), *Relevance Lost: The rise and fall of management accounting*, Boston, Mass: Harvard Business School Press.

Kaplan, R. S. and Cooper, R. (1998), *Cost and Effect: Using Integrated Cost Systems to Drive Profitability and Performance*, Boston: Harvard Business School Press

Kaplan, R. S. and Norton, D. P. (1992), "The Balanced Scorecard – Measures That Drive Performance", *Harvard Business Review*, Vol. 70, No. 1, pp. 71–79.

Kaplan, R. S. and Norton, D. P. (1996), *The Balanced Scorecard: Translating Strategy into Action*, Boston, M.A. Harvard Business School Press.

Kaplan, R. S. and Narayanan, V. G. (2001), "Measuring and managing customer profitability", *Journal of Cost Management*, Vol. 15, No. 5, September/October 2001, pp. 5-15.

Kotler, P. (2003), *Marketing Management, International Edition*, 11th edition, Upper Saddle River, New Jersey: Prentice Hall, Pearson Education International.

Langfield-Smith, K. et al. (2003), *Management accounting an Australian perspective*, 3rd edition, Australia: McGraw-Hill.

Longman, D .R. and Schiff, M. (1955), *Practical Distribution Cost Analysis*, Homewood, Il.: Richard D. Irwin,

Moorman, C. and Rust, R. T. (1999), "The Role of Marketing", *Journal of Marketing*, Vol. 63, (Special Issue), pp. 180-197.

Mulhern, F.J. (1999), "Customer Profitability Analysis: Measurement, Concentration and Research Directions", *Journal of Interactive Marketing*, Vol. 13, No.1, Winter, pp. 25-40.

Niraj, R., Gupta, M. and Narasimhan, C. (2001), "Customer profitability in a supply chain", *Journal of Marketing*, Vol. 65, No. 3, pp. 1-16.

O'Sullivan, O. (1997), "Some of Your Customers Are Unprofitable. OK, Now What?", *ABA Banking Journal*, Vol. 89, No. 11, pp. 42-46 and 93.

Pfeifer, P. E., and Carraway, R. L. (2000), "Modelling Customer Relationships as Markov Chains", *Journal of Interactive Marketing*, Vol. 14, No. 2, Spring, pp. 43-55.

Pfeifer, P. E., Haskins, M. E. and Conroy, R. M. (2005), "Customer Lifetime Value, Customer Profitability, and the Treatment of Acquisition Spending", *Journal of Managerial Issues*, Vol. 17, No. 1, pp. 11-25.

Reichheld, F. F., (1996), *The Loyalty Effect*, Boston: Harvard Business School Press.

Raihall, D. and Hrechak, A. (1994), "Improving Financial Institution Performance Through Overhead Cost Management", *The Journal of Bank Cost and Management Accounting*, Vol.7, No.1, p. 44.

Reinartz W. J. and Kumar V., (2000), "On the Profitability of Long-Life Customers in a Noncontractual Setting: An Empirical Investigation and Implications for Marketing", *Journal of Marketing*, Vol. 64, No. 4, pp.17-35

Reinartz W. J. and Kumar V., (2002), "The Mismanagement of Customer Loyalty.", *Harvard Business Review*, Vol. 80, No. 7, July, pp.86-94.

Reinartz W. J., Thomas J. S. and Kumar V. (2005), "Balancing Acquisition and Retention Resources to Maximize Customer Profitability", *Journal of Marketing*, Vol. **69**, No. 1, pp. 63-79.

Roslender, R. and. Hart, S. J. (2003), "In Search of Strategic Management Accounting: Theoretical and Field Study Perspectives", *Management Accounting Research*, Vol. **14**, No. 3, pp. 255-279.

Rust R. T., Lemon K. N. and Zeithaml V. A. (2004), "Return on Marketing: Using Customer Equity to Focus Marketing Strategy", *Journal of Marketing*, Vol. **68**, No. 1, January, pp. 109–127.

Sevin, C. H. (1965), *Marketing Productivity Analysis*, McGraw-Hill, New York.

Shank, J. K. and Govindarajan, V. (1989), *Strategic Cost Analysis,* Homewood, Illinois: Irwin Inc.

Shank, J. K. and Govindarajan, V. (1993), *Strategic Cost Management: the New Tool for Competitive Advantage*, New York: Free Press.

Shields, M. D. (1997), "Research in Management Accounting by North Americans in the 1990's", *Journal of Management Accounting Research*, Vol. **9**, pp. 3-61.

Simmonds, K. (1981), "Strategic Management Accounting", *Management Accounting,* Vol. **59**, No. 4, pp. 26-29.

Simmonds, K. (1982), "Strategic Management Accounting for Pricing", *Accounting and Business Research,* Vol. **12**, No. 47, pp. 206-214

Smith, M. (1993), "Customer profitability analysis revisited", *Management accounting (UK)*, Vol. **71**, No. 8, pp. 26-28.

Smith, M. and Dikolli, S. (1995), "Customer Profitability Analysis: and activity-based costing approach", *Managerial Auditing Journal*, Vol. **10**, No. 7, pp. 3-7.

Snow C. P. (1998), *"The Two Cultures"*, (1993 edition), Cambridge: Cambridge University Press.

Stahl, H. K., Matzler, K. and Hinterhuber, H. H. (2003), "Linking Customer Lifetime Value with Shareholder Value", *Industrial Marketing Management*, Vol. **32**, No. 4, pp. 267-279.

Storbacka, Kaj. (1997), "Segmentation Based on Customer Profitability- Retrospective Analysis of Retail Bank Customer Bases", *Journal of Marketing Management*, Vol. **13**, No. 5, pp. 479-492.

Storbacka K. (2006), *Driving Growth with Customer Asset Management*, Helsinki: WSOYpro.

van Raaij E. M., Vernooij M. J. A. and van Triest S. (2003), "The implementation of customer profitability analysis: A case study", *Industrial Marketing Management*, Vol. **32**, No. 7, pp. 573-583.

Wang H. and Hong W. (2006), "Managing customer profitability in a competitive market by continuous data mining", *Industrial Marketing Management*, Vol. **35**, No. 6, pp. 715-723.

Ward, K. (1992), *Strategic Management Accounting*, Oxford: Butterworth-Heinemann.

Ward, K. (2004), *Marketing Finance*, Oxford: Elsevier, Butterworth Heinemann.

Weiner, J. (1995), "Activity based costing for financial institutions", *The Journal of Bank Cost and Management Accounting,* Vol. **8**, No. 3, p.19.

Williams J. B. (1997), *The Theory of Investment Value*, (Originally published 1938, Boston: Harvard University Press), Fraser Publishing.

Wilson, R. (1990), Strategic Cost Analysis, *Management Accounting*, Vol. **68**, No. 9, p. 42-3

Wilson, R. M. S. and Gilligan, C. (2005), *Strategic Marketing Management: planning, implementation and control*, 3rd edition, Oxford: Elsevier Butterworth-Heinemann.

Zimmerman, J.L. (2003), *Accounting for decision making and control*, 4th edition, Boston: McGraw-Hill/Irwin

Determining the indirect value of a customer

Lynette Ryals, *Cranfield School of Management, UK*

Abstract The issue of accountability in marketing has led to a substantial and growing body of work on how to value customer relationships. Net present value methods (customer lifetime value / customer equity) have emerged as generally preferred ways to assess the financial value of customers. However, such calculations fail to take account of other important but indirect sources of value noted by previous researchers, such as advocacy. This paper examines the development and application of three processes to determine indirect value in business-to-business and business-to-consumer contexts. The research shows that indirect value has a measurable monetary impact not captured by conventional financial tools, and that understanding this changes the way in which customers are managed.

INTRODUCTION

The advent of relationship marketing has had a profound impact on the marketing /finance interface. Relationship marketing focuses on customers and long-term relationship building rather than on products (Christopher, Payne and Ballantyne 2003). A major implication of relationship marketing is that marketing decisions should be about optimising the long-term value of the customer (Berger and Bechwati 2001). Consequently, accounting for marketing has shifted from the traditional product profitability approach (Grant and Schlesinger 1995) to a customer profitability focus.

The new focus has revealed that customer profitability is principally determined not by the cost of the products that the customer buys, but by the costs of managing the customer relationship (Kalwani and Narayandas 1995; Reinartz and Kumar 2002).

This is particularly an issue in business-to-business markets, in which substantial proportions of sales and marketing resources may be allocated to individual customers (Bowman and Narayandas 2004). Overspending on customer retention can mean that retained customers are not necessarily more profitable (Thomas, Reinartz and Kumar 2004), and the influence of customer management activities on the profitability of customers is well-attested (Bowman and Narayandas 2004; Ryals and Knox 2004; Ryals 2005).

Focusing on the profitable management of customer relationships has also helped to address the calls for greater accountability in marketing (Doyle 2000), since the value of customers is related to the value of the firm (Gupta, Lehmann and Stuart 2004). Previous research has found two sources of value from customers: financial (measured by the profitability or lifetime value of the customer) and indirect (other value from the relationship that is not directly related to the financial value of that customer). A review of the literature on the financial value of the customer reveals that mainstream methods for valuing customers do not take indirect value sufficiently into account, despite its acknowledged importance. The paper goes on to examine how two companies have addressed this issue and determined the indirect value of their customers, and how this information changed their customer management strategies.

CALCULATING THE DIRECT FINANCIAL VALUE OF A CUSTOMER

The growing requirement to monitor how investments in customer management pay off over time has meant that customer lifetime value and customer equity approaches to valuing customers have become widely accepted (Jain and Singh 2002; Gupta and Lehmann 2003; Ambler and Roberts 2005). Customer lifetime value is the value of a customer relationship over the course of the relationship lifetime (e.g. Reichheld and Sasser 1990; Reichheld 1996; Reichheld and Schefter 2000). Customer equity is the total lifetime value of a company's customer base (e.g. Blattberg, Getz and Thomas 2001; Lemon, Rust and Zeithaml 2001; Rust, Lemon and Zeithaml 2001).

Table 1 sets out a definition of each financial approach, its advantages and disadvantages, and its application to marketing practice.

To calculate customer lifetime value, marketers must forecast the likely length of the relationship lifetime and then the customer profitability or cash flow each year (Ryals and Knox 2004). Customer acquisition costs for an existing customer are generally disregarded (Berger and Nasr 1998), although they may be included for a new or returning customer (Calciu and Salerno 2002). These future profits are then discounted back to present day monetary amounts (Jain and Singh 2002). Thus, in accounting terms, calculating customer lifetime value is about forecasting the net present value of a customer.

Where the lifetime value relates to a number of customers and takes potential value into account, it is known as customer equity (Blattberg, Getz and Thomas 2001). 'Potential value' involves forecasting likely additional future purchases, increase in share of spend etc. Because of the larger sample numbers, customer equity is amenable to the use of forecasting tools such as acquisition / retention modelling (Berger and Bechwati 2001), decision calculus, regression analysis, neural networks (Berger and Bechwati 2001), Delphi panels (Story, Hurdley, Smith and Saker 2001), or Markov techniques (Rust, Lemon and Zeithaml 2001).

TABLE 1 Financial approaches to the value of the customer

Approach	Definition	Advantages	Disadvantages	Application to marketing practice
Customer lifetime value	Remaining value of customer relationship (forecast).	Takes future into account. Returns can vary according to levels of investment.	Forecasting difficulties and issues with treatment of discounting and risk. Treatment of lost customers problematic. Indirect sources of value from customers not included.	Matching customer management to payback (supports asset management approach). Customer segmentation and differentiated strategy.
Customer equity	Remaining plus potential value of customer base [∑customer lifetime value].	Looks at whole of customer base (portfolio management). Linked to value of firm.	Forecasting difficulties and issues with treatment of discounting and risk. Treatment of lost customers problematic. May still need to look at individual customers in business-to-business settings. Indirect sources of value from customers not included.	Customer portfolio management / maximising customer assets. Balancing customer acquisition and retention budget. Evaluating communication strategy / marketing campaigns.

Applying customer lifetime value / customer equity to marketing decision-making

Marketing managers are increasingly interested in understanding customer lifetime value as a guide to the way they manage customer relationships (EIU 1998). Lifetime value is affected by the way in which the relationship is managed but may also be affected by exogenous factors such as the actions of competing suppliers or changes in the customer's own circumstances. Generally, however, customers with high lifetime value will be preferred targets for retention strategies; customers with low or negative lifetime values might be better managed through cheaper channels or via a third party such as a distributor, or offered a lower service package (Booz Allen and Hamilton 2002).

Since the way in which the customer is managed has a major impact on lifetime value (Kalwani and Narayandas 1995; Reinartz and Kumar 2002), calculating customer lifetime value should not be seen as a one-off exercise but as dynamic (Jain and Singh 2002). Resource allocation decisions should aim to optimise returns on the marketing investment.

Customer equity is a portfolio-based measure and is associated with the notion of customers as assets (Blattberg and Deighton 1996; Blattberg, Getz and Thomas 2001; Hogan, Lemon and Rust 2002). The marketing applications of customer equity relate to budget setting and allocation (Berger and Bechwati 2001), balancing customer acquisition and retention activities (Thomas, Reinartz and Kumar 2004) and profitable customer management (Zeithaml, Rust and Lemon, 2001).

Weaknesses of customer lifetime value / customer equity tools

Recent research has revealed three weaknesses that affect both tools – forecasting, discounting, and whether the tools really do measure all the value generated by customers.

The first two difficulties have been explored elsewhere. It is known that forecasting difficulties have limited the take-up of customer lifetime value by practitioners (Gupta and Lehmann 2003). On the discounting issue, some marketers have become concerned that the use of a single discount rate may not reflect the risk in certain customer relationships and have developed additional techniques, either adjusting the discount rate or assessing the relationship risk and thus the probability of future profits (Dhar and Glazer 2003; Ryals and Knox 2004; Malthouse and Blattberg 2005).

The third issue is that these tools do not fully reflect the value of customers to the firm (Hogan, Lemon and Rust 2002; Ambler and Roberts 2005; Haenlein, Kaplan and Schoder 2006). For example, customer equity calculations do not usually include the value of potential customers (those yet to be acquired), yet advocacy from existing customers may help attract them. Even where the value of potential customers is included in the customer equity calculation (Rust, Lemon and Zeithaml 2004), the customers acting as advocates are undervalued. Advocacy, and other indirect sources of value from customers not captured by conventional tools, will now be discussed.

THE INDIRECT VALUE OF A CUSTOMER

The indirect value of a customer is the additional value (over and above the direct financial value measured by customer lifetime value / customer equity) that accrues to the firm through their relationship with that customer. Perhaps the most-explored area is advocacy, or word of mouth, early identified as an important element of relationship marketing (Christopher, Payne and Ballantyne 1991) and associated not just with satisfaction but also with relationship duration (e.g. Reichheld 1996). Advocacy has repeatedly been shown to have a strong impact on purchasing behaviour (Murray 1991; East et al. 2005; Keaveney 1995) and can be influenced by marketing strategies (East et al. 2005). Consequently, it is positively correlated with company growth (Reichheld 2003; East et al. 2005; Marsden, Samson and Upton 2005).

The advocacy concept has been extended to include customer reputation or referenceability (Doney and Cannon 1997; Stahl, Matzler and Hinterhuber 2003). Burnett (1992:12) describes this as *"the kudos of being a supplier to Harrods"*. Advocacy and referenceability positively impact firm performance by reducing customer acquisition costs and by increasing sales through the attraction of new customers (Stahl, Matzler and Hinterhuber 2003).

Further relational benefits from customer relationships include learning (Womack et al. 1990; Wilson 1996; Hope and Hope 1997; Srivastava, Shervani and Fahey 1998; Stahl, Matzler and Hinterhuber 2003) and innovation (Wilson 1996; Thomke and von Hippel 2002). Learning and information benefits contribute slightly differently to the value of the firm. Rather than reducing the costs of customer acquisition, they enhance the overall competitiveness and revenues / efficiency of the firm (Cravens, Piercy and Prentice 2000; Stahl, Matzler and Hinterhuber 2003).

It is difficult to account for indirect value. For example, the impact of advocacy or reference benefits is to reduce the cost of customer acquisition, which increases the financial value of the acquired customer but does not affect the value of the referring customer. Learning and innovation benefits may or may not increase the financial value of the customer generating them, through increased sales or reduced costs, but they can also increase the overall revenues or improve the overall efficiency of the supplier (Table 2).

TABLE 2 The financial impact of indirect benefits

Indirect benefit	Financial impact on value of customer asset	Financial impact on firm
Advocacy (Referrals)	None	Reduced customer acquisition costs; higher lifetime value on acquired customers
Reference	None	Reduced customer acquisition costs; higher lifetime value on acquired customers
Learning	May reduce costs	May reduce overall costs, or increase revenues if learning opens up new markets
Innovation	May increase revenues (product innovation) or reduce costs (process innovation)	May increase overall revenues if product innovation is wider than customer-specific innovation; may reduce overall costs through process efficiencies

FIGURE 1 Two sources of value from a customer

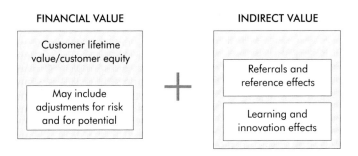

Table 2 illustrates the difficulty of evaluating indirect value in financial terms. Jenkinson (1995) suggests adding the revenues generated from relational benefits to the calculation of the value of the customer, although it is unclear how this is to be done without double counting (Ryals 2002). Since the indirect value of a customer relationship is usually described as additive to the financial value (e.g. Wilson 1996; Stahl, Matzler and Hinterhuber 2003), current financial valuation models based solely on net present value using customer lifetime value or customer equity probably understate the value created by customers. To find out how serious this understatement is, companies need to determine the indirect value of their customers. Figure 1 illustrates these two sources of value from customer relationships, financial and indirect.

The purpose of the current research was to explore how marketing and account managers could place a value on indirect benefits and whether the results would change the way in which those customer relationships were managed.

METHODOLOGY

The research approach was exploratory and descriptive, so a case study method was chosen (Patton and Appelbaum 2003). Two participating companies were selected to explore the process of valuing indirect benefits (Eisenhardt 1989; Yin 2002). Both participating companies were large international corporations from the financial services industry, one business-to-business and the other business-to-consumer. The companies met the theoretical sample requirements (Patton and Appelbaum 2003) which, in this case, were acceptance of the need for measurement of indirect value; an established customer management operation; good data-gathering processes; and a relative familiarity with the financial valuation of customers using customer lifetime value or customer equity approaches. Case study 1, a business-to-business case study, examined indirect value for major customers whose individual lifetime value had already been forecast. Case study 2, a business-to-consumer example, examined a set of customers whose customer equity had already been forecast.

The methodology was inductive, using one-on-one interviews and team-based workshops (Gummesson 2000) to collect both quantitative and qualitative data (Yin 2002). These data were used to develop pro-formas or produce provisional results that were then discussed at further interviews and workshops. Multiple iterations were carried out and, at each stage, the participating marketing and account managers were asked about the results and the implications for customer management practices.

The research produced interesting results relating both to processes for measuring the indirect value of customer assets and to the impact on customer management of applying these processes.

RESULTS: CASE STUDY 1

Case study 1 (business-to-business) focused on a small number of individual customers all having high customer lifetime value and where the indirect value was thought to be important. Eight customers who accounted for 47% of the customer portfolio by revenue were selected for study. Two processes for calculating indirect value were explored, one subjective and the other monetary. The first process used a weighting and scoring system (WSS); the second process imputed additional financial value directly to the relationship with individual customers.

The WSS process began with a workshop to explore whether, unprompted, the managers would identify the same relational attractiveness factors that had been identified in the literature. In fact, only one factor overlapped. This was Profile, identifiable as referenceability (Table 3).

These results suggest that indirect value is not well understood, even for more important customers. Three of the four 'indirect value' factors identified by the account managers during the first iteration (Relationship, Resources, and Skill Demands) turned out to affect costs to serve and ought therefore to be considered under the heading of direct financial value.

Figure 2 (overleaf) shows the results of the second iteration. Financial attractiveness was based on customer lifetime value, and the size of the circle indicated whether the customer was relatively high, medium or low revenue.

Figure 2 is suggestive of a relationship between financial and indirect attractiveness. There are some practical reasons that this might be true: larger customers are likely to be bigger, better-known companies with higher referenceability and greater learning and innovation value. However, the initial outputs of the WSS process (Table 3) also indicated a tendency for managers to confuse financial and indirect value. More research would be needed to establish the relationship between financial and indirect value, using an objective valuation method such as those discussed in the following section.

TABLE 3 Indirect attractiveness factors identified using unprompted WSS process

Relational attractiveness factors (unprompted)	Definition
Profile (referenceability)	Size of customer / Standing in industry / degree to which relationship enhances supplier's reputation
Relationship	Access barriers / depth of relationship (no. of contacts)
Resources	Time and people required to resource relationship
Skill Demands	Level of people required

FIGURE 2 Financial versus Indirect value

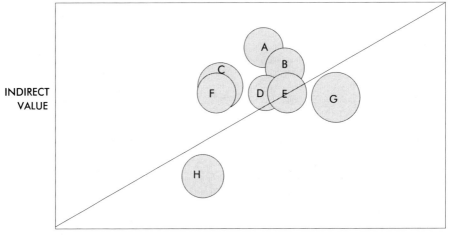

FINANCIAL VALUE (CUSTOMER LIFETIME VALUE)

FIGURE 3 Key customer matrix

	High	Low
High	Definitely a key account ✓	Decide case by case ?
Low	Probably a key account ✓	Probably not a key account ✗

INDIRECT ATTRACTIVENESS

FINANCIAL ATTRACTIVENESS

Although the WSS process for determining indirect value suffered from some drawbacks as described above, it did help the managers in this team to resolve a current business issue relating to how they could identify their company's key accounts (Figure 3). Figure 3 uses the convention for customer portfolios of a reversed X axis (e.g. McDonald, Rogers and Woodburn 2000).

Figure 3 illustrates an additional finding from this case study, which was that the identification of a key account might take account of both financial and indirect value. Although high financial value was a strong identifier of key account status, high indirect value might also be sufficient for key account status. This was the case for customers such as C and F shown in Figure 2, whose indirect value was considerably higher than their financial value. The WSS process also resulted in managerial action in the case of low-scoring customer H, shown towards the bottom of Figure 2. Examining the results, the managers felt that H's relatively low financial and indirect value meant that it should no longer be considered a key account. They made a decision to reduce its status; service levels and customer management practices were adjusted accordingly. The analysis summarised in Figure 2 enabled the team to make clearer decisions about which customers should – and should not – be considered as key accounts.

The second process tested in case study 1 was whether specific financial amounts could be attributed to indirect value.

Putting a financial value on indirect value

Following consultations with the research company finance managers and with finance academics, a probabilistic forecasting process was selected to put an expected monetary value on relational benefits. The probabilistic process reduced the problem of double counting noted by Jenkinson (1995) and Ryals (2002) whilst still resulting in a noticeable difference to the value of the customer.

For trialling purposes, major customer G was considered. The managers felt that the most likely type of relational benefit from G, which is a large and high-profile drinks company, was customer attraction through referenceability and advocacy. The managers forecast that their relationship with customer G was certain to help them win one new customer the following year and likely to help them win two new customers in year 2 and a fourth in year 3. Without customer G, there would be a zero probability of acquiring these customers. Moreover, probabilities of benefits in future years would be contingent on the relationship in earlier years, so conditional probabilities were used to calculate the monetary impact. Assuming a discount rate of 10%, the net present financial value of the increased probability of customer acquisition thanks to the relationship with customer G was £468,538 (Table 4).

In all, this exercise was repeated for four of the eight customers and resulted in an increase of 6.4% in the total net present value of those four customers. There were considerable differences in the perceived indirect benefits, with fully 76% of relational benefits identified as relating to customer G. Determining the expected

TABLE 4 Probabilistic valuation of Customer G's indirect value

	Item	Yr 1	Yr 2	Yr 3	Yr 4
a	**Profit on additional business**	112,220	561,100	1,009,980	1,458,860
b	% Probability without G	0%	0%	0%	0%
c	% Probability with G	100%	40%	16%	6%
d	Increase in probability (c-b)	100%	40%	16%	6%
e	**Expected Monetary Value (a x d)**	112,220	224,440	161,597	87,532
g	Discount Factor	.909	.826	.751	.683
h	**Net Present Value (e x g)**	102,008	185,387	121,359	59,784
	TOTAL				£468,538

monetary amount of G's indirect value resulted in an increased focus on continuing this relationship; as one key account manager commented:

If we build up positive relationships with customers and learn from them, those customers also wish to learn from us and then we continue to work together and grow...

The probabilistic forecasting method necessitates a series of assumptions about the acquisition timing and financial value of potential customers. The case demonstrates empirically that managers were able to apply the process and generate financial numbers that seemed realistic to them as a proportion of the value of customer G. The findings also suggested that indirect value might differ considerably between customers. This differential would be an interesting topic for future research.

RESULTS: CASE STUDY 2

The second case study, also in financial services, was in a very different context. Here, business-to-consumer research was carried out within the retail loans department of a bank. This case study was based on an examination of 123,442 loan applications by customers representing 100% of applications during a three-month period.

An initial workshop with the marketing managers quickly established that the WSS process was not viable with this sample size. Moreover, there were limited indirect benefits because the lender did not identify its customers publicly or exploit its relationships. At the time of the case study the bank was not collecting formal data about advocacy because it was not believed to be financially valuable, even though the bank's own research data suggested reasonably high intention to advocate. As one of the senior marketing managers observed at the beginning of the process:

If I'm honest, I'm a bit sceptical about whether there will actually be sufficient numbers to make it worthwhile but, unless you investigate it ... you'll never know.

The data in Table 5 were drawn from a re-analysis of marketing research data over the three-month period and based on the responses of 300 customers per month (900 responses in total).

Table 5 shows that customer satisfaction within the loans department was higher than for the company as a whole, although complaints were also substantially higher. This dichotomy illustrates a known problem with customer satisfaction as a predictor of repurchase (Reichheld 2003). A subsequent regression analysis carried out by the

TABLE 5 Satisfaction, advocacy and complaints

	Satisfaction*	Very likely to refer	Quite likely to refer	Complaints**
Loans dept %	55	39	39	16
Company overall %	53	33	42	<10

* Percentage of respondents describing themselves as 'delighted' or 'completely satisfied'
** Percentage of respondents who had complained within the previous year

bank determined that advocacy was a more useful predictive measure than customer satisfaction, supporting Reichheld's (2003) contention. As one of the marketing analysis commented:

A very large chunk of the people who say they are completely satisfied, it is simply because we haven't done anything wrong. It's not because they are delighted with us.

Putting a monetary value on advocacy

As the bank had no data on the actual incidence of referrals, the research focused on estimating the monetary value of advocacy based on triangulating an output measure (proportion of advocates) drawn from live data, with input measures (proportion of customers where advocacy was a declared reason influencing purchase) generated from two sources: research estimates and manager interviews. First, the marketing and database managers made estimates of the value of advocacy based on analysis of customer records and behaviour. These estimates were then triangulated through primary research with managers who were selling loans.

Having identified those customers most likely to refer, the marketing and database managers estimated the proportion of those saying that they were 'very likely' to refer who would actually do so (one third). This yielded a figure of 8,500 customers per month who were predicted to be advocates and a further estimate that one in 10 recommendations resulted in an application. Given that the company rejected 46% of loan applications, this would represent 457 converted customers per month. Multiplied by the average value of a customer, this would yield an estimate of the financial value of advocacy of £188,100 in revenue per quarter (0.75% of total revenue) and £81,140 in profits per quarter (just over 0.7%).

These estimates of the financial value of advocacy made by the marketing managers were triangulated against interviews with six loan managers and branch managers in four typical branches. These interviewees, who all spend the majority of their time selling loans to customers, estimated that advocacy accounted for 2% to 3% of incoming customers which translated into 440 to 660 customers per month. This estimate was noticeably higher than the projections of the marketing managers, suggested that the impact of advocacy had been understated by the central marketing team. Moreover, the loans managers were only reporting on the customers who had volunteered information about advocacy during the application process. As there was no formal requirement to ask loan applicants why they had applied, it is likely that many more incidents of advocacy went unreported.

However, in financial services it is not just revenues but risk that is important, and the branch office interviews produced some intriguing observations about the types and risk profiles of the customers arriving as a result of recommendation (Table 6).

As Table 6 (overleaf) shows, the managers identified three categories of referral: Family (thought to be most prevalent); Peer; and Colleague. Moreover, an interesting observation was that the risk profile of the customer was felt by the managers to be similar to, or the same as, that of the advocate.

The managers noted several implications of this research for their marketing strategy. The first was that advocacy was sufficiently prevalent to make it worthwhile tracking which customers had come through referral by including a specific question to that effect on the loan application form. The second was that the risk profile of the family, not just of the applicant, might be taken into account when making a loan to the close relative of an existing customer. Third, the firm could analyse its

TABLE 6 Advocacy sources and risk profile

Relationship to advocate	Source of referral	Risk profile and application behaviour
Family	Usually, parents referring children*	Same. Children's risk profile felt to be same as that of parents. Thought to be the most frequent type of referral.
Peer	Friends (tended to be younger customers)	Similar. Friends may even accompany one another into the branch to apply for loans at the same time.
Colleague	Workmates	Similar. Can result in multiple customers - several customers from same workplace may follow shortly after one customer recommends. Loans may be for same purpose (e.g. car buying), and purpose of loan is known to influence risk.

* 'Children' here merely indicates the relationship to the referrer, as all the customers under discussion are adults.

database to identify clusters of customers all working for the same company; this would be indicative of advocacy by a business colleague. Finally, if the firm wanted to encourage referrals, it would have to ensure that its pricing strategy was consistent with its advocacy strategy. The branch managers commented that sometimes they only became aware that a customer was there as a result of advocacy when the customer queried the rate (price) for the loan and complained that their relatives, friends or colleagues had got better deals:

> If they're not getting the same rate as their friends or whoever they've been talking to is getting, that can be a little bit difficult.

The research resulted in a change in advice to branch managers about how customer relationships were to be managed:

> While we still look at satisfaction, in terms of driving the things that we want staff to do with customers there is much more that is actually under their control in terms of relationship building with recommendation [referrals] than there is with satisfaction.

DISCUSSION

In recent years there has been considerable exploration of the financial value of customers. The need for net present value approaches (customer lifetime value and customer equity) is now widely accepted. However, research has also indicated that customers can create additional indirect value (e.g. Stahl, Matzler and Hinterhuber 2003). This research used a case study approach to identify and test three processes for evaluating the indirect value of a customer. The three methods, and their advantages and disadvantages, are summarised in Table 7.

In case study 1, two processes were used. The indirect value of customers was

TABLE 7 Three methods for valuing indirect benefits

Method	Process	Advantages	Disadvantages
Case Study 1:			
1. WSS	Identify attractiveness factors, apply importance weighting, score each customer.	Conceptually straightforward, may help identify key accounts.	Managers may tend to conflate financial size or profitability of customer with high indirect value.
2. Probabilistic	Change in probability of benefit multiplied by financial value of benefit.	Reduces double counting issue and problem of 'would have happened anyway'; results in substantial differences to value of customer.	Requires a series of assumptions about timing and financial amount of relational benefits.
Case Study 2:			
3. Triangulated, based on advocacy rates and incoming	Collect data on intent to refer, compare this with predicted actual referral and conversion rates, check against incoming customers where they indicate they came through referrals	Minimises need for forecasting even where actual referrals are not recorded. May encourage recording of referrals. Produced indication that referred customers may have similar risk profile to their advocates.	Collecting advocacy data from incoming customers may be cumbersome.

measured first with a WSS and then using a probabilistic forecasting approach. The WSS approach resulted in a managerial tool for the identification of key accounts and a decision to downgrade one company to non-key account status, changing the way that it was managed. The second, probabilistic approach indicated that relational benefits could be substantial and might be positively associated with financial value, although more research would be needed to determine the accuracy of probability estimates. Managerially, the findings confirmed the importance of one particular customer that was already known to be financially attractive. The discovery of substantial indirect benefits increased the customer management team's investment in this account.

In case study 2, the indirect value of customers was thought to consist entirely of advocacy. In the event, three sources of advocacy were identified: Family, Peer, and Colleague. Of these, Family advocacy was thought to be the most frequent although Peer or Colleague advocacy could result in the acquisition of multiple customers and so might be more valuable overall. Managers also noted that the source of referral might indicate the risk of the acquired customer. These findings led to a reassessment of the importance of advocacy to the company that also affected pricing and loan acceptance decisions.

The wider applicability of this research is to supplement and extend the concept of customer lifetime value / customer equity. Typically, such calculations incorporate the stream of future value from one customer or group of customers, usually measured in terms of future product or service purchases. It is rare for such calculations to include consideration of the value of advocacy, referenceability, learning, or innovation. This research demonstrates three methods for calculating indirect value and attributing it to the customers who are generating that value. The empirical testing of these methods reveals that indirect value can be substantial, and may result in changes to customer management.

Limitations and future research

The limitations of this research relate to the generalisability of the results from two case studies, both in financial services and both examining contractual relationships. In the first case study, only eight customers were studied and detailed financial evaluation of indirect value was completed on just four. However, these were major customers and the monetary value attributed to the relational aspects of the relationship was considerable. In the second case study, the sensitive nature of the product (personal loans) and the firm's existing customer management practices meant that indirect value was confined to advocacy. It is uncertain whether other sources of indirect value could be obtained from these relationships if they were managed differently.

Several questions for future research are set out in Table 8.

TABLE 8 Summary of findings and future research directions

	Case study 1	Case study 2
	Business-to-business	**Business-to-consumer**
Financial valuation process	Customer lifetime value	Customer equity
Relational valuation process	1. WSS: intuitive and easy to use but may tend to conflate financial and indirect value. 2. Probabilistic approach: increase in probability of obtaining benefit multiplied by value of benefit.	3. Estimated value of advocacy based on previous research and behaviour, triangulated with branch manager perception.
Impact on perceived value of customer	Considerable for some customers, less for others.	Small but potentially profitable incremental business, especially if risk taken into account.
Additional issues raised	a. Are financial and indirect value positively related? b. How can predictive accuracy in probabilistic method be gauged?	c. Is the risk / return profile of referred customers similar to that of the referrer? d. Is indirect value in business-to-consumer confined to advocacy?

The first question for future research is whether financial and indirect value are positively related. If customers with a higher lifetime value also have a higher indirect value, this would provide further substantiation for customer management practices such as key account management and CRM. A second question relates to the subjectivity of probability evaluations by account managers; it is not clear whether the change in probability of a relational benefit can accurately be measured.

Additional future research questions are raised by case study 2, which raised the intriguing possibility that the risk/ return profiles of referred and referring customers might be similar. If this is generally the case, companies need to think carefully about which customers they target for referrals (Reichheld 2003), particularly in sectors such as financial services. This case study also suggests that the main indirect value in business-to-consumer services might be advocacy. There are some indications of this in East et al. (2005), although they find a much higher impact of advocacy in other service industries than was the case in the current research.

CONCLUSION

The contribution of the paper was to propose and empirically test three processes for evaluating the indirect value of a customer, demonstrating that these processes produced managerially useful results that 'fill a gap' in conventional tools that measure the financial value of customers. The first process (WSS) needed care in application to prevent overlap between financial and indirect value, but produced a tool that helped the managers identify key accounts. The other two processes enabled the companies to impute a monetary amount to indirect value. This information was then used to shape customer acquisition and management strategies.

Overall, this research has demonstrated that managers can put a value on advocacy. It has also demonstrated that determining the indirect value of a customer is not only feasible but is managerially useful, as it leads to changes in the way that the customer is managed. Indirect value may influence the identification of key accounts. It may also, through like-for-like advocacy, affect the risk profile of the customer base as well as its returns.

The research provides an extension to the widely-used tools of customer lifetime value and customer equity, demonstrating that there are substantial indirect benefits from customers that are not usually captured in conventional financial calculations.

REFERENCES

Ambler, T. and Roberts, J. (2005), "Beware the Silver Metric: Marketing Performance Measurement has to be Multidimensional", Centre For Marketing Working Paper, 05-207 (September), London Business School.

Berger, P. D. and Bechwati, N. N. (2001), "The allocation of promotion budget to maximise customer equity", *Omega,* Vol. **29**, No. 1, pp. 49-61.

Berger, P. D. and Nasr, N. I. (1998), "Customer lifetime value: Marketing models and applications", *Journal of Interactive Marketing,* Vol. **12**, No. 1, pp. 17-30.

Blattberg, R.C. and Deighton, J. (1996), "Manage marketing by the customer equity test", *Harvard Business Review,* Vol. **74**, No. 4, pp.136-144.

Blattberg, R. C., Getz, G. and Thomas, J. S. (2001), *Customer Equity: Building and Managing Relationships as Valuable Assets,* Boston: Harvard Business School Press

Booz Allen Hamilton Inc (2002), "The Customer Profitability Conundrum: When to Love 'Em or Leave 'Em", *Strategy + Business / Knowledge@Wharton*, 10th April 2002.

Bowman, D. and Narayandas, D. (2004), "Linking Customer Management Effort to Customer Profitability in Business Markets", *Journal of Marketing Research*, Vol. 41, No. 4, pp. 433-447.

Burnett, K. (1992) *Strategic Customer Alliances: How to win, manage, and develop key account business in the 1990s*, London: Pitman.

Calciu, M. and Salerno, F. (2002), "Customer Value Modelling: Synthesis and extension proposals", *Journal of Targeting, Measurement and Analysis for Marketing*, Vol. 11, No. 2, pp. 124-147.

Christopher, M; Payne, A and Ballantyne D. (1991), *Relationship Marketing*, Oxford: Butterworth Heinemann.

Christopher, M; Payne, A and Ballantyne D. (2003), *Relationship Marketing*. 2nd edition, Oxford: Butterworth Heinemann.

Cravens, D. W., Piercy, N. F. and Prentice, A. (2000), "Developing market-driven product strategies", *Journal of Product and Brand Management*, Vol. 9, No. 6, pp. 369-388.

Dhar, R and Glazer, R. (2003), "Hedging Customers", *Harvard Business Review*, Vol. 81, No. 5, pp. 86-92.

Doney, P. M. and Cannon, J. P. (1997), "An Examination of the Nature of Trust in Buyer-Seller relationships", *Journal of Marketing*, Vol. 61, No. 2, pp. 35-51.

Doyle, P. (2000), "Valuing Marketing's Contribution", *European Management Journal*, Vol. 18, no. 3, pp. 233 – 245.

East, R. Hammond, K. Lomax, W. and Robinson, H (2005), "What is the Effect of a Recommendation?", *Marketing Review*, Vol. 5, No. 2, pp.145-157.

Eisenhardt, K. M. (1989), "Building Theories from Case Study Research", *Academy of Management Review*, Vol. 14, No. 4, pp. 532-550.

EIU (1998), "Managing customer relationships", *The Economist Intelligence Unit, Report with Andersen Consulting*, London: EIU

Grant, A. W. H. and Schlesinger, L. A. (1995), "Realise your Customers' full profit potential", *Harvard Business Review*, Vol. 75, No. 5, pp. 59-72.

Gummesson, E. (2000), *Qualitative Methods in Management Research*, 2nd Edition, London: Sage.

Gupta, S. and Lehmann, D. R. (2003), "Customers as Assets", *Journal of Interactive Marketing*, Vol. 17, No. 1, pp. 9-24.

Gupta, S., Lehmann, D. R and Stuart, J. A. (2004), "Valuing Customers", *Journal of Marketing Research*, Vol. 41, No. 1, pp. 7-18.

Haenlein, M., Kaplan, A. M. and Schoder, D. (2006), "Valuing the Real Option of Abandoning Unprofitable Customers When Calculating Customer Lifetime Value", *Journal of Marketing*, Vol. 70, No. 3, pp. 5-20.

Hogan, J. E. Lemon, K. N. and Rust, R. T. (2002), "Customer Equity Management: Charting New Directions for the Future of Marketing", *Journal of Service Research*, Vol. 5, No. 1, pp. 4-12.

Hope, J and Hope, T. (1997), *Competing in the Third Wave*, Boston: Harvard Business School Press.

Jain, D. and Singh, S. S. (2002), "Customer lifetime value research in marketing: a review and future directions", *Journal of Interactive Marketing*, Vol. 16, No. 2, pp. 34-46.

Jenkinson, A. (1995). *Valuing your Customers: From quality information to quality relationships*, London: McGraw Hill.

Kalwani, M. U. and Narayandas, N. (1995), "Long-term manufacturer-supplier relationships: do they pay off for supplier firms?", *Journal of Marketing*, Vol. 59, No. 1 (January) pp. 1-16.

Keaveney, S. M. (1995), "Customer switching behavior in service industries: an exploratory study", *Journal of Marketing*, Vol. 59, No. 2, pp. 71-82.

Lemon, K., Rust, R. T. and Zeithaml, V. A. (2001), "What drives customer equity", *Marketing Management,* Vol. **10**, No. 1, pp. 20-25.

Marsden, P., Samson, A. and Upton, N (2005), "Advocacy Drives Growth", *Brand Strategy,* Vol. **198**, (Dec-Jan), pp. 45-47.

Malthouse, E. C. and Blattberg, R. C. (2005), "Can We Predict Customer Lifetime Value?", *Journal of Interactive Marketing,* Vol. **19**, No. 1, pp. 2-16.

McDonald, M., Rogers, B. and Woodburn, D. (2000), *Key Customers: How to Manage them Profitably,* Oxford: Butterworth-Heinemann

Murray, K. B. (1991), "A Test of Services Marketing Theory - Consumer Information Acquisition Activities", *Journal of Marketing,* Vol. **55**, No.1, pp. 10-25.

Patton, E. and Appelbaum, S. H. (2003), "The case for case studies in management research", *Management Research News,* Vol. **26**, No. 5, pp. 60-71.

Reichheld, F. F. (1996), *The Loyalty Effect,* Boston: Harvard Business School Press.

Reichheld, F. F. (2003), "The One Number You Need to Grow", *Harvard Business Review,* Vol. **81**, No. 12, pp. 46-54.

Reichheld, F. F and Sasser Jr,, W. E. (1990), "Zero Defections: Quality Comes to Services", *Harvard Business Review,* Vol. **68**, No. 5, pp. 105-111.

Reichheld, F. F. and Schefter, P. (2000), "E-loyalty: Your Secret Weapon on the Web", *Harvard Business Review,* Vol. **78**, No. 4 (July/Aug), pp. 105-113.

Reinartz, W. J. and Kumar, V. (2002), "The Mismanagement of Customer Loyalty", *Harvard Business Review,* Vol. **80**, No. 7, pp. 86-94.

Rust, R. T., Lemon, K. N. and Zeithaml, V. A. (2001), "Where should the next marketing dollar go?", *Marketing Management,* Vol. **10**, No. 3, pp. 24-28.

Rust, R. T., Lemon, K. N. and Zeithaml, V. A. (2004), "Return on Marketing: Using Customer Equity to Focus Marketing Strategy," *Journal of Marketing,* Vol. **68** No. 1, pp. 109-127.

Ryals, L. J. (2002), "The Total Value of the Customer and Targeted Marketing Strategies", PhD thesis, Cranfield School of Management, Cranfield.

Ryals, L. J. (2003), "Making Customers pay: Measuring and Managing Customer Risk and Returns", *Journal of Strategic Marketing,* Vol. **11**, No. 3, pp. 165-176.

Ryals, L. J. (2005), "Making Customer Relationship Management Work: The Measurement and Profitable Management of Customer Relationships", *Journal of Marketing,* Vol. **69**, No. 4, pp. 252-261.

Ryals, L. J. and Knox, S. D. (2004), "Measuring Risk-adjusted Customer Lifetime Value and its Impact on Relationship Marketing Strategies and Shareholder Value", *European Journal of Marketing,* Vol. **39**, No. 5/6, pp. 456-472.

Srivastava, R. K., Shervani, T. A. and Fahey, L. (1998), "Market-Based Assets and Shareholder Value: A Framework for Analysis", *Journal of Marketing,* Vol. **62**, No. 1, pp. 2-18.

Stahl, H. K. Matzler, K. and Hinterhuber, H. H. (2003), "Linking customer lifetime value with shareholder value", *Industrial Marketing Management,* Vol. **32**, No. 4, pp. 267-279.

Story, V., Hurdley, L., Smith, G. and Saker, J. (2001), "Methodological and Practical Implications of the Delphi Technique in Marketing Decision-Making: A Re-Assessment", *The Marketing Review,* Vol. **1**, pp. 487-504.

Thomas, J. S., Reinartz, W. and Kumar, V. (2004), "Getting the most out of All your Customers", *Harvard Business Review,* Vol. **82**, No. 7/8, July/August pp. 116-123.

Thomke, S. and Von Hippel, E. (2002), "Customers as Innovators: A New Way to Create Value", *Harvard Business Review,* Vol. **80**, No. 4, pp. 74-85.

Wilson C. (1996), *Profitable Customers,* London: Kogan Page.

Womack, J. P., Jones, D. T. and Roos, D. (1990). *The machine that changed the world,* New York: Rawson Associates

Yin, R. K. (2002), *Case Study Research - Design And Methods,* Thousand Oaks: Sage Publications.

Zeithaml, V. A., Rust, R. T. and Lemon, K. N. (2001), "The Customer Pyramid: Creating and Serving Profitable Customers", *California Management Review,* Vol. **43**, No. 4, pp. 118-142.

The marketing / accounting synergy: a final word but certainly not the last word

Robin Roslender, *Heriot Watt University, UK*
Richard M. S. Wilson, *Loughborough University, UK*

Abstract In this closing essay we take the opportunity to briefly recount our understanding of the history of work at the marketing/accounting interface, and equally briefly to review its current state as evidenced by the various contributions to this collection. While agreeing the importance of focusing increased attention on the customer, the accounting perspective that promises to be of greatest utility in this process is that of managerial accounting. The prospects for any breakthrough via the continued employment of a predominantly financial accounting and reporting emphasis are argued to be limited, whilst the current vogue for its near neighbour, a finance emphasis, seems to us to be in fundamental contradiction of what characterises customers.

INTRODUCTION

From an accounting perspective, the longest established cooperative practice with marketing would seem to have been the introduction and acceptance of financial management disciplines within the marketing function. This strongly reflects popular stereotypes of both groups: profligate marketers being reeled in by penny-pinching accountants. And yet if we move forward to the C21st interface between them, many who are attracted to it, be they academics or practitioners, would be hard pressed to deny that customer profitability analysis (CPA) is the most popular exemplar of this synergy.

Briefly reprising CPA, which has been extensively discussed in other contributions to this collection, many people are familiar with it as a highly visible, and widely practised derivation of activity accounting, activity-based costing (ABC) applied to 'doing business with customers'. From a traditional cost accounting perspective, CPA potentially identifies which customers to divest, although those more managerially-oriented accountants might remind us of the merits of the short-term relevant costing corrective to such impulses. Conversely, from a contemporary cost management perspective, CPA promises to identify cost management opportunities that might be pursued for mutual benefit. To those with a longer, and wider familiarity with the accounting/marketing interface, the origins of CPA (and ABC) actually lie in the 1920s and 1930s, while there was significant interest in Customer Account Profitability in the 1960s, at the very time that Johnson and Kaplan (1987) suggested managerial accounting was rapidly losing its relevance within the business enterprise.

Rather than debate the genesis and evolution of CPA, it is more useful to observe that, as an instance of segmental analysis, it is the principal exemplar of accounting/marketing cooperation, and very distinctly a *managerial* accounting technique. In truth there is very little possibility of developments that combine marketing and financial accounting and reporting, at least as they continue to prevail. Marketing expenditures have traditionally been expensed as incurred, in the name of prudence. As discretionary expenditures they can readily be slashed quickly, removing them from the income statement at one fell swoop (in the pursuit of increased earnings with a short-term focus – although this is a myopic view of the importance of investing in markets).

Brands continue to remain a serious problem to financial accounting and reporting practitioners, unless they are acquired in a business transaction when they may be included in the purchaser's balance sheet (nowadays) at their fair value, with any excess outlays being designated and accounted for as goodwill. Unfortunately, once a stock of brands is purchased, any enhancement expenditures must be expensed – there is no accounting for 'home-grown' brands. There is provision for capitalising the expenses entailed in creating customer databases or customer lists but this again is constrained by a set of demanding requirements designed to conform with the established practices of financial accounting and reporting rather than contribute to the challenge of creating and delivering value to customers and shareholders. Brand equity, which marketing management researchers have explored since the early 1990s, and with no little success (Aaker 1991, 1995), presently has the appearance of being a step too far. But this is to get ahead of the story.

In the absence of much prospect of creating a fruitful *financial* accounting/marketing interface, the question that begs itself is whether CPA, as a popular managerial accounting development, provides the basis on which to promote further accounting/marketing synergy? A number of contributors to this collection are not persuaded that it does, suggesting alternative approaches that draw on parallel developments in marketing management. Unfortunately, there seems to be little will to identify what it is about CPA that ultimately restricts its appeal. Today there is much more to managerial accounting than identifying techniques of varying degrees of sophistication that amount to little more than identifying where it is possible to contain marketing expenditures. Least it be overlooked, those who initially commended ABC did so because they believed it furnished more accurate product costs. As such, those of a sceptical disposition might conclude that it is little more than an improved approach to absorption costing, which has its roots firmly in financial accounting and reporting requirements. The subsequent recognition of ABC's and CPA's cost management potential, with its value creation emphases, is welcome. At the same time the subtle distinctions between cost reduction and cost management are easily dismissed by practitioners in particular as merely playing with words. Whether, in the role of the management accountant, you ask a marketing colleague to reduce her/his costs or manage them, it amounts to importing the same thing: the application of a financial management discipline within the marketing function.

At an early stage in the debate about how managerial accounting might be made more relevant to the challenges faced by senior management, Bromwich and Bhimani (1989) identified strategic management accounting (SMA) as a possible alternative to developments such as ABC. The term SMA was initially coined by Simmonds in 1981 to identify a form of management accounting that he believed held out great promise for the profession. Where managerial accounting was traditionally represented as internal reporting, SMA was characterised by its external orientation (Wilson 1995). Simmonds argued that some management accountants were beginning to recognise the value of assembling information about their competitors, hence the subsequent designation of SMA as competitor-focused accounting (Guilding 1999). This did not exhaust the alternative nature of SMA, Simmonds arguing that it was now desirable to collect information on sales volumes, market shares, cash flows and resource utilisation as well as on costs and prices. SMA did not privilege accuracy of information as much as the contribution it made to a business's strategy formulation. Simmonds freely acknowledged that, because of its departure from mainstream accounting emphases, SMA might also become part of the toolkit of marketing managers or business planning professionals, although in his view management accountants were better placed to make this new approach their own. Simmonds subsequently published further papers on SMA (Simmonds 1982, 1986) but it largely failed to capture the attention of practitioners during the 1980s. A case study on something akin to SMA practice was published by Rickwood, Coates and Stacey in 1990, a notable feature of which was that it suggested a significant degree of cooperation between management accountants and marketing managers.

In some respects, Shank and Govindarajan's strategic cost management framework (Shank 1989; Shank and Govindarajan 1989, 1992a, 1992b, 1993, 2000) is the closest descendent of Simmond's approach. It is an externally oriented approach focusing on competitors with the intention of generating comparative insights that are designed to inform the strategy process. Shank and Govindarajan have Porter's work on value chains to inform their conceptualisations of competitor performance (Porter 1980, 1985), as well as the early work within the activity-based (cost) management field (Cooper and Kaplan 1991). On the critical question of the quality of any strategic cost information Shank and Govindarajan are less convinced of the need to depart too radically from the accounting mainstream, a difficulty that ultimately suggests that, counter to Shank's own founding assertion, what is on offer here remains old wine. The link is evident in the set of customer-focused accounting techniques identified by Guilding (1999).

Following the publication of their CIMA research monograph: *Management Accounting: Evolution not Revolution* in 1989, in a series of outputs published during the next five years Bromwich and Bhimani outlined a second variant of SMA that remained fundamentally faithful to Simmonds' founding idea (Bromwich 1990, 1991; Bromwich and Bhimani 1989,1991,1994). Like Shank and Govindarajan, Bromwich and Bhimani also had the benefit of Porter's competitive advantage theory to aid them. More importantly perhaps, they incorporated insights from work on target costing, the Japanese counterpoint to ABC and a development that was itself more multidisciplinary in its foundations, as well as explicitly outward looking (Hiromoto 1988, 1991; Sakurai 1989; Kato 1993).

The centrepiece of Bromwich and Bhimani's SMA approach was the attribute costing technique. On the basis of their assertion that the real drivers of cost were the benefits that customers sought in products, Bromwich and Bhimani advocated costing the benefits of products. While continuing to commend attempts at competitor costing, for Bromwich and Bhimani the central focus of SMA should be on markets and customers. Bromwich defined SMA as:

The provision and analysis of financial information on the firm's product markets and competitors' costs and cost structures and the monitoring of the enterprise's strategies and those of its competitors in these markets over a number of periods.

(Bromwich 1990: 28)

subsequently arguing that the adoption of SMA will:

....help focus management efforts on their markets where customers have to be won and retained and competitors repulsed.

Bromwich 1991: 2)

Attribute costing is based on the application of a strategic cost analysis matrix in which the many attributes associated with a particular product are to be subject to systematic costing, using a typology of four cost categories. In the spatial representation of this matrix (p127) it is possible to see how its effective utilisation implies a high degree of cooperation between management accountants and their marketing management colleagues, an observation reinforced by Bromwich's concept of an efficient product:

Only efficient products, each of which yield the maximum amount of a specific bundle of characteristics for the amount of money the customer wishes to spend, will survive in a well organised market. Whether a product represents an efficient way for the consumer of buying the bundle of characteristics depends on product prices as well as the quantities of characteristics offered by products.

(Bromwich 1991: 9)

Despite these very persuasive arguments for developing the SMA concept, little more than a couple of years later the project seemed to peter out. A collection of papers exploring the state of the art of SMA practice published in *Management Accounting Research* (Tomkins and Carr 1996a,b) was largely decoupled from Bromwich and Bhimani's work, affirming the editors' opening observation that there still remains little consensus about what the term SMA means. Coad (1996) and later Dixon (1998) provide case studies of what they identified as SMA practice, although both papers were content to rehearse its earlier conceptual foundations. In many respects, however, it was Lord's 1996 paper that signalled the end of the road for SMA. Drawing on a wider set of developments than outlined above, she identified the principal attributes of SMA, which she then argues do not form part of the stock of contemporary management accounting in New Zealand. In the second half of her paper, Lord discusses Cyclemasters, an organisation in which something akin to SMA was practised but, unfortunately, not by the accountants. This leads her to conclude that SMA may not be anything more than just a figment of academic imagination. Conversely, from our perspective the observation that this was part of the marketing functions' jurisdiction only served to reinforce the conclusion that there was still considerable mileage left in a multidisciplinary approach to SMA.

Roslender and Hart have been in the vanguard of continuing to promote SMA in recent years. They have done so using a particular conceptualisation that represents it as a development incorporating managerial accounting and marketing management insights. Informed by a study of patterns of interaction between management accounting and marketing management practitioners in UK organisations, they identify three stages of increasing cooperation between them (Roslender and Hart 2002, 2003). At the initial, most rudimentary stage, the two groups are involved in the implementation of budgetary control processes within the sales and marketing function. Such cooperation has been conceptualised as the pursuit of marketing controllership (Wilson 1999), being very close to the imagery invoked in the opening paragraph of this essay. Stage two entails the two groups cooperating in the exploration of a range of managerial accounting developments, including CPA, which seem to be more progressive and potentially beneficial than budgeting and responsibility accounting. For Roslender and Hart, however, developments such as SMA and VBM constitute a further, significantly more fruitful instance of interfunctional coordination (cf Narver and Slater 1990), which is referred to as the *synergistic* stage of development.

In a later paper, Roslender and Hart (2006) present the case for viewing brand management accounting (BMA) as a further development of the generic SMA concept (Roslender 1995). BMA is identified as a means of finally dissociating accounting for brands from the financial accounting and reporting model briefly described earlier in this essay. It is also argued to be a continuation of work begun in the early 1990s by Guilding and various associates, parallel to that of Bromwich and Bhimani's thinking on SMA but seemingly quite distinct from it. The significance of (management) accounting for brands lies in the rapidly growing importance of brands in everyday life and, as a result, their cruciality to the creation and delivery of value to market savvy customers by business enterprises to their customers. Roslender and Hart take as axiomatic the position that unless the accountancy profession, in close cooperation with marketing management, is able to successfully account for brands, its contribution to accounting for strategic positioning (Roslender 1995) may be seriously undermined.

Rereading the 2006 paper, there are some grounds for acknowledging that what is being proposed amounts to a potential Trojan horse, in that Roslender and Hart seem prepared to gift a significant part of the traditional jurisdiction of accounting, if not necessarily management accounting, to marketing managers. Frankly, Roslender and Hart had been persuaded that there was more to be learned from some marketing management contributions on strategic brand management than from managerial accounting. As a consequence, the brand equity concept presented little difficulty, since what is being proposed is a multi-metric approach to accounting for brands. They were also gratified to learn at the time that something similar was being proposed by Ambler and Roberts (2006) in the case of the customer equity concept, and affirmed in their paper in this collection. Moreover, given the rise and rise of the balanced scorecard reporting framework, in its more sophisticated iterations (Kaplan and Norton 2004, 2006), Roslender and Hart also felt assured that some at the leading edge of managerial accounting developments were also thinking along parallel if not identical lines.

What did trouble Roslender and Hart were the observations of one reviewer, who continually insisted that the paper was saying nothing new in advocating brand management accounting. This was very largely true, of course, something admitted in both the various iterations of the paper and in responses to reviews. Although not obvious at the time, this position is about as profound as saying that what is new about a particular cocktail, given that none of its ingredients is new? What is new, surely, is how the various constituents are first selected and then mixed together. To our knowledge there is no contribution to the managerial accounting literature that replicates the BMA cocktail. It is still much too early to determine whether we have indeed produced a palatable cocktail in Roslender and Hart (2006), although if the present collection is any indication, it appears not. In the interests of balance, however, it should also be observed that, for whatever reason, despite their increasing encroachment into everyday life, brands still do not appear to have attracted the attention of those working at the accounting/marketing interface, with the contribution to this collection by El-Tawy and Tollington being a welcome exception.

Conversely, the collection does seem to suggest that many of those who are interested in the accounting/marketing interface are focused on customers. This should come as no great surprise following two decades during which relationship marketing has emerged as a core perspective within marketing management, one consequence of which has been that many marketing academics and practitioners loudly assert that 'our customers are our most important asset' (Peppers and Rogers 2005). Intriguingly, this claim is challenged by their counterparts in human resource management, who prefer to identify employees in this way. Ironically, identifying either customers or employees as assets is guaranteed to make accountants in general, and financial accounting and reporting specialists in particular, more than a little uncomfortable. By comparison, accounting for brands is pretty straightforward stuff – at least you can buy a brand asset, unlike either customers or employees (though you can buy customer lists......).

So how is it possible to account for customers? Obviously they can't easily be put on the balance sheet, which to the purists might mean it is wrong to even refer to them as assets. Earlier considerable doubt was cast on whether accounting for customers via the mechanism of CPA or customer account profitability exercises is of much significance. If customers really are the most important asset for any business (and we are not prepared to discount this out of hand, in this essay at least), accounting for them must surely have more weight associated with it.

With the realisation of the importance of customers to the continued commercial success of the business has come the emergence of a new concept much in evidence in the previous pages: customer equity. And with the concept of customer equity has come the project to revisit attempts to determine the financial value of marketing assets using the principles of discounting. Arguably the best known example of this approach, developed in the case of brands in the early 1990s by Interbrand, entailed applying a composite brand strength multiplier to discounted short-to-medium term income streams for a brand. While still a successful consultancy, the model commended by Interbrand failed to find much favour with the UK accountancy profession, which thereafter felt sufficiently comfortable to quietly forget about it. This time around, much of the customer equity literature emanates from the USA and is largely the work of financ(e)ially oriented marketing management academics who feel confident that they can begin to go it alone to some extent, a risk that Foster and Gupta (1994) warned against in their seminal paper on the accounting/ marketing interface. Although not widely involved as yet, some sections of the financial accounting and reporting fraternity will take comfort in the observation that their marketing management colleagues have eventually begun to recognise the superiority of the accountancy profession's jurisdiction and the credibility of what some like to refer to (albeit disparagingly) as "hard numbers".

The authors are neither sufficiently well equipped nor inclined to debate the merits of the different approaches to determining the financial value of customer equity. If readers have not as yet grasped that we have little confidence in financial accounting and reporting approaches, and most especially those which embrace the scientificity associated with what in the accounting research literature is termed market-based accounting research, then we have summarily failed in our task. What specifically interests and challenges us is to develop a managerial accounting approach to accounting for the customer, and one that is rather more ambitious than CPA or similar developments. It must also reflect the direction in which managerial accounting has been developing over the past couple of decades, i.e. towards a much softer emphasis evidenced by a greater acceptance of non-financial metrics that are reported in their variety, with an appreciation that more maybe better than less information, *inter alia* via a balanced scorecard or some such performance reporting framework. Besides, there is also something wholly incongruous about visualising customers using what might be designated as the hardest of hard numbers.

It is axiomatic that this new management accounting for customers is the result of cooperation by managerial accounting and marketing management academics working in tandem. Therefore, what initially needs to be agreed upon is the purpose of the exercise. For us there is little doubt that their joint objective should be to contribute to *the creation and delivery of value to customers*. This returns us to the erstwhile focus on the market orientation concept, as articulated by Narver and Slater:

> *Creating value for buyers is much more than a "marketing function"; rather a seller's creation of value for buyers is analogous to a symphony orchestra in which the contribution of each subgroup is tailored and integrated by a conductor......When there is no tradition of interfunctional coordination within a business, effective advocacy and leadership are needed to overcome each functional area's isolation from the other functions. Achieving effective interfunctional coordination requires, among other things, an alignment of the functional areas' incentives and the creation of interfunctional dependency so that each perceives its own advantage in cooperating closely with the others.*

(Slater and Narver 1990: 22)

If this is the fundamental challenge that faces all businesses (and many other organisations beyond), then it is incumbent on all parties to make a contribution towards meeting it (see also Wilson and Fook 1990). This is at odds with the overarching objective attributed to financial accounting and reporting, which remains focused on the interests of shareholders, nowadays referred to as creating and delivering shareholder value. Reporting increased customer equity (and before it, brand equity) would seem to be consistent with this latter notion. By contrast, the creation and delivery of value to customers doesn't seem to sit easily with the intentions of CPA, which, once again, can probably be best understood as being shareholder oriented in the last analysis, whether used in tandem with cost management or not.

What we have in mind is some form of customer-focused accounting (CFA), although not with the same constituents as Guilding and McManus' (2002) designation: customer profitability analysis; customer segment profitability analysis; lifetime customer profitability analysis; and valuation of customers/customer groups as assets. As the term suggests, CFA needs to focus on the customer; it must provide information about customers. More specifically it must provide information on value as sought by the customer. From a managerial accounting perspective, the image that this immediately conjures up is the creation and delivery of "value for money" to customers. Here customers are being characterised as always seeking value for money, wanting the most for a given outlay. If we return to Porter (1985), however, we find that this is more commensurate with a cost leadership strategy, which strongly resonated with those who advocated a strategic approach to cost management.

Porter also identified a second generic strategy, that of differentiation, whereby customers were prepared to pay more for a different product, perhaps best conceptualised in the form of branded offerings. While not entirely oblivious to the need for some semblance of value for money in the case of many branded offerings, sizeable numbers of customers are prepared to pay more for the offerings they seek. Value, therefore, is not simply about financial value (as in value for money, shareholder value, economic value added, etc). It also encompasses a range of subjective, emotional, associational, significatory, i.e. qualitative, dimensions that are sufficiently powerful to subordinate the rational person in most of us. Such ideas are, not surprisingly, already well-documented in parts of the strategic brand management literature.

CFA should, therefore, be oriented to providing information on *customers as sources of income streams*, rather than as income streams, current or future discounted. Some of this information will be of the most basic sort, and widely associated with market research, e.g. numbers of customers or growth in numbers of customers, for both the business and its principal competitors, much in the manner intimated by the founder of SMA, Simmonds. Customer satisfaction measures are already well-established, and with varying levels of sophistication, as are measures of customer loyalty, customer retention, customer turnover and customer referrals. There is no necessity to attempt to place any financial value on these data. They are simply alternative representations of customers as assets, representations which to us are more relevant than those normally furnished by the accountancy profession. The observation that such exercises effectively relieve management accountants of their comparative advantage over marketing managers misses the point, that of different expertises being combined in the pursuit of creating and delivering value to customers. At its simplest, what is being commended to management accountants is that they refocus some of their priorities from providing information to senior management as the representatives of the shareholder within the organisation to providing information to senior managers as the representatives of the customers.

Unfortunately, for some readers a rather uninspiring image of management accountants and marketing managers cooperating in 'counting customers' may come to mind. Some in the former group might find consolation in having the opportunity to teach the latter how they might count better and more systematically. Correspondingly, marketing managers might conclude that they have at last begun to grasp the tricky nettle of marketing accountability (Shaw and Mazur 1997)

So to end with a more radical proposal: there is something unconvincing about linking the notion of customer value to the practice of counting. By the same token, it seems to us that there should be rather more to accounting than 'counting'. What is an account? It is a story, a representation, a visualisation. We are all familiar with the 'account' provided by the eye witness at some incident or the newspaper article on the same incident produced by a journalist. Both of these accounts employ words (and sometimes pictures) to tell their stories. Likewise the accountant has traditionally told her/his story using numbers, in a highly prescribed way in some cases, which links back to the idea of counting. To the extent that marketing managers wish to fashion their own accounts (of customers) they may be readily seduced by the kudos that continues to be attached to accounting.

Is it possible to capture the subjective, emotional, associational, significatory or similar qualitative attributes of customer value by counting? A much more promising avenue to explore is that of *recounting*, where customers fashion their own accounts of their links with particular offerings and the organisations that provide them. This process would need to be pursued in a systematic way in order to enhance its credibility, with the array of stories generated being combined with other information sets to provide a more balanced, richer understanding of customer value expectations. Would the accountancy profession be prepared to consider such excursions? The leading edge of intellectual capital reporting, in the form of the Danish intellectual capital statement approach, suggests this may not be so far away (DATI 2001; DMSTI 2004). Similarly the exploration of Health Statements in Scandinavia (Grojer and Ahonen 2005; Mouritsen and Johanson 2005; Almqvist, Backlund, Sjoblom and Rimmel 2007), and recent work done in connection with the definitions/valuation of information as an asset (Oppenheim, Stenson and Wilson 2003a,b, 2004), as well as the continuing interest in the role of narrative reporting within a business reporting model (AICPA 1994; ICAS 1999; IASB 2005). In our view, it seems to merit at least the same level of interest and exploration that the marketing management community seems to be being urged to pay to its antithesis, the heavily counting oriented customer equity concept.

REFERENCES

Aaker, D. A. (1991), *Managing Brand Equity*, New York: The Free Press.
Aaker, D. A. (1995), *Building Strong Brands*, New York: The Free Press.
AICPA (1994), "Improving Business Reporting- A Customer Focus: Meeting the Information Needs of Investors and Creditors", Report of the special committee on financial reporting, American Institute of Certified Public Accountants (chaired by E.L. Jenkins)
Almqvist, R., Backlund, A., Sjoblom, A. and Rimmel, G. (2007), "Management control of health – the Swedish example". In: Johanson, U. , Ahonen, G. and Roslender, R., (eds.), *Work Health and Management Control*, Stockholm: Thomson-Fakta, pp. 291-316.
Ambler, T. and Roberts, J. (2006), "Beware the silver metric: marketing performance measurement has to be multidimensional", *Report 06-113*, Cambridge, MA.: Marketing Science Institute.
Bromwich, M. (1990), "The case for strategic management accounting: the role of accounting information for strategy in competitive markets", *Accounting, Organizations and Society*, Vol. 15, No. 1, pp. 27-46.
Bromwich, M. (1991), "Accounting for strategic excellence", mimeo, London School of Economics and Political Science.
Bromwich, M. and Bhimani, A. (1989), *Management Accounting: Evolution not Revolution*, London: Chartered Institute of Management Accountants.
Bromwich, M. and Bhimani, A. (1991), "Strategic investment appraisal", *Management Accounting (US)*, Vol. 72, No. 9, pp. 45-48.
Bromwich, M. and Bhimani, A. (1994), *Management Accounting: Pathways to Progress*, London: Chartered Institute of Management Accountants.
Coad, A. (1996), "Smart work and hard work: a learning orientation in strategic management accounting", *Management Accounting Research*, Vol. 7, No. 4, pp. 387-408.
Cooper, R. and Kaplan, R. S. (1991), "Profit priorities from activity-based costing", *Harvard Business Review*, Vol. 69, No. 3, pp. 130-135.

DATI (2001), *A Guideline for Intellectual Capital Statements*, Copenhagen: Danish Agency for Trade and Industry.

Dixon, R. (1998), "Accounting for strategic management: a practical example", *Long Range Planning*, Vol. 31, No. 2, pp. 272-279.

DMSTI (2004), *Intellectual Capital Statements: the New Guideline*, Copenhagen: Danish Ministry for Science, Technology and Innovation.

Feldwick, P. (1996), "What is brand equity and how do you measure it?", *Journal of the Market Research Society*, Vol. 6, pp. 43-77.

Foster, G. and Gupta, M. (1994), "Marketing, cost management and management accounting", *Journal of Management Accounting Research*, Vol. 6, pp. 43-77.

Grojer, J-E. and Ahonen, G. (2005), "Social accounting in the Nordic countries – from social accounting to accounting in a social context". In: Jonsson, S. and Mouritsen, J. (eds.), *Accounting in Scandinavia – The Northern Lights*, Malmo/Copenhagen: Liber/Copenhagen Business School, pp. 43-60.

Guilding, C. (1999), "Competitor-focused accounting: an exploratory note", Accounting, *Organizations and Society*, Vol. 24, No. 7, pp. 583-595.

IASB (2005), *Management Commentary: A Discussion Paper*, London: International Accounting Standards Board.

ICAS (1999), *Business Reporting: The Inevitable Change?*, edited by V.A.Beattie, Edinburgh: Institute of Chartered Accountants of Scotland.

Johnson, H. T. and Kaplan, R. S. (1987), *Relevance Lost: the Rise and Fall of Management Accounting*, Boston, MA: Harvard Business School Press.

Kaplan, R. S. and Norton, D. P. (2004), *Strategy Maps: Converting Intangible assets into Tangible Outcomes*, Boston, MA: Harvard Business School Press.

Kaplan, R. S. and Norton, D. P. (2006), *Alignment: Using the Balanced Scorecard to Create Corporate Synergies*, Boston, Ma: Harvard Business School Press.

Lord, B. R. (1996), "Strategic management accounting: the emperor's new clothes?", *Management Accounting Research*, Vol. 7, No. 3, pp. 347-366.

Mouritsen, J. and Johanson, U. (2005), "Managing the person: human resource costing and accounting, intellectual capital and health statements". In: Jonsson, S. and Mourisen, J. (eds), *Accounting in Scandinavia – The Northern Lights*, Malmo/Copenhagen: Liber/ Copenhagen Business School Press, pp. 139-157.

Narver, J. C. and Slater, S. F. (1990), "The effect of a market orientation on business profitability", *Journal of Marketing*, Vol. 54, No. 4, October, pp. 20-35.

Oppenheim, C., Stenson, J and Wilson, R. M. S. (2003a), "Studies of information as an asset I: definitions", *Journal of Information Science*, Vol. 29, No. 3, pp. 159-166.

Oppenheim, C., Stenson, J. and Wilson, R.M.S. (2003b), "Studies of information as an asset II: repertory grid", *Journal of Information Science*, Vol. 29, No. 5, pp. 419-432.

Oppenheim, C., Stenson, J. and Wilson, R. M. S. (2004), "Studies of information as an asset III: views of information professionals, *Journal of Information Science*, Vol. 30, No. 2, pp. 181-190.

Penrose, N. and Moorhouse, M. J. (1992), *The Valuation of Brands*, London: Interbrand Group plc and Ranks Hovis McDougall.

Peppers, D. and Rogers, M. (2005), *Return on Customer: Creating Maximum Value from Your Scarcest Resource*, New York: Currency-Doubleday.

Porter, M. E. (1980), *Competitive Strategy: Techniques for Analysing Industries and Competitors*, New York: The Free Press.

Porter, M. E. (1985), *Competitive Advantage: Creating and Sustaining Superior Performance*, New York: The Free Press.

Rickwood, C. P., Coates, J.B. and Stacey, R. J. (1990), "Stayplton: strategic management accounting to gain competitive advantage", *Management Accounting Research*, Vol. 1, No. 1, pp. 37-49.

Roslender, R. (1995), "Accounting for strategic positioning: responding to the crisis in management accounting", *British Journal of Management*, Vol. **6**, No. 1 pp. 45-57.

Roslender, R and Hart, S. J. (2002), *Marketing and Management Interfaces in the Enactment of Strategic Management Accounting Practices: An Exploratory Investigation,* London: Chartered Institute of Management Accountants

Roslender, R and Hart, S. J. (2003) "In search of strategic management accounting: theoretical and field study perspectives", *Management Accounting Research*, Vol. **14**, No. 3, pp. 255-79.

Roslender, R and Hart, S. J. (2006), "Interfunctional cooperation in progressing accounting for brands: the case for brand management accounting", *Journal of Accounting and Organizational Change*, Vol. **2**, No. 3, pp. 229-247.

Shank, J. K. (1989), "Strategic cost management: new wine or just new bottles?", *Journal of Management Accounting Research*, Vol. **1**, pp. 47-65.

Shank, J. K. and Govindarajan, V. (1989), *Strategic Cost Analysis*, Homewood, Ill.: Irwin Inc.

Shank, J.K. and Govindarajan, V. (1992a), "Strategic cost management: the value chain perspective", *Journal of Management Accounting Research*, Vol. **4**, pp. 179-197.

Shank, J. K. and Govindarajan, V. (1992b), "Strategic cost analysis of technological investments", *Sloan Management Review*, Vol. **34**, No. 1, pp. 39-51.

Shank, J. K. and Govindarajan, V. (1993), *Strategic Cost Management: the New Tool for Competitive Advantage*, New York: The Free Press.

Shank, J. K. and Govindarajan, V. (2000), "Strategic cost management and the value chain". In: Reeve, J. M. (ed.), *Readings and Issues in Cost Management*, London: Thomson Learning, pp. 185-203.

Shaw, R. and Mazur. L. (1997), *Marketing Accountability*, London: Financial Times/Pearson International.

Simmonds, K. (1981), "Strategic management accounting", *Management Accounting* (UK), Vol. **59**, No. 4, pp. 26-29.

Simmonds, K. (1982), "Strategic management accounting for pricing: a case example", *Accounting and Business Research*, Vol. **12**, No. 47, pp. 206-214.

Simmonds, K. (1986), "The accounting assessment of competitive position", *European Journal of Marketing*, Vol. **20**, No.1, pp. 16-31.

Tomkins, C. and Carr, C. (eds.) (1996a), "Special issue on strategic management accounting", *Management Accounting Research*, Vol. **7**, No. 2.

Tomkins, C. and Carr, C. (1996b), "Reflections on ....", *Management Accounting Research*, Vol. **7**, No. 2, pp. 271-280.

Wilson, R. M. S. (1995), "Strategic management accounting". In: Ashton, D., Hopper, T. and Scapens, R. W., (eds.), *Issues in Management Accounting*, 2e, London: Prentice Hall, pp. 159-190.

Wilson, R. M. S. (1999), *Accounting for Marketing*, London: Thomson Business Press.

Wilson, R.M.S and Fook, N.Y.M (1990), "Improving market orientation", *Marketing Business*, Issue 11, (June), pp. 22-3.

Index

Page numbers in *Italics* represent tables.
Page numbers in **Bold** represent figures.

ROUTLEDGE

Key Issues in Marketing Management

New Horizons in Arts, Heritage, Nonprofit and Social Marketing

Edited by Roger Bennett, Finola Kerrigan and Daragh O'Reilly

Arts, heritage, non-profit and social marketing today comprise key components of the contemporary marketing management scene. Governments, charities and voluntary sector organisations throughout the world are increasingly involved in the development of marketing campaigns, and more and more of these organisations are likely to utilise the latest marketing methods. Research in the arts, heritage, non-profit and social marketing fields is intellectually rigorous, relevant for user communities, and has a great deal to offer to marketing theory as well as to promotional practice.

This book presents a collection of stimulating articles that report some of the freshest and most innovative empirical and conceptual research in arts, heritage, non-profit and social marketing. They explore new ideas, challenge pre-existing orthodoxies, develop knowledge, and demonstrate the epistemological importance of current research in these critical areas.

This book was originally published as a special issue of the *Journal of Marketing Management*.

June 2012: 246 x 174: 192pp
Hb: 978-0-415-62889-1
£85 / $135

www.routledge.com/9780415628877

Key Issues in Marketing Management

New Developments in Online Marketing

Edited by Jim Hamill, Stephen Tagg, Alan Stevenson and Tiziano Vescovi

The Internet has had a profound impact on all aspects of business over the past decade. It is now widely accepted that we have entered a new and even more revolutionary phase in the development of the Net as a global marketing and communications platform. New generation Web-based communities and hosted applications are beginning to have a major impact on customer behaviour across a diverse range of industries. Success in this new online environment, characterised by people and network empowerment, requires new 'mindsets' and innovative approaches to marketing, customer, and network relationships. This book examines recent and future developments in online marketing, including the revolutionary impact of new media, and covers a wide range of topics: information exchange; Web 2.0 and 'New-Wave Globals'; online tribal marketing; co-creation; industry impact; privacy issues; online advertising effectiveness; and practitioner prognostics for the future of online marketing.

This book was originally published as a special issue of the *Journal of Marketing Management*.

June 2012: 246 x 174: 216pp
Hb: 978-0-415-62887-7
£85 / $135

For more information and to order a copy visit
www.routledge.com/9780415628877

Available from all good bookshops

www.routledge.com/9780415628907

Key Issues in Marketing Management

Multicultural Perspectives in Customer Behaviour

Edited by Maria G. Piacentini and
Charles C. Cui

With globalisation taking centre stage in the business
world and multiculturalism affecting markets and
societies, there is a need to understand the ways that
customers respond to the changing marketplace from
both international and multicultural perspectives. This
book addresses important themes raised in marketing
literature such as: global consumer culture, and the
impact of Western culture on consumer behaviour in
other countries; consumer acculturation processes, and
the impact on identity conflicts and the strategies people
use to manage them; globalisation vs. localised strategies,
and the interaction of local and global influences on
customer behaviour; climate change and global warming,
their impact on consumer behaviour, and the implications
for social responsibility; and cross-cultural customer
research, including important methodological questions
around the application of sociological, group-level
measures to psychological, individual-level phenomenon
in marketing contexts.

This book was originally published as a special issue of
the *Journal of Marketing Management*.

June 2012: 246 x 174: 184pp
Hb: 978-0-415-62890-7
£85 / $135

For more information and to order a copy visit
www.routledge.com/9780415628907

Available from all good bookshops

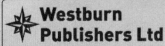